The Journal of Contemporary Heathen Thought

The Journal of Contemporary Heathen Thought

Edited by

Christopher A. Plaisance
Ben McGarr
Vincent Rex Soden

Volume I

2010

The Journal of Contemporary Heathen Thought
Volume 1, 2010
Editors: Christopher A. Plaisance, Ben McGarr and Vincent Rex Soden

© 2010, Heiðinn Publications. Copyrights for individual articles, poems and images rest with their respective creators. All rights reserved. No part of this book, either in part or in whole, may be reproduced, modified, stored in a retrieval system, transmitted or utilized in any form or by any means, electronic, mechanical, or otherwise, without prior written permission from the publisher and/or authors, except for brief quotations embodied in literary articles and reviews, or those works designated by their author as being in the common domain.

Note: The ideas expressed herein belong to the individual contributors and are not necessarily representative of the contributors as a whole nor the editorial staff.

Contributors: Asseling, Xenia Bakran-Sunic, Alain de Benoist, Stephen M. Borthwick, Dan Cæppe, Juleigh Howard-Hobson, Henry Lauer, Loddfafner, Ben McGarr, Christopher A. Plaisance, Jennifer Roberge-Toll, Steven "Piparskeggr" Robinson, Kris Stevenson, Jordan Turner, Troy Wisehart and Hunter Yoder.

Front cover painting, *The Wishing Tree*, by Diana Plaisance.
Cover design by Christopher A. Plaisance with special assistance from Lissa Haas.

ISBN: 1452883718
EAN-13: 9781452883717

The Journal of Contemporary Heathen Thought may be reached at
Email: heathen.editor@gmail.com
Web: http://www.heathenjournal.com

Table of Contents

Editorial Preface	vii
Dedication	xiii

Essays and Poems

Why I am a Heathen *Christopher A. Plaisance*	1
Hermann Awakened: Folkishness vs. Racism *Stephen M. Borthwick*	35
Folkways (a kyrielle) *Juleigh Howard-Hobson*	41
Cognitive Bias and Contemporary Heathenry *Henry Lauer*	43
When the Gods Speak Back: A Heathen Perspective on Gardening *Loddfafner*	63
Descendants of the Sun *Xenia Bakran-Sunic*	67
Magic Plants Used Symbolically in Germanic Heathen Hexology *Hunter Yoder*	69
To Vinland *Steven "Piparskeggr" Robinson*	83
Thoughts on Poetry *Steven "Piparskeggr" Robinson*	87
The Feminine in the Post-Modern Age: How Feminism Negates Folkways *Juleigh Howard-Hobson*	91

Sommer
Juleigh Howard-Hobson   103

Wandering the Nine Worlds:
Heathenism's Shamanic Origins
Dan Cæppe   105

Baldr's Temple
Troy Wisehart   127

Intolerance and Religion
Alain de Benoist   129

An Interpretation of Germanic Mythology
Kris Stevenson   137

Book Reviews and Interviews

The Decline of the West
Ben McGarr   205

New Lands, New Faith
Asseling   219

Primordial Traditions Compendium 2009
Juleigh Howard-Hobson   221

The *EDDA* as Key to the Coming Age
Christopher A. Plaisance   223

Confessions of a Radical Traditionalist
Henry Lauer   227

Freyja: Great Goddess of the North
Jordan Turner   233

Songs of Sun and Hail:
A Conversation with Sonne Hagal   237

Editorial Staff   245

Contributors   247

Editorial Preface

Like a snake, who bites its own tail, we shall sun ourselves in the warmth of what is to come.

—K.S.

Background

We are in the midst of a great reawakening—a reawakening the likes of which have not been seen since the height of the Germanic Revivals of the 19th century. At the close of this first decade of the 21st century, we bear witness to the power of the resurgent atavism that is Heathenry. With each passing year the pre-Christian religion of our Teutonic forefathers is strengthened and vivified by increases in the quantity and quality of Heathen folk, organizations and publications. From the initial phases of the revival to the current day, Heathenry has been the subject of dozens of periodicals. From the turn of the century with *Das Deutsche Buch* of the Germanische Glaubens-Gemeinschaft or Guido von List's *Iduna* all the way to the gambit of contemporary magazines and journals, periodicals have served as nodes in the continuum of Heathen thought—focal points through which Heathen minds have sought to develop the ways we think about our religion and its place in the modern world.

Like all organisms, this journal has a genealogy, and it is from the origins of an entity that insight into its nature and the initial trajectory of its life-course can best be gained. Unlike most publications within the Heathen community, our journal springs not from an organization, but—like the journal from which ours drew its initial inspiration—from an idea. Although many of our contributors do belong to large Heathen groups such as the Odinic Rite or Ásatrú Folk Assembly, this journal is not an official organ or reflection of any of these. At its core, our publication is a response to the critiques leveled at the current state of Heathen thought in the journal *TYR: Myth—Culture—Tradition*. Although not specifically a Heathen publication,[1] *TYR*'s focus on Radical Traditionalism overlaps in quite a few instances with Heathenry. In its second volume, Stephen McNallen wrote that we are besieged by a "lack of philosophical depth."[2] He goes on to note that

---

1 "*TYR* was never intended to be an 'Ásatrú' or 'Odinist' publication," (Joshua Buckley and Michael Moynihan. "Editorial Preface." *TYR: Myth—Culture—Tradition* 2 [2003-2004]: 9-10).
2 Stephen A. McNallen. "Three Decades of the Ásatrú Revival in America." *TYR* 2: 217.

> it is an error to think that we can simply pick up where we left off a thousand years ago. The Christian interregnum must be addressed using the intellectual tools that have developed in the intervening time—and this means examining our beliefs and expressing them in intellectually compelling ways.[3]

Likewise, in volume three, Collin Cleary ventured that what Heathenry "seems to desperately need...is something like a theology...that would address...basic philosophical questions."[4] And it is thus that *The Journal of Contemporary Heathen Thought* begins as a journal of profound discontent. We begin as a publication which is ultimately *untimely*—in that our focus is neither to recreate that which was, nor to propagate that which is, but rather to strive towards the actualization of that which is to come. What we seek to do is take steps towards rectifying the vast gap that separates the depth and sophistication of contemporary Heathen thought from that of the world's major religions. What is currently absent is the kind of systematic, multi-disciplinary, academic treatment that comprises Religious Studies.[5] What we lack, in other words, is a distinct discipline that could be called Heathen Studies.

Mission

What then would this type of treatment of Heathenry entail? What disciplines and methodologies does the journal seek to promote? In what way is our mission distinct from those of other Heathen publications? To be sure, there are many books, dissertations and essays that have been written about the historical Heathenry by academics both within and without the Heathen community. Indeed, this branch of the Religious Studies tree seems to be practically *the only one* that has received the appropriate amount of attention! It is for that reason that this journal is decidedly not interested in gathering essays from researchers working within that sub-discipline. There are more than enough dedicated outlets that exist in connection with the Scandinavian Studies departments of various universities that the inclusion of such material here would be redundant. Within the other divisions of Religious Studies, however, the field is more or less wide open.

---

3 Ibid., 218.
4 Collin Cleary. "Paganism Without Gods." *TYR* 3 (2007-2008): 429.
5 The discipline of Religious Studies can be defined as the academic study of religion as informed by the methodologies of fields of study such as Philosophy, Anthropology, Sociology, etc. The point of departure from Theology lies in the perspective from with the research is carried out. Religious Studies is generally carried out from an external, belief-neutral position, whereas theological work is done from within that religion's paradigm.

Excepting treatments of the following subjects *as historical phenomena* (relegating such works, ultimately, to the History of Religion), the remaining subdivisions of Religious Studies as it pertains to Heathenry are all but untapped. The explanation for this dearth may lie in a phenomenological concept that appears to be unique to Neopaganism: unverified (or unverifiable) personal gnosis (UPG). If this term is unfamiliar to those who have studied philosophy or religion in an academic setting, there is a good reason for it. UPG is an idea unique to reconstructionist streams of Neopaganism. As it is not a part of any formal terminology, there is no standard definition, but the general meaning refers to any knowledge (*gnosis*) gained from sources other than archaeological investigation and textual exegesis.[6] While it seems to have been originally formulated to act as a bulwark against the inclusion of personal theophanies in religious canon—a function it has performed quite well—it has also had the side-effect of stifling forays into any non-exegetically grounded thought from reaching print or gaining widespread acceptance.

Now, this is not to say that we intend on publishing the type of material that the UPG concept *specifically* is designed to inhibit; what we *are* interested in are the ideas that have been *incidentally* obfuscated as a result of the prominence of the UPG construct. What this means specifically is that we seek to encourage the development and assist in the promulgation of rational inquiry into Heathenry as expressed in the domains of Philosophy, Theology, Psychology, Sociology Anthropology, and other disciplines generally included under the umbrella of Religious Studies.

One point should be immediately clarified, lest potential contributors be put off by the seeming academic specialization of the aforementioned disciplines. The Psychology of Religion, for example, is *not* Psychology proper, and is not a topic that is generally covered by psychologists. Religious Studies in general, and the coming Heathen Studies, is not a domain restricted to professionals in specified fields of study; it is within the grasp of any thoughtful, educated—formally or otherwise—individual with a thorough understanding of Heathenry who is willing to engage in penetrating research on a specific topic. At this time there are no universities or professors who teach Heathen Studies as there are with many other large religions; that means it is up to us as Heathens to develop this on our own. We cannot wait for it to be formulated by outsiders, but must spearhead this with the tenacity and erudition the subject deserves.

---

6 Exegesis, the critical examination and analysis of an historical—particularly religious—text, often utilizing linguistic and archaeological data.

That being said, what manners of questions, one might ask, would be pertinent to Heathenry in this field? As so little has been published outside of works on the History of Heathenry, mythographical studies and introductory expositions, there are a plethora of possible topics for consideration. Within Anthropology of Religion and its related sub-fields, we have the ethnobotanical works of Christian Rätsch[7] and Stephen Flowers' semiotic work on the Runes,[8] but not much else. What do we make of Ludwig Feuerbach and Émile Durkheim's theories on religion as a societal projection, or Max Müller and Ernst Cassirer's ideas about the linguistic roots of myth? Contributions tackling such questions are exactly the kind of material we hope to receive for our future volumes.

In Sociology of Religion we have a myriad of texts that amount to historical studies of the subject,[9] but what of Heathen societies today? Mattias Gardell's study, *Gods of the Blood*, is perhaps the first full-scale sociological text on Heathenry, but is geared towards the sensationalism of fringe elements and the politics of certain Heathen groups. What of the rest? How do our ideas of the *innangarð* and *útangarð* relate to Benedict Anderson's concept of imagined communities? What sociological comparisons can be drawn between us and extant polytheistic cultures? In Psychology of Religion the field is even more open, with no major published texts. How do we respond to the theories of religion put forth by evolutionary psychologists such as John Tooby and Leda Cosmides, or to the critiques of authoritarianism leveled by the Frankfurt School? What do we think of Richard Dawkins' memetic explanation of the transmission of religious ideas?

Works in Philosophy of Religion and Theology are similarly scarce. Alain de Benoist's *On Being a Pagan* and Collin Cleary's works on phenomenology[10] and Hegelianism[11] are excellent starting points, but, given the breadth of these two fields, this is not even the tip of the iceberg. We have articulated *what* our ethical platform is, but have failed to provide a philosophically coherent explanation of *why* it is so; are our ethics grounded in relativism, deontology, constructivism or

---

7 *The Encyclopedia of Psychoactive Plants: Ethnopharmacology and Its Applications*. (South Paris, ME: Park Street Press, 2005).
8 Stephen E. Flowers. "A Semiotic Theory of Rune Magic." *Studia Germanica*, vol. I (Smithville, TX: Rûna-Raven, 2000), 9-27.
9 Georges Dumézil's trifunctional hypothesis of early Indo-European cultures being a prime example.
10 "Knowing the Gods" (*TYR* 1 [2002]: 23-40) and "Summoning the Gods: The Phenomenology of Divine Presence" (*TYR* 2: 25-64).
11 "Philosophical Notes on the Runes," parts one and two in vols. 21 and 22 of *Rûna Magazine*.

something else? We have Anthony Winterbourne[12] and Paul Bauschatz's[13] works on temporality, but Bauschatz fails to articulate his ideas in the vocabulary of contemporary philosophy and Winterbourne is an avowed Kantian; what of Martin Heidegger's, Alfred North Whitehead's or even John McTaggart's ontologies[14] of time—might they be appropriate for Heathen Philosophy? What manner of hermeneutics[15] might rightfully be applied to our primary sources? What modes of epistemology[16] explain our knowledge of the Gods? All of these and *so many more* are the kinds of questions that this journal is interested in answering. The doors of inquiry are already open—we need only to enter.

Submissions

Regarding guidelines for submissions, there are several points that bear mention. First, we would like to emphasize that, in spite of the seeming scholasticism of the above outline of Religious Studies as it applies to Heathenry, we are not solely interested in soliciting essays and dissertations of an academic nature. The Heathen community is not comprised entirely of scholars, and nor is Heathen thought uniformly scholastic in nature. Within Heathendom and within the pages of this journal there is ample room for short essays, poems and art whose function is neither didactic nor dialectic, but is meant to inspire, provoke and enthuse. Secondly, we seek to collect review essays of material pertinent to the journal's mission and interviews with prominent Heathens. Thirdly, beginning with volume two, we hope for the journal to host a "letters" section, where comments and constructive critiques of the journal's form and content can be aired. It is our hope that some of the more philosophically oriented pieces presented in the journal will elicit formal response essays of comparable depth and quality to the original work—thus allowing the journal to function as something similar to an online discussion forum, albeit in a more rigorous and penetrating manner.

It is worth mentioning that more than a few of the authors featured in this volume have spent the last few years debating the ideas at the core of their respective works on various internet discussion forums. Thus, in the interest of furthering the very mode of discourse responsible for some of the journal's central themes,

---

12 *When the Norns Have Spoken: Time and Fate in Germanic Paganism.* (Cranbury, NJ: Associated University Press, 2004).
13 *The Well and the Tree: World and Time in Early Germanic Culture.* (Amherst, MA: University of Massachusetts Press, 1982).
14 Ontology, the branch of philosophy concerned with the nature of being.
15 Hermeneutics, the science of interpretation—particularly as applied to religious texts.
16 Epistemology, the philosophical study of the nature and limits of knowledge.

we are pleased to host an online forum[17] wherein similar dialectic idea building may occur. Being a journal of ideas, it ought also be noted that *The Journal of Contemporary Heathen Thought* is not an ideological journal. There is no litmus test that submissions must pass in order to be considered for publication. Any well researched and articulated essay that falls within the domains discussed above will be given due consideration regardless of the particular ideas in question or the association of the individual contributor (or lack thereof) with any Heathen organizations. The journal is also apolitical and will not be pushing *any* political agenda. We recognize that one's political outlook is oftentimes just as central to one's *Weltanschauung* as is religion, but submissions that overtly politicize their topics will not be recommended by the review panel for publication.

With all of this in mind, if you are a thinker, poet or artist that would like to join us and submit material for consideration, please contact the staff. We are accepting essays, dissertations, poems, artwork, reviews and interviews on a continual basis. Inquiries regarding the suitability of a topic can be addressed via email or our internet discussion forum. If our work resonates with you, please, join us. *Wæs þu hæl!*

—The Editors
Spring, 2010

---

17 Accessible with registration at: http://www.heathenjournal.com/forum/

Dedication

This journal is an offering.

It is an offering to all of our Gods, whose inspiration permeates every page.

It is an offering to our Folk, both without whom its assemblage would be impossible and for whose benefit it was created.

It is an offering to Heathendom, to the myriad of physical and online webs of interconnection in which the origins of the journal lie.

It is an offering to Heathenry itself, so that we might progress towards becoming that which we are not yet—that which we might become as we actualize our potential to the fullest.

Hail to Thee!

Essays and Poems

For it is not a God that is coming, but *Gods*. They are taking shape; their gravity is inescapable.

—K.S.

Why I am a Heathen

Christopher A. Plaisance

The Christian missionary may preach the gospel to the poor naked heathen, but the spiritual heathen who populate Europe have as yet heard nothing of Christianity...Christian civilization has proved hollow to a terrifying degree: it is all veneer, but the inner man has remained untouched and therefore unchanged... Inside reign the archaic gods, supreme as of old...[1]

—C.G. Jung

Introduction

"Why do you believe what you do?" It is a question we have all been asked and is a question which is often met with stuttering and half-answers. For those of us who adhere to the pre-Christian ways of our ancestors, it becomes even more difficult to provide rational explanations for *why* we follow this religion while we are at the same time attempting to impart *what* exactly Heathenry is. This is not, however, a question whose asking should first be done by an outsider, nor is the answer one to be intuited on the fly. This is a question that each and every one of us should, with deep forethought, examine and actively seek to reconcile within ourselves. This is exactly what I have been doing, more or less constantly, for the last six years since I began transitioning into a Heathen. This essay is meant to be an exploration of the philosophical schools and strains of thought that have come together, in my mind at least, to provide a rational, self-consistent reasoning for the adoption and practice of Heathenry. This is not meant to speak for any other person, or any organization that I belong to; these are my thoughts and my thoughts alone. They are not *necessarily* a reflection of the greater Heathen community, although I do hope that they can be of use to others. Lastly, this essay is not, I hope, a final resting place. Like all things, systems of thought are *in process* (as Whitehead[2] would say), and are ever changing and evolving.

---

[1] C.G. Jung. *Psychology and Alchemy.* trans. R.F.C. Hull. (New York: Bollingen Foundation, 1993), 12.

[2] Alfred North Whitehead (1861-1947) was a mathematician and philosopher whose views revolved not around enduring, substantial entities, but around what he termed *actual occasions* which are in the process of becoming. Of understanding, he said that it "is never a completed static state of mind. It always bears the character of a process of penetration, incomplete and partial," (*Modes of Thought*. [New York: The Free Press Company, 1968], 43).

While I am currently satisfied with the arguments this essay provides, I sincerely hope that the ideas contained herein can, in the future, be further refined, grown, and transformed into something that is more true and effective.

Now, before we get into a discussion about the motivations one might have for embracing Heathenry, let us define our terms. The word Heathen is the contemporary form of the Old English *hæðen* and cognate to the Old Norse *heiðinn*; both words stem from a Proto-Germanic word close to the Gothic *haiþno*, meaning "one who lives in the country or on the heaths and in the woods."[3] Throughout the essay, Heathenry is the term I will be using to refer to the pre-Christian tribal religions of Northern and Western Europe. There are plenty of other terms[4] used today to describe what is basically the same set of beliefs, but terminological quibbles have no real place here. It is worth noting, however, that our ancestors did not really have a specific term to describe their religion, or religion *per se*. Prior to the Medieval conversions, what we now single out as religion was not thought of as a separate entity, but as a limb of an *integral* culture which encompassed not only "religion," but also the ancestry, land and language of the tribe.[5] So, for our ancestors, religion was less about what one *believed* and more about who one *was*.[6] This distinction, or lack thereof, was lost with the faith-based focus of Christianity, but is slowly being recovered by contemporary Heathens.

To dig a little deeper into what Heathenry is, without going overboard, we can break it out into a three-fold definition. These are not in any particular order of precedence, and different Heathens will emphasize different aspects in their personal practice. Expanding on our preliminary definition of Heathenry as a tribal religion, most contemporary practitioners agree that it is an ethnic faith and that the practice of it is tied to our ancestry, both in that the religion is a modern revival of that of our ancestors and in that the veneration of those same ancestors

---

3 Heathen. Dictionary.com. *Webster's Revised Unabridged Dictionary*. MICRA, Inc. http://dictionary.reference.com/browse/heathen (accessed: June 23, 2009).

4 Aside from Heathenry, the most common terms are *Ásatrú* (a recently constructed Old Norse term literally meaning "holding troth with the Æsir"), Odinism (almost exclusively used by members of the Odinic Rite), *Forn Siðr* (an Old Norse term, meaning "old custom") and Theodism (derived from the Anglo-Saxon term *þeod*, meaning "people" or "tribe").

5 Stephen Flowers. "The Idea of Integral Culture: A Model for a Revolt Against the Modern World." *TYR: Myth—Culture—Tradition* 1 (2002): 12.

6 Stephen A. McNallen. *The Philosophy of Metagenetics, Folkism and Beyond*. (Nevada City: Asatru Folk Assembly, 2006), 14.

is a fundamental practice within it.[7] On the other side of the *Blut und Boden*[8] equation, we look to Nature for the second component of Heathenry. Traditionally, this took two forms, as veneration of natural entities and of phenomena such as the Sun, Moon, Dawn, etc., and of the spirits of the land (*landvættir*). Many of the traditions and holidays connected to these continued well after the Christian conversion and are still in practice today, albeit under a Christian facade as with Easter.[9] Lastly, we come to the most well known facet of Heathenry, the Æsir and the Vanir; deities such as Óðinn (Odin) and Þórr (Thor) who, largely thanks to Richard Wagner and Marvel Comics, are at least somewhat known to most Westerners. It was, and is, the sacrifices to these deities that comprised the bulk of the high holy days of our ancestors.

Materialism

Now that we have a simple, working definition of what Heathenry is, we can dig into why anyone would practice such a thing. Let us begin by confronting the first of two guardians that attempt to block our path: the specter of materialism. It is my opinion that the explanation of *what* the universe is is best provided by the physical sciences, and thus it is not at all my intent to provide justifications for Heathenry that fly in the face of what is known about the world around us. Religion tells us less about what the world is and more about how we should experience and interact with it. Just so we are clear on what is meant by materialism, we will use Hugh Elliot's[10] three point definition. First, materialism posits the uniformity of natural law, meaning that there is one overarching system of physical laws that all phenomena are governed by. There are not natural laws and separate supernatural laws that govern qualitatively different types of occurrences. Second, materialism involves denying that teleology[11] exists on a cosmic scale. Thus, the universe is not developing under the guidance of some deity. It does not exist for any reason or purpose. It simply is. Ideas of meaning are human constructs that are quite useful in imbuing that sense of purpose into our own lives, but are foreign to the cosmos at large. Third, materialism is

---

7 Ibid, 1-4.
8 A German phrase meaning "blood and soil." It signifies a concept of identity based on both ancestry and homeland.
9 H.R. Ellis Davidson. *Myths and Symbols in Pagan Europe: Early Scandinavian and Celtic Religions.* (Syracuse: Syracuse University Press, 1988), 102.
10 Hugh Elliot. *Modern Science and Materialism.* (London: Longmans, Green and Co., 1919), 138-141.
11 Teleology, from the Greek *telos* (goal), is "the philosophical doctrine that all of nature…[is] goal-directed and fundamentally organized," (Robert Audi, ed. *The Cambridge Dictionary of Philosophy.* 2nd ed. [New York: Cambridge University Press, 2006], 905-906).

monistic. There is but one substance in the universe and that substance is matter. Some would point to the dyadic nature of matter and energy as evidence that the Cartesian[12] split between the body and the spirit still has some credence, but as general relativity unequivocally has shown: mass and energy are but two sides of the same coin.[13] They are both states of matter, just as water and ice are two states of the same substance. So, in summary, materialism presents us with a picture of a universe whose homogeneous elementary substance is governed by a law of similar uniformity, with the whole system being devoid of intrinsic teleology.

There is an immediate and almost visceral reaction to this type of stark materialism. The yawning gap between it and what is generally thought of as religion is indeed vast and can appear insurmountable. It is as if by making this pronouncement, that science is telling us that the religions of the past are naught but silly stories created by superstitious primitives to explain a world that they were incapable of understanding. But is this *necessarily* so? There are three types of generalized responses to the materialist revelation: fundamentalism, atheism and reconciliation.

Religious fundamentalism is an all too common phenomenon throughout the world. There are churches and mosques without number whose intent is "to renounce science, to maintain that it is false, and to insist that the religious teachings are literally true."[14] The consequences of this kind of willful ignorance hardly need any exposition. The centuries of persecution that European scientists faced from the Catholic Church are all but legendary; and yet, the blatant denial of basic scientific facts persists. It is not my place here to launch into a complete critique of fundamentalism. I think it is enough to note that it is a "completely unphilosophical way of responding" to materialism and that it will in no way serve the Heathen revival.[15] Thankfully, those who espouse a fundamentalist interpretation of our ancestors' cosmologies are rare, and most Heathens with whom I have met have a positive perspective towards science and do not feel threatened by its advances in the way that adherents of the Abrahamic[16] faiths tend to be.

---

12 René Descartes (1596-1650) was a French philosopher and mathematician known for espousing a type of qualitative dualism between the mind and body (Audi, 223-227).
13 Per Einstein's $E=mc^2$ equation (Albert Einstein. *Relativity: The Special and the General Theory.* [New York: Three Rivers Press, 1961], 54).
14 Yeager Hudson. *The Philosophy of Religion.* (Mountain View: Mayfield Publishing Co., 1990), 149.
15 Ibid., 148.
16 The Abrahamic religions are those who treat Abraham as a patriarch: Judaism, Christianity and Islam.

On the polar opposite end of things, let us turn our attention to atheism, which can be seen as both a reaction against fundamentalism and as a logical expression of materialism. Atheism as simply the lack of belief in God (as it is defined by most theists) is certainly a conclusion that can be drawn from the data of contemporary science. Our current cosmogonic and anthropogenic theories do not include a creator deity because the evidence before us does not support that as a theory. Those who purport the so-called Intelligent Design theory are, by and large, members of the same fundamentalist groups discussed above. Their motivations for interpreting the data in the way they do are unscientific and skewed by their *a priori*[17] belief in the truth of their religion.[18] However, objections to theism are almost always made in specific response to the conceptions of monotheistic deities. The nature of monotheism, and the type of universalism that it breeds, demands a very specific definition of God. Since Heathenry is bound by none of this, it allows us to explore avenues of thought that are outside the purview of materialism's limitations.

As I said before, it is not my intent to provide any justification that *contradicts* accepted scientific theory, but what we are free to do is find theologies that *supplement* it to provide a reconciliation. What sparked this differentiation was, oddly enough, not a school of theology, but of fiction. In the so-called "weird fiction" of H.P. Lovecraft and his circle, entities that in other types of fiction might be termed "supernatural," were depicted not as existing or operating in contradiction with the *known* laws of physics, but rather *in addition* to them.[19] They presuppose that there are heretofore undiscovered vistas of reality, governed by similarly unknown laws—laws that encompass both those we know and those yet to be discovered. While this type of thought is obviously unscientific in and of itself, it can, nonetheless, be of use to us in an attempt to set the parameters of our religious thought. Now, what I mean by this is not that we, for example, set about and decide *once and for all* that the Gods are any one thing. What I am suggesting is that this provides us the opportunity to develop a plurality of *possible* explanations which we are then free to examine, adopt and disregard as we see fit. These models may or may not be ultimately true, but they are, for our purposes of justifying Heathenry, useful fictions.

---

17 An *a priori* belief is one whose justification "does not depend at all on sensory or introspective or other sorts of *experience*" (Audi, 35-36).
18 David Mu. "Trojan Horse or Legitimate Science: Deconstructing the Debate Over Intelligent Design." *Harvard Science Review* 19, no. 1 (Fall 2005): 23
19 S.T. Joshi. *H.P. Lovecraft: The Decline of the West.* (Gillette: Wildside Press, 1990), 54.

Traditionalism

We will get along to expanding on the concepts of fictions and fictionalism in depth in just a bit, but there is presently a question that must be addressed before we proceed any further: why are we going through all of these philosophical contortions to justify Heathenry at all? Is it not better to just adopt atheism and be done with religion all together? Suppose for a moment that we assent to this suggestion; let us see where that takes us. Imagine a universe that is too old and too big to fully conceive of; a universe governed by the cold, uncompromising laws of nature; a universe in which man is nothing more than a biochemical accident. In this universe we are alone, completely and utterly. We are born, we live our meaningless lives and we die. The universe neither notices nor cares that we exist at all. We are naught but a temporary phenomena on a tiny planet, circling a tiny star within a cosmos that is all but without end—a fleeting speck of life in an otherwise dead expanse. In such a world, there is no hope. Not only will each and every human die, but our sun too will die. Our world, our civilizations, our achievements will be dust on a cold rock "in the midst of black seas of infinity."[20] Our world will pass, unmourned, unloved, and unremembered; for there is no God looking down on us to care. It is a picture that is as bleak as can be imagined; a vision so desolate that it is unlivable. It is from this understanding of the universe's and of man's nature and fate that nihilism is born. Through this train of thought the spirit of man is driven as low as it can possibly go, but

> what has happened, at [the] bottom? The feeling of valuelessness was reached with the realization that the overall character of existence may not be interpreted by means of the concept of "aim," the concept of "unity," or the concept of "truth." Existence has no goal or end; any comprehensive unity in the plurality of events is lacking: the character of existence is not "true," [it] is *false*. One simply lacks any reason for convincing oneself that there is a *true* world.[21]

This is not a livable paradigm, regardless of its truth or falsehood. Few would ever be content to live their lives with this misery constantly hanging over their heads. Thankfully, even Nietzsche recognized that "nihilism represents a... transitional stage" in our development.[22] It need not be our final philosophical

---

20 H.P. Lovecraft. "The Call of Cthulhu." *Tales of the Cthulhu Mythos*. (Sauk City: Arkham House Publishers, Inc., 1990), 3.
21 Friedrich Nietzsche. *The Will to Power*. Trans. Walter Kaufman and R.J. Hollingdale, ed. Kaufman (New York: Vintage Books, 1968), 13.
22 Ibid., 14.

resting place. But, given the truth of materialism, as we outlined previously, and the lack of any "true" divine commandments with which to order ourselves, how can we possibly go about justifying one type of behavior over another, particularly a behavioral pattern as outlandish as Heathenry? How can morality, truth, honor or any of our most cherished ideals be defended against the kind of Epicurean[23] hedonism that *seems* to stem naturally from nihilism?

> In a cosmos without absolute values we have to rely on the relative values affecting our daily sense of comfort, pleasure, and emotional satisfaction. What gives us relative painlessness and contentment we may arbitrarily call "good," and vice versa. This local nomenclature is necessary to give us that benign illusion of placement, direction, and stable background on which the still more important illusion of "worthwhileness," dramatic significance in events, and interest in life depend. Now what gives one person or race or age painlessness and contentment often disagrees sharply on the psychological side from what gives these same boons to another person or race or age. Therefore "good" is a relative and variable quality, depending on ancestry, chronology, geography, nationality, and individual temperament. Amidst this variability there is *only one anchor of fixity* which we can seize upon as the working pseudo-standard of "values" which we need in order to feel settled and contented—and that anchor is *tradition*, the potent emotional legacy bequeathed to us by the massed experience of our ancestors, individual or national, biological or cultural. Tradition means nothing cosmically, but it means everything locally and pragmatically because we have nothing else to shield us from a devastating sense of "lostness" in endless time and space.[24]

The monolithic "truth" that we so desperately need, that our basic psychological makeup seems to crave may not exist on its own, as a natural, universal entity, but it is within this wellspring of tradition that we discover a plurality of *truths*. These truths may not apply to the universe at large, or even to humanity as a whole, but within the ethno-cultural matrix that they were born, they are potent. It is within a specific tradition that we are able to establish language, ethics, art, a mythos—all of the things that define us as distinct peoples. It is these facets of

---

23 The Epicureans were a group of Greek philosophers during the 3rd and 4th centuries BC whose ethics were purely hedonistic. For the Epicurean, "pleasure is our innate goal, to which all other values, including virtue are subordinated," (Audi, 269-271).
24 H.P. Lovecraft. *Selected Letters*. Vol. 2 (Sauk City: Arkham House Publishers, Inc., 1965), 356-357.

our traditions that bring meaning into our lives and permit the continuity of beliefs and behaviors that result in cultures and civilizations. They are the lens through which we view and interpret the world around us and project our values upon it. They are the raft that we must cling to as we sail through the vast oceans of meaninglessness; they are the rocks, the foundations upon which humanity is built. They are at once our ancestry, our progeny and our legacy. We define them by our very being, just as we ourselves are defined by them. It is through tradition, and only tradition, that we are what we are. Our traditions strike to the very core of our being in innumerable ways. They are our spirit—our soul—our fate.

Christianity

Having faced the specter of materialism and vanquished it into the night with the sword of tradition, let us turn to meet the next challenger who attempts to block our path: Christianity. Why must we face down Christianity here? Has this beast not been slain before, countless times even? We must, for we have raised this ghost ourselves by invoking traditionalism as a reason for Heathenry's adoption. Traditionalist defenses of Christianity, particularly of Catholicism[25] and Restorationism,[26] are legion in certain parts of the world—most notably in the Hispanosphere and the American South. Were it not for the critiques of the gentlemen we shall be discussing presently, the Christian Traditionalists would have a good argument. After all, what religion were your parents? How about your grandparents? Their parents? If you are of European descent, chances are your ancestors have been Christians for most of the last millennium. That being the case, what cause have we to deny a thousand years of Christian traditions? Is the case for Heathenry so strong that it can overpower *the Cross*?

One of the most common arguments within the Heathen community against the appropriateness of Christianity is that it is an alien faith which is fundamentally incompatible with Europeans.[27] The distinction between Christianity as an essentially Middle Eastern religion and Heathenry as natively European allows us to view 'European Christianity' as a divergent evolutionary path followed by our ancestors. A path that, for centuries, obscured and impeded the *authentic* traditions of our peoples. This would make Heathenry a type of resurgent

---

25 Avery Cardinal Dulles. *A History of Apologetics.* (San Francisco: Ignatius Press, 2005), 232.
26 Robert T. Handy. "Biblical Primitivism in the American Baptist Tradition." *The American Quest for the Primitive Church.* (Chicago: University of Illinois Press, 1988), 143.
27 McNallen, *Metagenetics*, 19-20.

atavism;[28] a hearkening back to an earlier aspect of our development in an attempt to correct our spiritual course, to allow our indigenous spiritual traditions to develop, unmolested, as they could have, had it not been for the Christian conversion. In this way, the tradition with which we ground ourselves is not based upon the myths and histories of a people not our own, the Hebrews, but on the ways of our own ancestors. This brings to our traditionalist argument a continuity and history that far predates Christianity's, and prevents us from having to justify the adoption or the continued practice of foreign traditions.

The primary adjective used to describe contemporary Heathenry is 'folkish.' This is an anglicization of the German term *völkisch*, a word intrinsically linked to the Germanic revival and Ariosophy of the late 1800s.[29] There is still much debate amongst modern Heathens[30] over both the meaning of the word and the place of this concept, but the views expressed here are clearly in the folkish vein of thought. Many authors will explain the folkish nature of Heathenry as we did above, in terms of ancestry, positing that Heathenry is only the *appropriate* religion for those within its ancestral continuum. I would like to expand on that and offer a tripartite definition that approaches a more holistic and organic perspective. It is my belief that Heathenry stems not only from our ancestry but that it is also a product of the *lands* in which our people originated and of the *languages* that developed during our ethnogenesis.

Landscape

Let us look to the Earth, to the landscapes that forged both our ancestors and the Hebrews, so that we may see the connection between the geographical features within which these peoples were born and the religions that they themselves birthed.

> A race has roots. Race and landscape belong together. Where a plant takes root, there it dies also. There is a certain sense in which we can, without absurdity, work backwards from a race to its "home," but it is much more important to realize that the race adheres permanently to this home with some of its most essential

---

[28] A resurgent atavism is, in biology, the reverting back to a more archaic, ancestral type. An atavistic trait is an evolutionary throwback.

[29] David Freis. *Völkische Religiostät und Antimodernismus in Deutschland (1871-1919)*. (Germany: Druck und Bindung, 2006), 25-28.

[30] For a mostly fair overview of the current state of the debate, see: Kveldúlf Gundarsson, ed. *Our Troth*. vol. 2 (North Charleston: BookSurge Publishing, 2007), 25-60.

characters of body and soul.[31]

Christianity, like its siblings Judaism and Islam, is a desert religion, and has an unshakable connection to the people of the desert. As Ernest Renan so famously wrote in his oft quoted *General History and Comparative System of Semitic Languages*, "nature holds little place in the Semitic religions; the desert is monotheist...There are monotheist races just as there are polytheist races, and this difference stems from an original diversity in the way they envision nature."[32] What Renan is saying here is that the monotheism that is so very particular to the Middle Eastern people, is a byproduct of their inhabitation of the desert—that landscape has such a powerful impact on the collective psyche of a people that, in the case of the Semites, it was able to transform their religiosity from the polytheistic animism of Paleolithic man into the monotheism that emerged alongside the Hebrews.

Similarly, Spengler proposed that it was the dome-like skyline of the vast and empty desert that developed in the Semites a cosmology and religio-cultural feeling of a *world cavern*.[33] It was this *cavern-feeling* that led to the creation of the domed heavens depicted in Genesis.[34] While this might, at first, seem like a trifle, Spengler argues that many of the peculiarities of Middle Eastern religious philosophy are a direct result of the cavern-feeling, which, itself, is born from the desert topography:

> In the World-Cavern persistent and unresolved struggles become that "Semitic" primary-dualism which, ever the same under its thousand forms, fills the Magian[35] world. The light shines through the cavern and battles against the darkness (John 1:5).[36] Both are Magian substances. Above and below, heaven and earth become powers that have entity and contend with one another. But these polarities in the most primary sensations mingle with those of the refined and critical understanding, like good and evil, God and Satan. Death, for the author of the John Gospel as

---

31 Oswald Spengler. *The Decline of the West.* eds. Helmut Werner and Arthur Helps, trans. Charles Francis Atkinson (New York: Vintage Books, 1990), 254.
32 This passage and several others are quoted by Alain de Benoist (*On Being a Pagan.* trans. Jon Graham, ed. Greg Johnson [Atlanta: Ultra, 2004], 150).
33 Spengler, 111.
34 Genesis 1:6-8 (KJV), "And God said, Let there be a firmament...and God called the firmament Heaven."
35 Spengler's term for the Middle Eastern spirit.
36 John 1:5 (KJV), "And the light shineth in the darkness; and the darkness comprehended it not."

Why I am a Heathen

for the strict Moslem, is not the end of life, but a Something, a death-force, that contends with a life-force for the possession of man.[37]

It is a direct result of this cavern-feeling that dualism plays so large a role in Zoroastrianism, Judaism, Islam and Christianity. And it is that very dualism that, from Plato to Descartes, has plagued Western philosophy and theology with innumerable problems—problems that we need not have faced had it not been for the imposition of this alien world-feeling. It is because of this primal seed of dualism that was cast into our collective unconscious that we, for so long, struggled with the illusory "problem" of reconciling the two "fundamentally different" substances of matter and spirit. This dualism was the cause of our consistently failed attempts at defining "good" and "evil," and basing universally applicable systems of morality upon these definitions. This dualism is what led to the identification of the body and woman as "evil" and of the spirit and man as "good." For nearly a millennium, we have intellectually and spiritually suffered from the needless vexations that the seed of dualism sprouted within our souls.[38]

Enough of the desert; what of Europa and its primal forests? What effect did this habitat have upon the burgeoning psyches of the Indo-European tribes of the vast oak woods, as they slowly developed into the Celts and Teutons of historical times? The forest, its shape, depth and darkness was one of the greatest influences on the development of the Heathenry of old. The tree is one of the most basic and elementary symbols of our mythology. It is from driftwood, ocean borne husks of trees, that Óðinn, Hœnir and Lóðurr are, in the *Völuspá*, depicted as creating man.[39] It was in the mighty oaks of Germania that our ancestors first found shapes for their Gods. The identification of deities with trees was one that continued into the time of Charlemagne with both the Irminsûl

---

37 Spengler, 299.
38 de Benoist, 22-30.
39 *Völuspá* stanzas 17-18 (All Eddic references, including the *Hávamál* and *Sigrdrífumál*, in this paper are from Lee M. Hollander, *The Poetic Edda*. [Austin: University of Texas Press, 2004]):

> To the coast then came, kind and mighty,
> from the gathered gods three great Æsir;
> on the land they found, of little strength,
> Ask and Embla, unfated yet.

> Sense they possessed not, soul they had not,
> being nor bearing, nor blooming hue;
> soul gave Óthin, sense gave Hœnir,
> being , Lóthur, and blooming hue.

Illustration 1: The nave and exterior of the Cathédrale Saint-Étienne de Bourges.

Illustration 2: Compare the shape of the forest with that of the cathedral.

Why I am a Heathen

and Donar's Oak of the Saxons.[40] For untold centuries, it was the tree that was the living, breathing body of the Holy; the vessel through which the Gods lived and made their presence known.[41] Cosmologically, it is the tree itself that was the center of the universe, the *axis mundi* which connects the whole multiverse of worlds that comprise the Northern cosmos.[42] Among both the Celts and the Teutons, "in Central and Northern Europe dark groves composed of ancient trees, and situated in the midst of gloomy forests, were...the only temples, but these had been rendered holy by the awe and reverence with which they had inspired in each succeeding generation."[43] It was the sacred grove that was the center of nearly all cultic practice within the Northern world.[44] In a blinding myriad of ways, the forest provides us with a wellspring of information relating to the foundations of the mythos of our ancestors.

Out of the forest, there arises, apart from the specific details above, "such a primary feeling...of the Divine immanent in the world-around."[45] Unlike the dualistic theology of the desert dwellers, with a God above and Devil below, the European cosmos is inhabited by a multitude of divine entities; it is a world teeming with Gods. This fundamental difference in the root of the religious impulse and conception of the divine can be most clearly seen by examining the disparities between the *native* religious architecture of the two peoples. The cavern-feeling of the desert soul is clearly represented in the "basilicas of Christianity, Hellenistic, Hebrew and Baal cults, and in the Mithraeum, the Mazdaist fire-temple and the Mosque."[46] It is "the definite roof that is emphasized" in the domes of these structures that mirrors the cosmology presented in their myths.[47] This is in stark opposition to the Gothic Cathedrals of the Celto-Germanic world—vast buildings whose "wooden beams...locked

---

40 Jacob Grimm. *Teutonic Mythology* vol. I, trans. James Steven Stallybrass. (London: George Bell and Sons, 1882), 115.
41 Swain Wodening. "Wóden Worhte Wéos: Idols in Germanic Heathenry." *The Runestone Journal* 1 (2007): 133-140.
42 *Völuspá* stanza 2:
    I call to mind the kin of etins
    which long ago did give me life.
    Nine worlds I know, the nine abodes
    of the glorious world-tree the ground beneath.
43 Alexander Porteous. *The Forest in Folklore and Mythology.* (Mineola: Dover Publications Inc., 2002), 48.
44 Names ending in *-leah* or 'woodland glade' form the greater part of English Heathen toponymy, where Tuesley, Wensley, Thursley bear witness to the intimate link between the landscape and divine worship.
45 Spengler, 200.
46 Ibid., 111.
47 Ibid., 112.

themselves into rib-vaulting" to form an interior that was able to "fulfill the idea of infinite space."[48]

> The word "God" has a different sound under the vaulting of Gothic Cathedrals...The character of the Faustian[49] cathedral is that of the *forest*. It is the architectural actualizing of a world-feeling that had found the first of all its symbols in the high forest of the Northern plains, the deciduous forest with its mysterious tracery, its whispering of ever-restless foliage high over the watcher's head, its treetops struggling to escape from earth.[50]

It is through the form of the Cathedral that, once forced from the grove, the Heathen soul wrapped in a Christian facade was able to express its arboreal nature. The limitless scope of the forest allowed European man to "lift his eyes to the worlds of space and consider his relation to infinity."[51] The forest and what it means to our psyche is an inescapable necessity of Heathenry. The sacred groves of old Europa, representations of them, and their character have always been and will always be linked to the mythos and practice of Heathenry. It is this connection between the soil and spirit of Europe that makes Heathenry an infinitely more fitting mode of religious expression than Christianity. The faith itself is a natural expression of the European landscape. The forests can be dressed in Christian clothing, but their roots will ever remain Heathen.

Language

Having tackled the issue of how landscape affects the development of religion, let us move to language and discuss how the speech of our ancestors shaped their faith. Theories relating to the connection between mythologies and language families have been put forth ever since linguists discovered the genealogical manner in which languages develop.[52] Max Müller, the seminal scholar of Indo-European linguistics went so far as to say that "there is nothing more ancient in the world than language. The history of man begins, not with rude flints, rock temples or pyramids, but with language."[53] This view was later developed by the proponents of linguistic relativism, who theorize that the disparate structures of

---

48 Ibid., 113.
49 Spengler's term for the Western European spirit.
50 Ibid., 199.
51 H.P. Lovecraft. *Selected Letters.* vol. 1 (Sauk City: Arkham House Publishers, Inc., 1965), 106.
52 Max F. Müller. *Contributions to the Science of Mythology.* Vol. 1 (London: Longmans, Green and Co., 1897), 178.
53 Ibid., v.

the world's languages affect the way in which the speaker *is able* to think about things.[54] They purport that language provides our minds with a filter through which all of our sensory data is analyzed. The most famous formulation of this concept was in the hypothesis of Edward Sapir and Benjamin Whorf, who claimed that "language embodies *an interpretation* of reality" and that it "involves a particular interpretation, not a universal one."[55] Thus, the vision of reality, the *Weltanschauung*, which a particular people is *capable* of having is, partially at least, *determined* by their native language.

This theory accounts for many of the differences, particularly those relating to the overall structures, between the religions that sprang from the speakers of Semitic and Indo-European language families. In particular, it appears that specific features of the Hebrew language itself have a tendency to unify similar ideas under collective terms.[56] It is this unifying linguistic feature that was partly responsible for the transformations from polytheism to henotheism[57] and finally to monotheism that Hebrew religion underwent. We see that

> the original bond between the linguistic and mythico-religious consciousness is primarily expressed in the fact that all verbal structures appear *also* as mythical entities, endowed with certain mythical powers, that the Word, in fact, becomes a sort of primary force, in which all being and doing originate.[58]

A prime example of this manifests itself when we examine solar deities. Although they sprang from the same Proto-Indo-European (PIE) mythological source, the sun Gods of the Germanics and Latins are gendered differently, with Germanic Sól being female and the Latin Sol being male. It is without doubt that these were at one point, prior to the Proto-Germanic and Proto-Italic split, one and the same God.[59] However, with the division, for whatever reason, the gendering of certain nouns shifted, thus causing a change in the gendering of certain deities. The exact same situation occurred with the Germanic Lunar God Máni, whose Latin equivalent, Luna, is female. Like the solar gods, these two derive from a common source, but, due to linguistic differences, ended up gendered differently. Examples like these abound throughout the mythologies of

---

54 John A. Lucy. "Linguistic Relativity." *Annual Review of Anthropology* 26 (1997): 292.
55 Ibid., 293-295.
56 de Benoist, 96.
57 Henotheism is, according to the *Random House Dictionary*, "the worship of a particular god, as by a family or tribe, without disbelieving in the existence of others."
58 Ernst Cassirer. *Language and Myth*. (Mineola: Dover Publications Inc., 1953), 45.
59 J.P. Mallory. *In Search of the Indo-Europeans*. (Germany: Thames and Hudson, 1992), 129.

the world and show, without question, just how powerful an influence language can be on a pantheon.

The particular mythology of a people can thus be viewed as a reinterpretation of the world and of the numinous experience of it *as it is translated* by the agency of language. As the father of the Germanic Revival, Guido von List, said in *The Religion of the Aryo-Germanic Folk*:

> If then, in the beginning was the word (*language*) in which the feelings and knowledge of the human soul were expressed, then this language must have been so deeply bound to what is generally termed "religion"…that a division was, and is, impossible.[60]

The connection between the language and mythos of a tribe is so deep and fundamental that it is difficult to even talk about one without heavily involving the other. Just as Semitic mythology is tied to the Semitic languages, so are the myths of the Indo-Europeans tied to their tongues. An intimate understanding of the myths of a people is not possible without a correspondingly intimate understanding of their language. Therefore, we, as both speakers of a Germanic language and inheritors of the linguistic legacy of the same, will naturally understand the fundamentals of the Germanic cosmos with greater ease than we will the Semitic. It is hardwired into our minds through a lifetime of speaking English. Through this seemingly simple act of learning and speaking the language descended from that of our forefathers we are imprinted with the skeleton of their religion. It is something that we have been taught from birth through the instrumentality of language itself—the Runes are etched upon our very souls.

Pragmatism and Fictionalism

Before we continue, let us recap our journey together up to this point. We set out to provide a reason for the adoption of Heathenry. In doing so we were immediately beset by materialism, which was countered by traditionalism. Traditionalism then raised Christianity as a challenger, but this was met with an examination of the geographic and linguistic origins of Heathenry, thus showing its intrinsic connection to the ethnogenesis of its creators. This being done, we must answer the all too obvious question of *why*, out of all the discarded traditions of our ancestors, is Heathenry something that we should revive. After

---

[60] Guido von List. *The Religion of the Aryo-Germanic Folk: Esoteric and Exoteric.* trans. Stephen Flowers (Smithville: Rûna-Raven Press, 2005), 1.

all, there are a great many specific practices and beliefs our ancestors held that few, if any, would argue are viable today. What is it about their religion that is particularly worthy of resurrection? I would argue that the *utility* of Heathenry is so great that the difficulties presented both in rekindling and justifying it are, without doubt, warranted.

In putting forth a utilitarian defense of Heathenry, we must evoke both the schools of pragmatism and fictionalism to aid us. Both of these were hinted at earlier and are fundamentally tied to the traditionalist response. The view that religion need not be defined by or adhere to the same type of absolutist epistemology[61] as do the physical sciences was touted by William James around the turn of the century. In his address, "The Will to Believe," James states that

> since we are all absolutists by instinct, what...ought we do about that fact? Shall we espouse and endorse it? Or shall we treat it as a weakness of our nature from which we must free ourselves, if we can? I sincerely believe that the latter course is the only one we can follow as reflective men. Objective evidence and certitude are doubtless very fine ideals to play with, but where on this moonlit and dream-visited planet are they found?[62]

What James is arguing here is that the absolutism of the physical sciences, the belief that *truth* is universal and monolithic, may be acceptable for the particulars of physics and chemistry, but that this outlook does not translate into a livable paradigm for mankind. By viewing religion as something which is *possibly* true absolutely, but is *definitely* of pragmatic value, we free ourselves from constantly having to battle with scientists over *the truth*. It allows us to treat scientific truths as existing in a *qualitatively* different manner than do religious truths. However, to be able to capitalize upon the utility of religious beliefs, James stresses, we must ensure that they are not so patently absurd as to defy our sensibilities.[63] This is where Lovecraft's doctrine of *supplements* over *contradictions* comes into play.[64] Since we are, in essence, making a conscious choice to believe in and to practice Heathenry, we must do what we can to ensure that the beliefs we are adopting do not run counter to things that we "know" to be true, for that will do nothing but make our adoption of that belief all the more difficult. Thus, it is in theological models that *supplement* the known laws of physics that we will find

---

61 "Epistemology (from the Greek *episteme*, 'knowledge,' and *logos*, 'explanation'), the study of the nature of knowledge and justifications," (Audi, 272-273).
62 William James. "The Will to Believe." *Pragmatism and Other Writings*. ed. Giles Gunn (New York: Penguin Books, 2000), 207.
63 Ibid., 217.
64 Joshi, 54.

the greatest solace; for it is these beliefs that will most easily be adopted without us having to commit the folly of denying science.

It is important here to note that we ought not, in proposing theological models in this manner, succumb to making an *argumentum ad ignorantiam*[65] by allowing our definitions of the divine to fall into the "God of the gaps"[66] pattern. Rather, we should heed Whitehead's enjoinments spread throughout *Modes of Thought* that philosophy's place is not to fill in *current* gaps in scientific knowledge that are likely to be addressed in the future, but to ask meta-scientific questions that the scientific apparatus is simply not capable of handling.[67] Thus, while it would be unwise to theorize, as some have, that the Gods are made of dark matter,[68] or that they exist in the fourth dimension[69]—it would certainly be in keeping with the spirit of philosophical inquiry to propose, as Whitehead does, that notions of panentheism[70] can be used to reconcile issues revolving around the seeming contradiction of divine immanence and transcendence.

To flesh out this doctrine of epistemological pluralism, of multiple types of categorically different truths, we will explore the fictionalism of Hans Vaihinger. Since it is such a recondite and, in ways, counterintuitive take on truth, let us hear Vaihinger define fictionalism in his own terms first:

> Fictionalism is [the premise that]...an idea whose theoretical untruth or incorrectness, and therewith its falsity, is admitted, is

---

65 The *argumentum ad ignorantiam* (argument from ignorance) is an informal logical fallacy often used to imply that simply because proposition *A* has not been disproved, that it is true (Audi, 434).
66 The "God of the gaps" refers to the method of defining God by means of currently unexplained natural phenomena.
67 Whitehead, 22.
68 The view that divine beings and realms are composed of dark matter, "a hypothetical form of matter invisible to electromagnetic radiation [but] postulated to account for gravitational forces observed in the universe," (dark matter. Dictionary.com *Dictionary.com Unabridged.* Random House, Inc. http://dictionary.reference.com/browse/dark matter [accessed: March 12, 2010]) was notably espoused by the founder of the International Society for Krishna Consciousness, A.C. Bhaktivedanta Swami Prabhupada in his *Easy Journeys to Other Planets* (Australia: Bhaktivedanta Book Trust, 1972).
69 P.D. Ouspensky in *Tertium Organum* (New York: Random House, 1970) posited that supernatural phenomena are the results of the actions of fourth dimensional entities upon those of three dimensions.
70 Panentheism, the position that "although nature and human consciousness are part of God or Absolute Being, the Absolute is neither exhausted in nor identical with them" (Audi, 476).

not for that reason practically valueless and useless; for such an idea, in spite of its theoretical nullity may have great practical importance.[71]

The reason that we must run our pragmatism through this fictionalist framework is that, no matter how plausible our theology might be, in the absence of a concrete religious experience, a veritable hierophany, we are, at the end of the day, working with a fictional schema. Granted, it is a fiction that has great utility, has a deeply entrenched history within our race, and is tied to the land we originated from and the language we speak; however, it is a fiction nonetheless. Now, before you give up at the notion that you should believe something that is "merely" fictional, let us take a look at just how prominent various types of fictions are in human thought and why that is the case.

When we really look at logical systems and fictions, it becomes apparent that it is not only religion and philosophy, but also various branches of science and mathematics whose very foundations rest, at least in part, on specific fictions. Both "analytic geometry and…infinitesimal calculus…[are] striking examples of methodic fictions."[72] Taxonomic and classificatory systems, as found in biology, are, as recognized by Lamarck himself, also a type of fiction.[73] Yet another type of commonly employed fiction is found in "the schematic drawings employed in many sciences."[74] Further, we see that juristic fictions, which subsume "a single case under a conceptual construct," are the fundamental basis of nearly all legal systems.[75] I could go on, but Vaihinger's examples are quite exhaustive. The point to be made is that fictions provide the bases for a wide array of disparate logical systems—that even though those systems are commonly employed, their ideationally contrived bases tend to go unnoticed even by professionals—fictions are simply *that* ubiquitous and invisible.

Why is it that fictions are so prevalent, you might ask. Why must we constantly resort to fictive *a priori* propositions on which to base our systems of thought? The answer "is that these boundaries of knowledge are not implicit in the specific nature of man…but that such limitations are part of the nature of thought itself."[76] This is a position that was formulated by the string of philosophers that led Vaihinger to construct Fictionalism, but was later conclusively proven to be the case with the infamous incompleteness theorem of Kurt Gödel, who showed that

---

71 Hans Vaihinger. *The Philosophy of "As If."* (Abingdon: Routledge, 2009), viii.
72 Ibid., xxxv.
73 Ibid., 17-19.
74 Ibid., 24-27.
75 Ibid., 33-35.
76 Ibid., xliii.

even a strictly logical system such as arithmetic cannot *prove itself* to be consistent.[77] Thus "whatever objective reality may be, one thing can be stated with certainty—it does *not* consist of [purely] logical functions."[78] It is only through the addition of externally posited, often fictive, data that such a system can be built at all. So, this way when we talk about the fictional basis of the epistemological pluralism that is being used to justify Heathenry, it is not as if we are talking about a fiction that is of the same order as a fantasy novel. Religious fictions certainly have a base that is *more largely* fictional than some other systems, but the overall rationale is not so different at all.

The foundations having been laid, we are now able to discuss the ways in which Heathenry proves itself to be a particularly utile fiction. The spheres of influence in which the utility of Heathenry is most apparent are, in my opinion, the ethical, social, and psychological. Although the ramifications of the adoption of the Heathen world view do provide a holistic change—and do affect nearly every facet of our experience of the world and the way we interact with it—it is these three areas in which the differences are most pronounced.

Ethos

It is in the ethical realm that we see, in Heathenry, one of the most abrupt departures from both Christian and contemporary secular morals. Since the ethical foundations of the West have developed under the yoke of Christianity for the last millennium and a half, an inspection of the nucleus of Judeo-Christian ideals responsible for this peculiar development is necessary. The core principle that underlies the Christian ethic is absolutism. It is an absolutism both in the moral primacy of God and in the definitude of good and evil. The story of Adam and Eve most clearly illustrates this, for their "transgression [consisted]...of wishing to determine for themselves the criteria of good and evil...[but] only Yahweh possesses this right. It is given that he alone defines what is good and what is evil and constitutes them into absolutes."[79] While this type of divine command ethic has been fought on purely logical grounds ever since the 5th century BC when Socrates won his verbal duel against Euthyphro,[80] the absolutist core continued on in a more or less unbroken chain from Plato's doctrine of the Forms, to the theology of Augustine and Aquinas, all the way to the immutable deontology of Kant and Hegel.[81] As pervasive as this moral absolutism and

---

77 Roger Scruton. *Modern Philosophy*. (USA: Penguin Books, 1994), 395.
78 Vaihinger, 8.
79 de Benoist, 61.
80 Plato. "Euthyphro." *Ethics: History, Theory and Contemporary Issues*. (New York: Oxford University Press, 2002), 5.
81 For a full treatment of this progression and its effect on the development of Western

dualism is, it is not, however, a philosophical inevitability. Rather, it is, as we have shown before, both a natural outgrowth of the Middle Eastern dome cosmology—which itself was conceived of as a result of the desert topography—and a logical manifestation of certain peculiarities of Hebrew grammar.[82]

So, if we are to abandon the view that ethical guidelines are absolutely true, why should we have them at all? The clear answer is that they are of immense utilitarian value. Without ethical parameters, no group can function at all. It is only by having some sort of behavioral rules that societies and civilizations are at all possible. But why, if morals are of such great utility, would an ancient ethic be preferable to that which has guided the West since the Dark Ages? Are Heathen ethics *really* that much more utile? In the words of its most famous critic:

> Christianity has taken the side of everything weak, base, ill-constituted, it has made an ideal out of *opposition* to the preservative instincts of strong life; it has depraved the reason even of the intellectually strongest natures by teaching men to feel the supreme values of intellectuality as sinful, as misleading, as *temptations*...it has waged a *war to the death* against [the] *higher* type of man.[83]

The very foundation of the Christian myth found in *Genesis* begins by proclaiming that man's natural impulses and desires are evil and that we are all sinners, born with the spiritual taint of Adam and Eve's guilt.[84] The denying of all that is natural eventually led to a wholly negative view of the body, sex and material comforts; it produced a faith which put forth asceticism, abstinence and poverty as the highest values.[85] It has produced a pervasive sense of shame and guilt regarding those wants that are most essentially human. It is anti-life,[86] anti-body,[87] anti-sex,[88] etc. The whole of Christian ethics is phrased in entirely

---

thought, see Bertrand Russell's *The History of Western Philosophy*, (New York: Touchstone Books, 1972).
82 de Benoist, 61.
83 Friedrich Nietzsche. *Twilight of the Idols and The Anti-Christ.* trans. R.J. Hollingdale (London: Penguin Books, 1990), 129.
84 Genesis 3
85 de Benoist, 159.
86 Genesis 3
87 Exodus 20:26 (KJV), "neither shalt thou go up by steps unto my altar, that thy nakedness be not discovered thereon," and Isaiah 47:3 (KJV), "thy nakedness shall be uncovered, yea, thy shame shall be seen."
88 Mark 12:25 (KJV), "for when they shall rise from the dead, they neither marry, nor

negative terms—endless lists of what 'thou shalt not' do.[89] If Christian ethics could be summed up with a single word, that word would be 'no.'

This moral is not fit to serve the proud children of Europa; it is an ethic of slavery and submission. It is an ethic under whose heel we have lain for centuries, but that we need suffer no longer. We can look beyond the naysaying of the Semitic Slave-God and take off the shackles of sin. We can get off of our knees, standing proud and tall, basking in the glory of our humanity. We can do as our Heathen ancestors of old did, looking not for commandments from the Gods, but for their advice, their wisdom. What we deserve is an ethic based not on slavery, but on honor, on nobility—an ethic that fosters an aristocracy of the soul. The ethic of our ancestors was one that said 'yes' to life,[90] 'yes' to love[91] and 'yes' to liberty.[92] Our Gods are not celestial overlords who, like the Semitic God,[93] are meant to be feared. They are our elder kin, the spiritual progenitors of our people. We look to them not with abasement and servitude, but with the reverence and respect that one shows to a wizened grandparent. In Heathenry,

---

are given in marriage," and 1 Corinthians 7:5 (KJV), "defraud ye not one the other, except *it be* with consent for a time, that ye may give yourselves to fasting and prayer; and come together again, that Satan tempt you not for your inconsistency."

89 Exodus 20:2-17, Exodus 34:11-27, Deuteronomy 5:6-21.

90 *Hávamál* stanza 70:
> Better alive (than lifeless be):
> to the quick fall ay the cattle;
> the hearth fire burned for the happy heir—
> outdoors a dead man lay.

91 Ibid., stanza 8:
> Happy is he who hath won him
> the love and liking of all;
> for hard is one's help to seek
> from the mind of another man.

And stanza 44:
> If friend thou hast whom faithful thou deemest,
> and wishest to win him for thee:
> ope thy heart to him nor withhold thy gifts,
> and fare to find him often.

92 Ibid., stanza 36:
> One's home is best though a hut it be:
> there a man is master and lord;
> though but two goats thine and a thatchèd roof,
> 'tis far better than beg.

93 Leviticus 25:17 (KJV), "thou shalt fear thy God," Deuteronomy 6:13 (KJV), "thou shalt fear the LORD thy God," and Luke 1:50 (KJV), "and his mercy *is* on them that fear him."

Why I am a Heathen

"man *elevates the deity by elevating himself*; he devalues it by considering it like an Eastern despot whose 'commandments' should be followed on penalty of punishment."[94] As Nietzsche said, "man is a rope, fastened between animal and Superman—a rope over an abyss."[95] The ethic of the Desert God is that of browbeating; it debases man, dragging him to the level of an animal. Ours is an ethic meant to inspire, to provoke us to surpass what we are and fulfill our potential. It is an ethic that seeks not to keep us as men, but to allow us to grow into Supermen. There is more danger in ours, for the abyss is treacherous, but ours is not a faith for the weak and the fearful; it is, if anything, a cult of strength and excellence. The Christian sentiment of the 'blessed meek'[96] has no place among us; for it is through overcoming what we are, creating beyond ourselves[97] that we approach the road to the Superman—a road that leads us to the very halls of Valhalla,[98] where we might see the Gods themselves as equals, and take our place among them. This was the ethic of Sigurðr[99] and Cú Chulainn,[100] of Arminius[101] and Vercingetorix;[102] it is a path made not for slaves, but for heroes.

It is thus that the ethics of Heathenry, rather than providing exhaustive lists of what not to do, put forth virtues that we aspire to embody. It is in this light that we can look to the Nine Noble Virtues of the Odinic Rite,[103] the Twelve Ætheling

---

94 de Benoist, 179.
95 Friedrich Nietzsche. *Thus Spoke Zarathustra.* trans. R.J. Hollingdale (London: Penguin Books, 1969), 43.
96 Matthew 5:5 (KJV), "blessed *are* the meek."
97 Nietzsche, *Zarathustra*, 91.
98 Valhalla (lit. "hall of the slain"), is the abode of Óðinn, and was believed to be where a portion of battle-slain warriors ended up (John Lindow. *Norse Mythology: A Guide to the Gods, Heroes, Rituals, and Beliefs.* [Santa Barbara: Oxford University Press, 2001], 308-309).
99 Sigurðr was the hero of the Old Norse *Völsunga Saga*, the German *Niebelungenlied*, as well as Wagner's opera, *Der Ring des Nibelungen* (H.A. Guerber. *Myths of the Norsemen: From the Eddas and Sagas.* [Mineola: Dover Publications, Inc., 1992], 251).
100 Cú Chulainn "is the epitome of the superhuman war-hero" from the Celtic mythos. His tales are found primarily in the Ulster Cycle of stories (Miranda J. Green. *Dictionary of Celtic Myth and Legend.* [London: Thames and Hudson, 1997], 70-72).
101 Arminius (c. 18 BC – AD 21) was a Cherusci leader who defeated the Roman troops at the Battle of Teutoburg Forest (AD 9), effectively halting the Roman incursions into Germania.
102 Vercingetorix (c. 82 BC – 46 BC) was a Gallic chieftain who, after unifying the disparate armies of the Gauls, led a revolt against Julius Caesar during the Gallic Wars that was nearly successful in stopping the birth of the Roman Empire.
103 The Nine Noble Virtues being: Courage, Truth, Honor, Fidelity, Discipline, Hospitality, Self Reliance, Industriousness, and Perseverance ("The Nine Noble

Thews of the Þéodisc Geléafa,[104] or even the chivalric codes of the Middle Ages[105] as a kind of magnetic North to which the needles of our moral compasses can be drawn. It is an ethic that does not base itself on the *a priori* belief that we are flawed creatures in need of salvation. It realizes that we are real people living in the world; its purpose is not, as is the Christian ethic's, to force us to live as monks and nuns, but to enable us to live meaningful lives—being the best that we can be at whatever it is we do in life. It is an ethic that has not one goal, but a multitude. Just as monotheism manifests itself ethically as one, immutable moral code, Heathenry's polytheism has an ethic that is correspondingly plural. It is our vast pantheon of Gods and heroes to whom we look to find models for our particular station in life. It is in them that we find the lights to guide us in the darkest hours of our lives—looking up, we see not a single sun, but a multitude of stars, leading us through the night.

Society

It is next to the social aspect of Heathenry that we look. Religions of all stripes have always played heavily in the social sphere and have been an integral ingredient in the glue that coheres a group. Although monotheisms have served this role as well, there is a fundamental difference that underlies the motivations for both familial and ethnic cohesion that Christianity and Heathenry have provided. This basic point of differentiation lies in what each faith considers to be the basic unit of its spirituality, and thus of society. Any discussion of Judeo-Christian metaphysics intrinsically revolves around the concept of an individual, immortal soul. It is this core component of individualism that is our point of departure. For, within Christianity, the fate of your soul is, ultimately, your business.[106] It is about a personal, private relationship between God and yourself. On a practical level, the Christian is still connected to both their family and community, but, when it comes down to it, their eternal salvation is a private matter that can, by definition, involve no one else. Priests, pastors, elders and relatives can all help the Christian to facilitate this personal relationship, but, come judgment day, it is every man for himself.[107]

Virtues," The Odinic Rite. http://www.odinic-rite.org/virtues.html [accessed June 24, 2009]).

104 The Twelve Thews are: Courage, Steadfastness, Loyalty, Generosity, Hospitality, Truthfulness, Vengeance, Equality, Friendship, Freedom, Wisdom, and Self-Discipline (Gundarsson, *Our Troth* vol., 525-544).

105 Matthew R. Holmes. "Chivalric Values and Social Religious Transformation in Early Medieval Europe." *The Runestone Journal* 1 (2007): 20-42.

106 Psalm 91:1-16.

107 John 14:12 (KVJ), "he that believeth in me..."

When we look at Heathenry, we see a very different picture. For our ancestors the soul was not a singular entity, but, like everything else was an organic plurality of 'spiritual organs,' all of which came together to create a person.[108] The biggest difference of all though, is that our ancestors' conceptions of the 'soul' included parts that were not individual, but familial as well. For example amidst the Anglo-Saxon conception of the soul, the aspects known as the *fetch*, *wyrd*, and *speed* were all seen as being "passed down through family lines."[109] With the Norse as well, the *hamingja*, *fylgja* and *ørlǫg* were seen as collective, familial components.[110] Thus, in the Heathen world, it is not only through our genes that we are tied to our ancestors and kin, but also through our souls. In this vision of the world, we are not singular spiritual entities but are the centers of ever expanding concentric spiritual circles, whose rings overlap and are shared by our families. Thus are we tied to our family—physically, emotionally and spiritually. It is in this way that we can view the family, not the individual, as the basic unit of spirituality in Heathenry. This gives our Heathen families a far greater sense of unity and cohesion—a singular spiritual identity that produces something far greater than an isolated soul is capable of experiencing.

I was fortunate enough to have begun my conversion while my wife was pregnant with our son. Prior to his birth, I had never thought at all about any kind of religious meaning to parenthood, or to there being any kind of spiritual significance to a child being born. I had done a bit of reading about the familial nature of Heathenry, but it was not until after his birth that it really sank in. The moment he entered the world, the word *family* had an entirely different meaning to me. I swiftly watched my actions and my concerns shift *naturally* from myself to my family. There arose in me an intrinsic desire for our family to be run along traditional lines, and for this to be done both my wife and I began the process stepping into traditional gender roles. Just as she became an earthly embodiment of the matron mother Frigga, so did I follow the Odinic path and enlist in the Army. The wonderful synchronicity of the cotemporality of our introduction to Heathenry and the conception of our child led to us both changing from very liberal, almost avant-garde people, into members of a more traditional and healthy family. It is my belief that it was, and still is, our identification with these primal archetypes of our ancestors that has enabled us to build the strong family ties that we have, and to maintain what traditions we are able to in an otherwise declining society.

Out of this sense of a shared spiritual identity with the members of our family,

---

[108] Edred Thorsson. *Runelore*. (York Beach: Samuel Weiser Inc., 1987) 167-173.
[109] Gundarsson, *Our Troth* vol. 1, 502.
[110] Ibid., 506-508.

grows something that, up until recently, was *practically* manifest in Christianity, but, as it was not a part of that faith's core, has now all but disappeared—the idea of religion being an instrument of ethnic cohesion. For the centuries between the conversion and the beginnings of the Asian proselytization by the Jesuits in the 16th century, the Christian identity was synonymous with the European identity. Although it is essentially not, and at its core cannot be, a folk religion, Christianity was *treated as such* from the time of Clovis[111] onward. The cross was the banner under which Europa gathered to defend against the Muslim hordes. It provided our people a sense of spiritual unity—a rallying tribal point of focus that allowed us to come together in that pivotal time leading up to the Battle of Tours.[112] However, this is much less a product of any part of Christian theology and much more a holdover of the tribalism under which European man had lived since time immemorial. The nature of Christianity is that it is a universal faith; it is believed by its adherents to be the appropriate faith for every man, woman and child on the face of the Earth, irrespective of their ethnic origin. Its proponents would see the entire globe Christianized.

Some have seen, and still do see this as a good thing; they believe that all of humanity can and will, at some point, come together in unity and brotherhood. Some of us, however, do not believe this to be either a desirable or even a possible goal—we see it as one that has already done nearly irreparable harm to the ethnic, cultural and spiritual diversity of the planet. We see the world, ideally, not as one of homogeneity, where everyone is of the same culture and creed; we believe that difference and diversity (*true* diversity, not the politically correct meaning of the word) is an essential feature of mankind that must be preserved.[113] A monolithically Christian world filled with monolithically encultured people speaking a monolithically standardized tongue sounds like a Hellish dystopia to me, but it would be the logical outcome of Christian principles followed through to their entirety. It is in standing up in opposition to the rise of this type of global monoculture that Heathenry proves itself an especially utile tool. Few things have the power to bring people together the way that faith does. It is my hope, as it is similarly of many folkish Heathens throughout the world, that the revival of our people's ancient ways can help wake them up—that it can help them *remember* where they came from. Our people have been brainwashed by a thousand years of Christianity and even more so by the last fifty years of multiculturalism to believe that cultural differences are regrettable and that it

---

111 Clovis I (c. 466-511) was the first of the Frankish Kings to convert to Christianity.
112 The Battle of Tours (October 10, 732) was the turning point in the attempted invasion of Western Europe by the Umayyad Caliphate. The winning of this battle by the Franks set the boundary for Muslim expansions and kept the bulk of European soil in the hands of Europeans.
113 McNallen, *Metagenetics*, 21-22.

would be a wonderful thing if the whole of humanity were spiritually unified. It is high time that we woke up and realized that we are not merely a collection of individuals who share a common genetic origin, we are a Folk. We are an organic ethno-cultural entity that is the physical, social, linguistic and spiritual expression of the seed our ancestors sowed so many centuries ago. We are our ancestors—we are Europa—we are the West. We are all of this and it is through the resurgence of the faith of our forefathers that we can raise this awareness within ourselves, our families and our folk. It is through Heathenry that Western man can regain his sense of ethnic, folkish spirituality. It is through Heathenry that our folk can save itself from dissolution.

Psyche

Lastly in our tour, we will inspect some of the psychological dimensions of Heathenry. Whereas the ethical and social spheres primarily deal with our interactions with others, it is in the realm of the psyche that we can take a look at how the adoption of Heathenry can affect our mental state. Now, while a complete paradigmatic shift from either Christianity or atheism to Heathenry would, in Nietzsche's words, result in a complete transvaluation of many aspects of oneself, there are two in particular that I would like to highlight here: the first being our experience of the external world and the second the inevitability of death.

As I sit outside composing this section, I feel the wind against my face; I see it play up on the grass; I see the trees sway gently in its embrace. I cannot help but allow this verse to loop in my mind as I take it all in:

> Here at the edge of this world
> Here I gaze at a pantheon of oak, a citadel of stone
> If this grand panorama before me is what you call God...
> Then God is not dead[114]

For me, one of the most apparent and powerful psychological shifts since my adoption of Heathenry has been in the way I experience the world around me. For our ancestors, the external world was no more dead and mechanistic than were they themselves; it was the living, breathing bodies of the Gods. For Heathens, the world

> is not simply a sacrality *communicated* by the gods, as is the

---

114 Agalloch. "In the Shadow of our Pale Companion." Lyrics. *The Mantle*. The End Records, 2002.

case, for example, with a place or an object consecrated by the divine presence. The gods did more; *they manifested different modalities of the sacred in the very structure of the world and of cosmic phenomena...the cosmos as a whole is an organism at once real, living, and sacred.*[115]

Not only were various groves, mountains, and rivers deemed sacred *to* a particular deity, but the very fabric of the world itself was conceived as a manifestation *of* the Gods themselves. We can see this sentiment most clearly expressed in the prayer of the valkyrie Sigdrífa:

> Hail to thee, day! Hail, ye day's sons!
> Hail, night and daughters of night!
> With blithe eyes look on both of us:
> send to those sitting here speed!
>
> Hail to you, gods! Hail, goddesses!
> Hail, earth that givest to all!
> Goodly spells and speech bespeak we from you,
> and healing hands, in this life.[116]

This is a powerful and moving vision of the world. While it could be argued that such a thing is "only" an aesthetic phenomena and relates not to the *truth* of the world, it is our *experience* of the world, not what it is, that has the potential to act upon our psyches. We can *choose*, through the mechanism of fictionalism, to experience the world as a Newtonian clock or as a divine organism. It may be a fiction, but it is a fiction that can enrich our lives with a sense of beauty, majesty and sheer numinosity that does not easily stem from purely mechanistic depictions of our universe. A living world of immanent divinity is simply *better* than one of brute matter. It provides us with a connection to nature by allowing us to interact with it as a *Thou*[117] rather than an *it*.

The second psychological aspect, and the final point in this essay deals with the finality of life itself—the certainty of death. From our perspective there is nothing more permanent than death. While every religion has its own pet theories about the possibility of an afterlife and what that might entail, all

---

115 Mircea Eliade. *The Sacred and Profane: The Nature of Religion.* (Orlando: Harcourt Inc., 1987), 116-117.
116 *Sigrdrífumál* stanzas 2-3.
117 The distinction between "I and Thou," is owed to Martin Buber (1878-1965). "The I confronts its Thou not as something to be studied, measured, or manipulated, but as a unique presence that responds to the I in its individuality," (Audi, 104).

biological evidence points to the death of an organism being a total termination of the body and mind's animating spirit. As mentioned before in the discussion on materialism, this is, however, a grim perspective that does not lend itself easily at all to mental well-being or emotional contentment. To believe, be it the truth or not, that our lives are strictly temporary and utterly meaningless is not at all a paradigm that more than a tiny minority of the Earth's populace is willing to hold. However, the specific beliefs relating to death and the afterlife that are held by the majority of Westerners have been shaped by Christianity for the last millennium and bear little resemblance to those of our ancestors.

It is the contention of Nietzsche that not only is the Christian idea of the afterlife false, but, furthermore it is downright harmful. The Afterworldsmen in *Thus Spoke Zarathustra*[118] are hypertrophied caricatures of those who hold the Christian tenets on death to be true. Their depiction is exaggerated, but it sheds light on the actual beliefs of many Christians. The basic argument is that Biblical teachings impel us to deny life while we are living so that we may secure a favorable afterlife.[119] *If* Christianity were literally true, and only if, this would be a reasonable course with which to chart one's life. But since the literal truth of the Bible is *assuredly* nonexistent, we can see whether Christianity's position on the afterlife is a useful or harmful fiction, and an examination through the lens of fictionalism reveals the position of an Afterworldsman to be detrimental in the extreme. After all, if all the evidence of our senses and sciences tells us that this life *is our only life*, then it should certainly not be lived in fear of punishment in an imagined Hell or lived for the promise of rewards in an equally fictional Heaven. Life must be lived for what it is. A life spent denying oneself pleasure, living as an ascetic, *for the sole purpose* of achieving a place in Heaven is a life wasted.

That being said, our ancestors *did* have beliefs about the afterlife. Thankfully, their beliefs were not singular or standardized. So, there exist a multitude of indigenous European beliefs about death for us to examine and judge the utility of. While both the Celts and Germanics held a wide array of beliefs about post-mortem states throughout their histories—to include reincarnation, celestial halls, and earthly underworlds[120]—the two that I would like to put forth here are exemplified in the *Hávamál*. The first deals with children:

---

118 Nietzsche, *Zarathustra*, 58-61.
119 1 John 5:15-19.
120 The Celtic views are discussed in Thierry Jolif's paper, "The Abode of the Gods and the Great Beyond: On the Imaginal and Post Mortem States in Celtic Tradition," (*TYR: Myth—Culture—Tradition* 3 [2007-2008]: 127-146), while the Germanic views are treated in pages 65-98 of Hilda Roderick Ellis' *The Road to Hel: A Study of the Conception of the Dead in Old Norse Literature* (New York: Greenwood Press, 1968).

> To have a son is good, late-got though he be,
> and born when buried his father;
> stones see'st thou seldom set by the roadside
> but by kith raised over kinsmen.[121]

It is first and foremost through our children that both our genetic legacy and our memories live on. It is through them that a biological continuance of ourselves is made manifest. It is in their hearts and minds that the memories of who we were are kept alive. This is why the cult of the ancestors plays so large in Heathenry. It is our duty to our ancestors to talk about them—to read and write about them—to think about them. And just as it is important to remember and honor the dead, so must we forge and maintain bonds with the living. For it is only through the next generation that we and the entire genealogical line that we are the culmination of will be remembered. This being the case, we must ask: what is it about our ancestors that is remembered and why?

> Cattle die and kinsmen die,
> thyself eke soon wilt die;
> but fair fame will fade never,
> I ween, for him who wins it.
>
> Cattle die and kinsmen die,
> thyself eke soon wilt die;
> one thing, I wot, will wither never:
> the doom over each one dead.[122]

There is a saying in modern Heathenry that is derived from this couplet—*we are our deeds*.[123] It is through our deeds, and the greatness thereof, that we can secure a place in the minds of both our descendants and, if our deeds are memorable enough, the world at large. It was through the magnitude of their achievements that the luminaries of history have been immortalized. It was not their faith in God, their piety or their asceticism that has made us remember and discuss them to this day; it was their works.

It could be said that this is, compared to the eternal bliss promised by Christianity, a petty kind of immortality. However, these two varieties of

---

121 *Hávamál* stanza 72.
122 Ibid., stanzas 76-77.
123 Culled from Eric Wódening's influential book, *We Are Our Deeds* (Watertown: Theod Press, 1988).

athanasia[124] are not only real and visible, but, more importantly, they inspire us to lead better lives. They impel us to remember where we came from and to honor that past. They force us to work at building lasting relationships with our children. They arouse in us a desire to do great things. It might be argued that given that the death of our species and planet is, at some point in time, immanent, even this type of "immortality" must fade, regardless of the greatness of one's deeds. However, the Germanic perspective on death still proves its utility. Similar to our contemporary scientific theories about the end of life on our planet due to star-death, our ancestors believed that their world too would end. Not only would humanity and the world die in the fire and ice from which it was born, but the Gods too would die. Although Óðinn would do what he could to prevent it, Ragnarök[125] *would* bring an end to all.

> This is the conception of life which underlies the Norse religion, as somber a conception as the mind of man has ever given birth to. The only sustaining support possible for the human spirit...is heroism...Like the early Christians, the Norseman measured their lives by heroic standards. The Christians, however, looked forward to a heaven of eternal joy. The Norseman did not. But it would appear that for unknown centuries, until the Christian missionaries came, heroism was enough.[126]

What we have is a choice. We can look at our doom and the doom of the universe as a death sentence—something to wail and gnash our teeth about; or we can look at it as a challenge—something that we strive to overcome. Although we know that we *will* die, we can still, in spite of it, live, love and fight! It might be futile in the end, but "heroism depends on lost causes."[127] A life lived in mourning for its eventual loss is no life at all. It is in our striving to overcome this inevitability and to make the most of what time we do have that we bring meaning into our lives. It is this laboring against all odds that makes our lives worthwhile at all. This is the lesson of Ragnarök and the *Völuspá*—in struggling to overcome that which we cannot, we truly approach the divine.

Conclusion

And so comes to an end my rambling attempt at providing a philosophical basis

---

124 Deathlessness.
125 Either spelled Ragnarök (lit. "judgment of the powers") or Ragnarøkkr (lit. "twilight of the gods"), it was thought by the Norsemen to be the violent end of the world.
126 Edith Hamilton. *Mythology: Timeless Tales of Gods and Heroes.* (New York: Mentor Books, 1942), 300-301.
127 Ibid., 300.

for the adoption of the ideology and practices of Heathenry. It has been a long and winding road, but I am glad that you followed it through to the end and I can only hope that you have found some of this to be of use. I cannot expect, nor would I even wish, for all Heathens to justify their beliefs in the same manner as I do. Part of the beauty of our faith is the pluralism that is inherent in it. Variety truly is the spice of life, and Heathenry would be *awfully* boring if our philosophy were to be as dogmatically rigid as Christianity's. What I *do* wish is that this essay can continue the veins of inquiries into the philosophic basis of our religion that has, until this point been carried our by very few individuals (Alain de Benoist and Collin Cleary being notable exceptions). As Stephen McNallen noted in his critical reflections on the Heathen revival, we are currently suffering from a "lack of philosophical depth," that "until we can hold our own in debate with the Jesuits or in the pages of the *New York Times Review of Books*, we will not be taken seriously."[128] It was, in part, in response to my reading of his critique back in 2005 that I vowed to do my best to help rectify the problem. We are on the edge of a precipice in our revival of the old ways. We are just now beginning to gain some semblance of notoriety and mainstream awareness. On the one hand, we must ensure that we do not sink into the morass of ridiculousness that is exemplified in Wicca and its related Neopagan ideologies. On the other hand we must not, as some Heathen groups already seem to be leaning, enact some type of rigid orthodoxy that leaves no room for innovation and philosophical development. It is a treacherous path, but we must forge ahead, for stasis will surely be our doom.

> We stand on a mountain pass in the midst of whirling snow and blinding mist, through which we get glimpses now and then of paths which may be deceptive. If we stand still we shall be frozen to death. If we take the wrong road we shall be dashed to pieces. We do not certainly know whether there is any right one. What must we do? 'Be strong and of a good courage.' Act for the best, hope for the best, and take what come [and]…if death ends all, we cannot meet death better.[129]

---

128 Stephen A. McNallen. "Three Decades of the Ásatrú Revival in America." *TYR: Myth—Culture—Tradition* 2 (2003-2004): 217.
129 Fitz James Stephen. *Liberty, Equality, Fraternity.* (Indianapolis: Liberty Fund, 1993), 353.

* OLD WAYS FOR A NEW DAY *

HEX
magazine

Radicalizing European Tradition since 2005

Folk Ways & Myth * Culture & Art * Seasonal Cycles
Sustainable Living * Earth Stewardship
Community * Ancestral Lore

Take your old beliefs and renew them...

HEX is a bi-annual journal and online community giving voice to radical traditionalism and the modern Heathen household

It's not enough to survive. We will thrive.
JOIN US

WE ARE ALWAYS ACCEPTING SUBMISSIONS ~ ARTICLES, ART, RECIPES, STORIES, POEMS

WWW.HEXMAGAZINE.COM

Hermann Awakened:
Folkishness vs. Racism

Stephen M. Borthwick

Probably the most common accusation levelled against the followers of Ásatrú, Odinism, and Heiðni who proudly call themselves "Folkish" is that of Racism. No term is so powerful in our modern society, no term has the ability to make pariah even the most upstanding member of a community. It is to moderns what cries of "witch!" and "devil-worshipper!" were to Europeans even to the 18th century. This power, a power which few words in the history of spoken language have possessed, is worth mention and contemplation but it is not the focus of this work. Rather, the very definite difference between what racism actually is and what one means when one says "Folkish" is what demands examination, and which this work shall explore. It is not the call of Ásatruar specifically to question and denounce the power of words, or the power of society: this is the call of all thinking people, no matter their Folk. What Ásatruar are specifically called to do is defend our Folk, our Faith, and our Families against both simple and innocent misconceptions as well as malicious slanders. This is an answer to that call—the call to remove an unjust and misapplied label, the call to denounce hurtful misconceptions, be they born from ignorance or malice, the call to separate Folkishness and Racism.

If one endeavours to remove a word from, or even to apply a word to, a certain group, philosophy, or practice, an adequate definition of the word is absolutely necessary. What, then, is "racism" and what is "Folkish?" Racism is the word which must be removed for the new word to be applied, and it therefore cries out in greater earnest to be defined. The social definition is of course one associated with superiority complexes, hatred, violence, and lesser minds. This is perhaps not so inappropriate when one reaches deeper into the realities which the most popular racist thought has spawned. Racist thought as an institution, i.e. as an active entity in Western civilisation, is defined by the belief in classifications—perhaps a better word is "ranks"—of humans based on purely biological traits. The existence of race as a biological fact is, of course, as undeniable and immutable as the existence of differently coloured eyes and hair (though, indeed, there is a great deal more to "race" than merely colour). There are some, however, who would seize upon the biological reality and alter it and use it to put forth theories, theories which give way to a worldview founded in biology and passing judgements of superiority and inferiority which can only be applied to the spiritual and mental realms. This misapplication of judgement and mismeasurement of inherent value and basic merit is what, at the core, defines racism. That which should not leave the realm of individual struggle is applied to entire people-groups on the basis of their biological make-up and origins. Then, given into the mixture is the distinctly Hebraic concept of the "chosen people," brought to the West by Christianity. This value judgement of superiority from Christianity overlaying the strict biological mindset spawned in modernity is the mother and father of all racist thought and tendencies: they are the primal source of the whole racist world-view. This alone should stand as proof that Ásatrú cannot be racist: its distinctly non-Christian basis coupled with the firm belief in individual struggle, sacrifice, and merit divorce it utterly from racism at the most foundational level. But Folkishness and Racism remain to be completely divorced, for Folkishness yet lacks definition and the two can therefore not be juxtaposed.

It should be made clear that there is no Folkish "world-view." "World-view" is far too limited a concept in our native tongue to contain the totality of Folkishness, for it is not a "world-view"—a mere set of opinions and beliefs—it is far more. The only word to truly contain within it the totality of Folkishness is *Weltanschauung*. *Weltanschauung* is a German term, formed from the words *Welt*, "world," and the verb *anschauen*, "to watch," which becomes the word *Anschauung* or "outlook" (somewhat more akin to our word "world-view"). The transfer of the literal meaning of "outlook" is very pronounced in the German: a **point** from which one looks out. To have a *Weltanschauung* is quite literally to have a **point** at which one stands to watch, or look out upon, the world. It is not a collection of opinions or beliefs roughly tied together, it is a **foundation**, a basis, a ground to stand upon which encompasses and defines all aspects of one's beliefs and actions. In brief, it is all-encompassing in the way a world-view is not and cannot be. Verily, such a departure into modern German linguistics seems somewhat misplaced in an essay of this nature, but it is necessary, for this totality of *Weltanschauung* is the beginning of the definition of Folkishness.

The Folkish *Weltanschauung*, simply put, is the belief that a people, or a culture, which serves as the foundation for a nation, has a native, primal spirituality inherently tied to it, a spirituality which that people, that Folk, discovered when the first gods cried out to the souls of men and were received in the fire and blood of sacrifice and in turn received those primeval shouts of prayer and quandary unique to our species. It is a spirituality tied to the physicality of the people, passed down from generation to generation amongst the Folk who originated it. It is this native, this ancient, this **organic** spirituality which is Mankind's truest faith, for it belongs to the most defining feature of human society: the clan, the tribe, the Folk, the first social order established by the most evolved social animal on Earth, just as natural to mankind as the intellect and willpower which first awoke this spirituality so many millennia ago. The Folkish *Weltanschauung* further holds that each individual culture, or Folk, of which there are hundreds, has a faith and spirituality native to it, and it is the call of the Folk towards the totality in their *Weltanschauung*, the axis upon which the Folk turns. There is no universalism, no "customised" religion that allows for a casual "faith;" it is a defined faith unique to each Folk, to which each individual Folk must as a whole return. However, where there is no universalism in Folkishness, nor is there value judgement attached to any Folk or that Folk's faith: each Folk's faith is its own, and equal in its superiority to universal faiths, and likewise each Folk's faith is more important to that Folk, and superior for that Folk, than any foreign faith which may seek converts from the Folk. This is as true for the Germanic *goði* as it is to the Siberian *shaman*: when the *goði* attempts to convert from a foreign Folk, he is inferior to the Siberian *shaman*, and when the *shaman* seeks to do the same so too is he inferior to the Germanic *goði*. It is action and character, not origin, unto which all value judgements are subscribed in the Folkish *Weltanschauung*. This alone should be enough to divorce Folkishness from Racism; this alone enough to defend Folkishness, but before those who would utter the cries of accusation, believers in the Folkish *Weltanschauung* must be prepared to fight with all possible weapons; let us, however, bear a sharp sword rather than a dull knife!

The first juxtaposition between Folkishness and Racism is that Folkishness recognises that there are categories—different "Folks"—and attaches no value judgement to these categories, while Racism cannot exist without value judgement attached to its categories (i.e. "races"). Where the racist man praises members of his race for their loyalty to their race because it is his native race, the Folkish man praises all members of all Folks for their loyalty to their Folk because it is their Folk—it is not their specific Folk, but their individual loyalty which decides whether they are to be praised or derided. To use a cliché, it is not the colour of their skin, but the content of their character upon which the Folkish man judges his fellow men. All Folkish faiths are brethren faiths, though they may be unique and different faiths, and the faithful Hindu is by far a better role model to the Folkish Ásatruar than a fellow Ásatruar who would see non-Germanics convert to Ásatrú, for Ásatrú is the spirituality native to the Germanic Folk, and no one else, just as Hinduism is the spirituality native to the Indic Folk and no one else. Is it racism to be loyal to one's Folk, and also praise and admire a foreigner for loyalty to his foreign Folk? This is the question all must ask themselves who would accuse Folkish faith of "racism", for this is the nature of true Folkishness.

For those to whom the answer to the above question is "yes," the subsequent question must be posed: is it racist to acknowledge the colour of a black man's skin? Is it racist to acknowledge the shape of an Asian man's eyes? Is it racist to acknowledge the absence of hair on a Native American's face? No, and again no, and it would be absurd to think that mere **acknowledgement** of these distinctly ethnic and racial traits is racist. Why, then, is the recognition of the existence of Folk racist? How, then, is loyalty to one's Folk, regardless of what Folk it is, racist? For is not this loyalty merely the recognition of the Folk's existence, for indeed does not each Folk by virtue of its existence demand loyalty? In a modern age, where exclusivity is evil, perhaps an explanation can be offered for the charges of "racism" in spite of the blatant absurdity of such accusations. For their distinct differences, Folkishness and Racism share something in common, something in common with all attitudes which have categories: they hold belief in exclusivity rather than universalism. To say there are Folks, to say there are Races, to say there are Peoples, Nations, Ethnicities, Cultures: all of these are to express there is exclusivity among groups, for without exclusivity none of these could exist. Each Folk, Race, People, Nation, Ethnicity, and Culture is distinct and exclusive from every other one. This is mere fact; not a deep philosophical quandary or amazing statement. Without the concept "that," there can be no concept for "this"—everything simply would be. If mankind had not seen and recognised "immorality," there would be no "morality," for all that we see as moral would simply **be**. If all men were German, there would be no "German," there would be only "man." This is a wonderful idealism to have, to wish that all men were the same and we had no need to say "German," "French," "English," "Indian," or "Chinese," but unfortunately for those idealists and singers of the *Internationale*, such a world does not exist and is quite incapable of existence.

Likewise for the idealist Christians who wish to see a world of only "morality;" they neglect that without immorality no such structure as morality would exist, and further they neglect that the morality as laid out by the Hebrew myths and folk-tales constructed into Christian Scripture is not world-morality, it is distinctly Hebrew morality. This is not to say that there is no universal right, no universal truth; nor is it to say that there is anything inferior or insufficient about Hebrew morality; it is perfect, in fact, for the Semitic people from whom it flows and to whom it was first given, just as the Germanic morality of our ancestors is perfect for our Folk, from whom it flows and to whom it was first given. Let no man be fooled, the two have much in common, since indeed there is a universal righteousness, but each is uniquely tailored to its Folk, and one cannot be properly applied to the other. This is what in action defines Folkishness: this recognition of the uniqueness and exclusivity of social institutions to each individual Folk, just as no two flowers have the same petals and colours, though they may be equal in beauty, they are tailored with a beauty unique to their species. This is why universalist movements like Christianity, Buddhism, Mohammedanism, and Atheism are so sternly opposed by Ásatrú and all Folkish faiths: they apply a universal morality without allowing for uniqueness and the inevitable cultural exchange that a natural (and truly *multi*cultural) world insists upon.

What, though, has this to do with Racism? Why even mention Christianity except as a self-gratifying effort to attack it further? Indeed, there is a deeper reason, and it lay in what the racist world-view has itself derived from Christianity. How ironic it is, that those fiercest anti-Semites of our world themselves would not exist if not for a Hebraic faith! For what is it that marks Christianity amongst the religions of the world if not the firm and foolish belief that it above all others is the superior faith? So their Christ proclaims: "I am the way, the truth, and the life: no man cometh unto the Father, but by me" (John 14:6). This is what has made Christians such adept imperialists: they insist upon their own superiority and the universality of their faith. So too the racist world-view, except it is the race in place of the faith; what remains the same, however, is the firm belief in self-superiority and universality. "White Power," "Black Power," all the Chicano-supremacy movements, and every other racist movement in the world uphold the same basic principle: the race which is superior should rule over all others, or, in some cases, even exterminate all others. The genocide of the Jews in Germany and surrounding states in the mid-twentieth century is a direct outgrowth of the very Christian sense of superiority that insists the world shall end with the conversion of all human beings to The Faith. Racism, therefore, aside from simply not being comparable to Folkishness, is itself amongst those things which Folkish faith, by virtue of its anti-Christian purism, actively seeks to drive from its midst.

The end result of all this juxtaposition is a revelation; a revelation of the utter divorce of racism and Folkishness by virtue of their very distinct and foreign origins and values. A racist values simple biology, and attaches spiritual significance to what is nothing more than an arrangement of chromosomes; the Folkish man reaches far deeper into his culture to find pride, and in so doing finds a pride which is understanding of itself and therefore understanding of the pride of other Folkish men, regardless of their origin. The Folkish man guards fiercely the uniqueness of his people against universalism, but if the foreigner's cause is the same as his own, he will join hands with the foreigner against the universalist and the uniculturalist, against the modern global ideology and against the assimilation of all cultures. But the Folkish man, regardless of his Folk, is passive and defensive. If none seek to harm his culture, his weapons remain in their hilt, unlike the racist who marches ever onward to the foolish goal of world dominion, a universalist who appears through Folkish lenses the same as a Christian crusader or modern uniculturalist. How can Folkishness, which stands firmly by exclusivity, not be racist? Racism itself is a quest for universality and global uniformity, and an extremely flawed and dangerous form of that quest. We who are Folkish, our battle cry is Folk and Faith, these we defend against those who seek to overrun and universalise them, for we know that if our Folk and our Faith becomes the uniform of all the world, we shall have no Folk or Faith. Ours is not a faith of conquest, nor one of domination, nor one of imperialism. As our ancestors, defenders of their Folk and Faith, stood at Teutoburg against the Imperialist aggressor, so too do we stand today against the legions who would see us fall to them, and there among them is universalism, there uniculturalism, there racism.

Folkways
(*a kyrielle*)

Juleigh Howard-Hobson

Harvest's home and hearth fires lit;
We raise the horn and hail with it—
We hail the ash, we hail the oak
We hail our gods, we hail our folk

With barnyard full from floor to bin
We thank the tompten and their kin
We give them oats with honey soaked
We hail our gods, we hail our folk

Our holly and our noble pine
Give us their green through winter time
While the world with snow is cloaked
We hail our gods, we hail our folk

With horns raised full of golden mead
We hail the ones who meet our needs
Winter's Nights these rites evoke:
We hail our gods, we hail our folk

And when the spring arrives again
We see the long cold winter's end,
And feel the turning of the spoke—
We hail our gods, we hail our folk

IRONWOOD
THE DEBUT ALBUM
:FIRE:WATER:ASH:

"Ein Meisterwerk ist „:Fire:Water:Ash:" ... 9/10."
- Chrischi, Burn Your Ears

"There is simply nobody out there doing what Ironwood is doing — certainly not with anywhere near this level of refinement and I urge you to support these warrior Antipodeans by purchasing this work of art."
- Geoff Birchenall, Asgard Root

WWW.IRONWOODSOUND.COM.AU
NEW ALBUM STORM OVER SEA COMING 2010

Elhaz Ablaze
Chaos Heathenism on the Web

We are a group of Heathen mystics and our internally contradictory philosophy is one of Chaos Heathenism.

On our site you will find articles on runes, seid/seidh/seidhr, Heathenism, history, philosophy, magic, trance, martial arts, altered consciousness, music, art, politics, and (lots of) practical experimentation. We are interested in creativity and wit. We hope to inform, entertain, annoy, and inspire Heathens, mystics, chaos magicians, berzerkers, martial artists, lovers, fighters, and trouble-makers.

Come join us - love us or hate us, our readers cannot get enough.

www.elhazablaze.com

Cognitive Bias and Contemporary Heathenry

Henry Lauer

In the Old Norse poem *Havamal*, Odin hangs on the tree for nine nights and embraces mystery in order to win wisdom.[1] This is an important symbol: Odin does *not* win the runes by reflecting on what he already knows and has experienced, but rather by embracing the limit point of his ignorance, namely death. Elsewhere in *Havamal*, Odin ruefully recounts a love affair gone wrong. Thinking himself well-armed with evidence to the effect that the woman he desires returns his affections, he gets into very severe strife when it turns out that she actually intends nothing but ill for him.[2]

These two vignettes from Odin's mythic life illustrate very different ways of dealing with the thorny question of knowing. The challenge of these vignettes has persisted well beyond the times when no one in the North disputed Odin's rightful place as a god. Indeed, I contend that this challenge poses itself to modern Heathens as well, and that we would do well to sort out for ourselves, as Odin did, how to frame a sound response.

> *Just because a scientist says something, even with lots of evidence, that doesn't mean we don't have to critically think about the experiments and the results.*[3]

One of the more fecund areas of modern psychological research is in the area of cognitive bias. It seems that human thinking processes can become confused, distorted, and dumbfounded in a myriad of marvelous ways. The list of types of cognitive bias is frighteningly long, and it would be impossible for me to discuss all of these, let alone in the context of Heathenry.[4]

As the above quote alludes, controlling for these kinds of bias is no easy feat, even with an entire institutional framework built just for that purpose, as is the

---

1 Ed. and trans. Lee Hollander. *The Poetic Edda*. (Austin: University of Texas Press, 1962), 36.
2 Ibid., 28.
3 Katherine Grobman. "Confirmation Bias." *Developmental Psychology.* (http://www.devpsy.org/teaching/method/confirmation_bias.html [accessed 23 December, 2009]).
4 For the intrepid, Wikipedia provides an exhaustive catalogue of cognitive biases (http://en.wikipedia.org/wiki/List_of_cognitive_biases).

case with modern quantitative science. Indeed, for all of the systems of knowledge in the world, it seems unlikely that it will ever be possible to eliminate the need for human circumspection. This is a point I will return to, because from observing the debates that run through historical, mythological, and archaeological domains (as well as through modern Heathenry) it seems that many folk forget just this consideration.

Confirmation Bias

Arguably the biggest and most troublesome of all forms of cognitive bias is *confirmation bias*: "a tendency to seek evidence that might confirm a hypothesis rather than evidence that might disconfirm it; a logical error."[5] It might not immediately be obvious why it should matter whether we seek evidence to confirm a hypothesis rather than disconfirm it. After all, are we not coming to a conclusion about the hypothesis either way?

Sadly, it does not work that way, for the simple reason that it is possible to find confirmation for any theory we might have, particularly in retrospect.[6] This is probably a major reason for why so many political debates persist without resolution. After all, if I am solely seeking to *confirm* my hypothesis then all of the evidence that I familiarise myself with will only convince me more of how right I am. The ironic fact that my opponent is in exactly the same predicament is likely to be lost on me. Under the sway of confirmation bias we ruthlessly seek out evidence that corroborates what we already believe and just as ruthlessly ignore anything that contradicts us.

These sorts of vicious cycles can have tremendously severe consequences. For example, it seems a major reason for the Global Financial Crisis was that analysts tended to only consider evidence of past patterns that appeared to *confirm* the theory that sub-prime mortgage tranches were perfectly safe investments. The few who were more methodologically sound in their approach, asking hypothetical, disconfirmatory questions that might have prevented the debacle, were mocked into submission.[7]

Similar problems occur in clinical mental health settings. It appears that when mental health professionals are given a client or patient's diagnosis before

---

5   Neil Carlson and William Buskist. *Psychology: The Science of Behaviour.* (Needham Heights: Allyn & Bacon, 1997), 363.
6   Nassim Nicholas Taleb. *The Black Swan.* (London: Penguin Books, 2007), 56.
7   "The Giant Pool of Money." *This American Life.* (http://www.thisamericanlife.org/Radio_Episode.aspx?episode=355 [accessed 23 December, 2009]).

meeting with them for the first time they tend to slot that person very neatly into the symptom profile they have already been primed to notice. As a consequence, clinician assessment of client prognosis without the assistance of objective measures (even something as arbitrary as the thickness of the patient's case note file) has a surprisingly low rate of accuracy.[8]

It is worth underscoring the point that confirmation bias affects even psychiatrists, the types of people who *know about it*, but who do not necessarily take personal action to counter it in their practice. This suggests that simple theoretical understanding is inadequate for the prevention of confirmation bias. Hence my point that personal agency is paramount: relying on the comfort of one's pre-existing knowledge easily leads highly trained and intelligent folk to reach horribly wrong conclusions.[9]

Confirmation bias seems to be the kind of reasoning that caused Odin his romantic difficulties. He has a hypothesis (*"she loves me"*) and therefore looks out (so it would seem) only for evidence that would confirm that hypothesis (for example her asking him to secretly visit her). Intent on confirming his preferred hypothesis (perhaps lover's hubris is clouding his reason), Odin never even bothers to consider whether some other situation—for example that she might intend to double cross him—could be the case.

The solution to the problem of confirmation bias lies in changing our behaviour and attempting to think in a more disciplined fashion. Specifically, the solution is to actively search for *negative evidence*; that is, to attempt to disconfirm one's preferred hypothesis.[10] This presupposes that we are conscious of what our preferred hypothesis is, which is often not the case, particularly if we succumb to the temptation of a dualist or very absolutist world view. A very effective attitude to adopt for such undertakings is one of curiosity—holding ourselves out into uncertainty rather than acquiescing to what is already familiar and therefore seemingly self-evident.[11]

---

8   Ian Bell and David Mellor. "Clinical judgements: research and practice." *Australian Psychologist* 44, 2 (2009): 115.
9   When I worked in a counseling centre where I received referral notes with each new client I quickly learned not to read these profiles until I had met each client and gotten to know them myself. For all of the very real and sometimes tragic challenges they faced, my clients were nevertheless almost invariably far more engaged, motivated, and agreeable than the miserable characters portrayed in the referral notes. I can only guess that the assessors had thought less about confirmation bias (and therefore been more vulnerable to its effects) than I had.
10 Taleb, 56.
11 Alice Morgan. *What is Narrative Therapy?* (Adelaide: Dulwich Centre Publications,

It is much easier to disprove something than to prove it. We can know much more easily when a claim is wrong than when it is right. For example, it is easy to disprove the claim that a person is always gentle if I witness them committing murder, whereas it is much harder to compile the endless evidence required to prove the claim that a person is always gentle.[12]

Here then is the fulcrum of the problem: it is easy to find confirmatory evidence, yet past a certain point finding more confirmatory evidence does not actually increase our chances of being correct—a single unexpected piece of disconfirmatory or negative evidence can instantly tear the whole edifice down. At some point, then, increasing the amount of information we have begins to impair our ability to comprehend the world, since it increases our overconfidence but not our understanding. The disparity between confidence and actual knowledge is a dangerous one. Our sense of certainty becomes grossly disproportionate to our actual grasp on reality.

Nassim Nicholas Taleb neatly sums up the whole problem in the image of the *black swan*.[13] For centuries it was believed that all swans were white: all of the evidence confirmed this theory, if you like. The considered scientific opinion held with conviction that with all this corroborative evidence—well, all swans were white! Then European explorers in Australia encountered *black swans* and all of that confirmative evidence was immediately overturned.[14] This is the problem: even the most seemingly secure point of knowledge can be hit with a black swan at any moment. Consequently: we must be cautious. Consequently: Odin turns to the embrace of mystery—uncertainty—in order to hone his fabled wisdom.

Whatever the Thinker thinks, the Prover proves.[15]

By now my reader may be quite curious as to why I am bothering to recount these considerations. Certainly in an elliptical way they are relevant to Heathenry —but why focus specifically on them in an essay written for a Heathen journal? The simple answer is that I think confirmation bias is rife in the writings I read by Heathens as they struggle to articulate exactly what Heathenry is and what

---

2000), 2.
12 Taleb, 56.
13 Ibid., xvii.
14 One wonders what the indigenous Australians of the day made of this sort of empirical shadow boxing.
15 Robert Anton Wilson. *Prometheus Rising*. (Reno: New Falcon, 1992), 25.

they believe. Not just among Heathens either: part of the problem is that confirmation bias also affects the academics, historians, and archaeologists whom modern Heathens are, to a greater or lesser extent, forced to rely on in elaborating their spiritual milieu.

Gimbutas & Metzner

Marija Gimbutas's theory that the Indo-Europeans were patriarchal brutes who came to Europe in Neolithic times and ruthlessly destroyed a pre-existing matriarchal culture is rife with confirmation bias.[16] Gimbutas, for example, sees the many female statuettes found in that time to be proof of the widespread goddess veneration; she ignores the volumes of non-female statues that have also been found which rather distinctly disconfirm her one-sided portrait of European prehistory.[17] Indeed, there is no compelling reason to assume that any of the Neolithic icons found are representations of the divine—only under the sway of confirmation bias could one become convinced of such an idea. This is not to say that they might not in fact be divine representations, but from our stand-point it is impossible to establish such a claim on any sound empirical basis.[18]

Furthermore, by painting the Indo-Europeans as hard patriarchs and the previous European culture as matriarchal hippies, Gimbutas leaves Ralph Metzner—who subscribes wholesale to her views—in a very difficult position for trying to understand Germanic mythology.

Metzner's interpretation of the Germanic mythic corpus is heavily determined by his Gimbutas-inspired confirmation bias. For example, he sees the stories of war between the Æsir and Vanir as a mythical memory of the conquest of the matriarchal Europeans by the evil patriarchal Indo-Europeans, who marched in and totally destroyed the old order with superior fire-power and a warrior ideology.[19] At first it seems like this myth might be a corroboration of Gimbutas's theory.

Of course, if we extricate ourselves from confirmation bias and look for negative evidence, we notice a number of flaws in Metzner's application of Gimbutas to Germanic myth. For example, it appears that the Æsir did not sweep in and crush the Vanir as the Indo-Europeans supposedly did to their predecessors. It seems

---

16 Ralph Metzner. *The Well of Remembrance*. (Boston: Shambhala, 1994), 31-32.
17 Wikipedia. "Marija Gimbutas." *Wikipedia*.
   (http://en.wikipedia.org/wiki/Marija_Gimbutas#Criticism [accessed 23 December, 2009]).
18 Jan Fries. *Helrunar*. (Oxford: Mandrake, 2006), 54.
19 Metzner, 43.

all they managed was to force a draw.[20] If we were to draw parallels between Norse myth and European Neolithic history we would have to conclude that the Indo-Europeans' arrival produced complex cultural interactions, some violent, some not, and that neither side can be adequately understood as a grab bag of patriarchal or matriarchal clichés. It is also worth noting that this myth has also been interpreted as a reflection of class conflict *within* a single culture and on this view does not reflect cross-cultural interactions at all.[21]

In other words, Metzner's confirmation bias leads him to only notice the aspects of this myth that fit his pre-existing theoretical expectation, and consequently his understanding of Germanic myth is deeply impaired. His book on Northern mythology, *The Well of Remembrance*, is filled with many examples of what amounts to double-think. For example, he struggles fruitlessly to explain why there is so much evidence attesting to the veneration of women by the supposedly ultra-patriarchal Celts and Germans. His recurring—and rather limp—implication that the patriarchs must have only partly suppressed the matriarchal current is an unacknowledged admission that Gimbutas's theory is too extreme to be accurate.[22]

Underlying the failure of Gimbutas's theories is a dualistic and disastrously absolutist understanding of cultures, gender identities, and their interactions. This understanding is itself anachronistic, as such intense dualism appears to have its birth only centuries after the Indo-European migration to Europe (another example of anachronistic thinking in the area of archaeology will be discussed below). Gimbutas is quite guilty of remaking the past in the light of present concerns, and confirmation bias seems to be an essential part of this error. Meanwhile Metzner, in adopting her notions without modification, is left in an impossible position for attempting to make sense of Germanic mythology.

Incidentally, none of this is to therefore suggest that I do not think the Indo-Europeans came from somewhere else into Europe, or that there would have been no conflicts between them and the people already dwelling in Europe. My concern is rather to highlight that confirmation bias makes us vulnerable to losing sight of the phenomenon for the sake of our theory. It is worth reflecting on the fact that Farley Mowat's interpretation of the character of the pre-Indo-European peoples—he calls them Albans—is notably different to Gimbutas' interpretation.[23] The evidence we find precipitates the beginning of a theory,

---

20 Rudolf Simek. *Dictionary of Northern Mythology.* trans. Angela Hall (Cambridge: D. S. Brewer, 1993), 352.
21 Ibid.
22 Metzner, 96-97.
23 Farley Mowat. *The Alban Quest.* (London: Phoenix, 1999), 46.

which channels our attention to evidence, which narrows the frame of our theory, and without great care we can easily get caught in a vicious cycle. The thinker who could square off Gimbutas and Mowat would be heroic (and perhaps foolhardy) indeed.

Dead Men in Drag

A classic example of confirmation bias interfering with our understanding of Northern European history relates to interpreting the gender of bodies found by archaeologists at burial sites.[24] Prior to the possibility of osteological and DNA analysis, the gender of such corpses was determined according to the dominant sex role assumptions held by the archaeologists—hence those buried with weaponry were assumed to be male, those with domestic equipment assumed to be female.[25]

With the recent advent of more sophisticated methods of determining gender, however, it appears that it was not uncommon for Heathen men to be equipped for the grave in rather *femme* ways, and the reverse held for female burials. Such surprising findings (surprising in that they violate our confirmation biases) have been made at burial sites in Denmark, Norway, Finland, Estonia, England, and Frisia.[26]

In short: all over Europe this sort of burial practice was occurring, but until recent technical advances we were denied these insights by our (or our researchers') confirmation biases, biases rooted in our own cultural mores about gender roles. These mores, having the invisibility of self-evidence, only begin to be exposed in the face of compelling contradictory evidence.

Though I am hesitant to make any cavalier claims, it seems very possible that these discoveries may disconfirm all sorts of ideas that have been entertained as near-certainties about the nature of gender roles among the Heathens of old. They also seem to echo Robert Ward's fascinating theory about the proliferation of female Germanic warriors, and certainly give impetus to the idea that Ward's theories deserve a fuller hearing than they have had hitherto.[27]

We can see that a great deal of what seemed certain about gender roles among the

---

[24] Tina Lauritsen and Ole Thirup Kastholm Hansen. "Transvestite Vikings?" *Idavallen*. (http://www.idavallen.org/artiklar/transvikings.html [accessed 22 December, 2009]).
[25] Ibid.
[26] Ibid.
[27] Robert Ward. "Were Valkyries Real?" *Hex* 2 (2007): 52.

Northern European Heathens—ideas informed by our own cultural biases—is made much less certain by these discoveries. Perhaps with this example my reader can begin to perceive why I think an appreciation of the effects of confirmation bias might be so important to our attempts to construct a Heathenry that has any kind of depth or credibility. All too easily we flow into the slipstream of seeing in our history and heritage what we (more or less arbitrarily) expect to see.

Incidentally, these archaeological findings represent a massive problem for the application of Gimbutas's theories to the Germanic peoples, since they suggest that gender roles were far less absolute than 20th century archaeology, shaped by quite rigid gender ideas itself, could have anticipated, and certainly much less absolute than Gimbutas's theories can permit.

Family Feuds

Many folk seem to regard the relationship between the giants and the Æsir as being fundamentally conflictual—even academically celebrated authorities like John Lindow and Margaret Clunies-Ross.[28] I suppose they make this argument on the basis of the extensive—here it comes—confirmatory evidence for that hypothesis. Apart from the constant scrapping between Æsir and Jotnar; Thor constantly venturing into Jotunheim; and the gods' difficult encounters with such characters as Suttung and Thjazi, there is the larger backdrop of Ragnarök itself. I am sure there is plenty of other evidence for this view as well. It seems open and shut: Æsir versus giants is a safe characterisation of the Northern myths and plenty of folk that I have encountered happily accept that.

Unfortunately, I think this is one of the most blatantly mistaken ideas about Germanic mythology that exists. Certainly, the relationship between Jotnar and Æsir is complex, trouble-riddled, and ends violently. Nevertheless, here are just a few black swans for this distinctly dualistic account of Germanic myth:

- Odin is himself descended from giant stock.[29]
- There are many giants who are welcome among or friends to the Æsir, such as Ægir[30] and Jord[31] (the *mother* of Thor the giant-killer, with Odin himself as the father no less).
- Mimir, one of Odin's best benefactors, is ambiguously either a god or a

---

28 John Lindow. *Norse Mythology.* (Oxford: Oxford University Press, 2001), 337.
29 Snorri Sturluson. *Edda.* trans. Anthony Faulkes. (London: Everyman, 1987), 11.
30 Hollander, 62.
31 Ibid., 101.

giant (or both!).[32]
- Jarnsaxa, a giantess, bears Thor's son Magni,[33] and is one of Heimdall's mothers.[34]

It seems that as soon as we attempt to properly test the simplistic vision of *Æsir versus Jotnar* it begins to crumble. We are left with a far more complex and subtle mythology, a series of stories about conflict and friendship between extended kin groups and *not* between radically alien cultures. I suspect that latent Christian dualism has influenced the simplistic *Æsir versus Jotnar* view of Germanic mythology, yet perhaps these ancient stories reflect a richer and more accurate vision of the world's workings than the kind of mentality that generally seems to be promulgated by Christianity.[35]

These comments bear particular relevance to the modern Heathen distinction of *innangarð* and *útangarð* which surfaces in various contexts. This notion conceptualises the Heathen world view in terms of ever widening concentric circles, from the immediate kin group out to the limits of creation, with very little permeability between circles.[36] It seems to be inspired by the ancient distinction between Midgard and Útgarð, although, as I have just discussed, it seems that this geographical distinction did not necessarily extend to groups and relationships, or at least that it worked in subtle, complex, semi-permeable ways rather than closed, strict, and rigid ways.

Unfortunately the more shallow application of the *innangarð* concept can lead to some very dualistic ideas, such as the notion that Heathens should always side with other Heathens. In my personal experience there are many Heathens with whom I have much less in common with than other individuals who are not Heathen. In one very difficult experience I made the, in my mind the utterly obvious, decision to stand with some responsible and honest non-Heathens against a Heathen individual whose behaviour could politely be described as deceitful, spiteful, and (ironically) self-destructive. Heathen social theory needs to be elastic enough to allow for such circumstances.

In contemporary Heathenry I have encountered applications of the basically

---

32 Simek, 216.
33 Sturluson, 79.
34 Hollander, 138.
35 Of course I am hesitant to make total generalisations about Christianity or its world-view—to do so might well make me guilty of the kinds of cognitive error discussed in this essay.
36 Wednesbury Shire. "The Sacred and the Holy." *Wednesbury Shire*. (http://www.englatheod.org/holy.htm [accessed 22 December, 2009]).

logical idea of concentric social rings that plunge into armoured dualistic thinking (a churlish "Us and Them" attitude), and I think this is strongly informed by a dichotomous misreading of the relationships between Æsir and Jotnar (or at the very least legitimates itself with such a misreading). This misreading is shaped by confirmation bias—if I funnel a dualist world view (shaped perhaps by the dominant Christian and modernist ideologies) into a seemingly binary model such as the *innangarð/útangarð* philosophy, it is thereafter very easy for me to "discover" evidence for a rigid interpretation of that philosophy in the old Heathen history and myths, and to ignore anything that inconveniently contradicts me.

It is worth noting that, despite their archaic inflection, historical Heathens did not seem to think in hard dualistic terms, and the basis for the more dualistic modern conceptions of the *innangarð* seems to largely lie in a failure to appreciate the porous lines of Germanic mythological geography. A more subtle and complex understanding of kinship, lineage, time, and space—and one that is likely more faithful to the historical Heathens—emerges once we cast off the shackles of confirmation bias and attempt to attend to mythology in its fullness and not merely as a relatively narrow theory would have us think it to be.

The old Heathens' fascination with lineage just as easily leads to an engagement with the vast interconnected matrices of wyrd as it does an attitude of rigid localisation.[37] Rather than being trapped within a monotheistic single focal point for the radiating concentric rings of the *innangarð*, it seems more likely that they saw the world as having a plenitude of such poles, each radiating rings that overlapped to create complex and dizzying patterns, like the splashes of multiple drops on the surface of a pond.[38] In truth it is likely that the old Heathens were unwilling to sacrifice either specificity *or* interconnection in their world view, and that we risk foisting a false dichotomy (inspired again by dualist monotheism) upon ourselves if we choose to focus on only one of these two elements (I will say more on this later).

Of course, by opening ourselves to a more complex understanding of these myths, we open ourselves to much richer possibilities for making sense of our own living Heathen spirituality. I believe that when we think through our understanding of Heathenry with a conscious awareness of the traps of

---

37 Bil Linzie. *Drinking from the Well of Mimir.* (Self Published: 2000), (http://www.angelfire.com/nm/seidhman/index.html [accessed 22 December, 2009]), 21.
38 Linzie's exploration of the metaphor of "Round River" in relation to the old Heathen world view bears particular relevance to this notion; see page 24 of Linzie's *Drinking from the Well of Mimir* for more on this.

confirmation bias we afford ourselves many more opportunities to genuinely understand the nature of our remarkable heritage and its place in our unfolding lives.

Euhemerism

An idea that has been touched on earlier in this essay is Euhemerism: the notion that mythology is merely the distorted remnants of historical events.[39] Euhemeristic accounts of Germanic mythology can be found in a range of medieval sources: in Saxo Grammaticus and in a number of Snorri Sturluson's works.[40]

In the clutches of confirmation bias it is easy to look for evidence that appears to corroborate Euhemeristic theory. More specifically, it is tempting for some folk to take these medieval accounts as solid evidence for Euhemerism. Yet as soon as we remember to also look for disconfirmatory evidence Euhemeristic theory loses its bright sheen: all the sources for this theory write at great temporal or spatial distance from Heathenry and all are Christian, with either defamatory or justificatory agendas blatantly woven into their work. These are hardly credible witnesses. Similar problems vex any attempt to use documents such as the sagas to understand Heathen culture.

More importantly, it seems very unlikely that an independent Germanic mythology, derived from historical events that occurred after the arrival of the Indo-Europeans in Europe, could have emerged that would nevertheless display such startling continuities with other branches of the same cultural tree (e.g. Celtic, Greek, Roman, Vedic). This factor alone makes it seem much more plausible to suggest that the Indo-Europeans brought a mythology with them—even if it subsequently underwent changes—rather than inventing a new one on their arrival.

Of course, there may be *some* truth to the Euhemeristic theory, but as an overall account of Germanic myth it remains compelling only so long as we allow confirmation bias to steer us away from the wide range of negative evidence that pertains to the subject.

Theory Countertransference & Group Polarisation

In many respects the underlying mechanism of confirmation bias lies in *theory*

---

39 Simek, 75.
40 Ibid., 76.

countertransference, a term first coined in the psychotherapeutic literature, and to which I have already alluded. The term countertransference refers to projections that the psychotherapist makes onto their client; theory countertransference, then, occurs when we project our theoretical expectations onto an individual or subject matter without adequately attempting to understand what is actually present before us first.[41]

Hence if, like Gimbutas, I expect to find a patriarchal Indo-European culture in my archaeological research...then chances are I will. It is all too easy to confuse my *theory* about ancient cultures with the cultures themselves, with the consequence that I no longer consider anything like the full breadth of relevant evidence or hypotheses available.

Of course, we cannot abandon theory altogether, since then inquiry would be reduced to random stabs in the night. However, it is necessary for us to seek to clarify where our own theory countertransference tends to lead us, and actively cultivate both tentativeness towards our preferred theories and an enthusiasm for the study of other perspectives. Only by disciplined thinking and energetic self-examination can we hope to avoid the worst excesses of this sort of error.

As soon as we attempt to undertake this challenge we encounter the other foe of a mature, fully realised Heathenry: *group polarisation,* which seems a natural bedfellow for dualistic misunderstandings of the *innangarð* concept.

Group polarisation occurs when, in order to assert their "rightness," a group begins to articulate their views in more exaggerated, absolute ways. Soon a leapfrog pattern emerges, and gradually folk allow the crucial determinants of their beliefs be things such as group cohesion or a defined sense of identity, things that can easily have little to do with fact or clear thinking. This, incidentally, is how messianic or doomsday cults often get started: it is a very typical facet of the Christian cult, and seems potentially able to run together very easily with dualistic readings of the *innangarð/ útangarð* concept.[42]

I have personally witnessed this very phenomenon in a Heathen community, partly over the kinds of ideological issues that Heathens tend to divide themselves into relatively artificial camps like "Folkish" or "Universalist" over. Indeed, the events in question saw the disintegration of the group integrity and a

---

41 For a discussion of the benefits and risks of theory in psychotherapy see: Barry Duncan, Scott Miller and Jacqueline Sparks. *The Heroic Client.* (San Francisco: Jossey-Bass, 2004), 121-123.

42 Neil Carlson and William Buskist. *Psychology: The Science of Behaviour.* (Needham Heights: Allyn & Bacon, 1997), 363.

great deal of harm done to a number of people as well as the loss of the momentum and the positive force that had initially been present.

Yet these sorts of hard-edged divisions, which are a fertile breeding ground for confirmation bias, theory countertransference, and group polarisation, are not immutable.

For example, Bill O'Hanlon describes a case where his colleagues instigated open dialogue between a group of rabid Pro Life folk and a group of rabid Pro Choice folk.[43] It turned out that once each group stopped playing out their confirmation bias scripts about how horrid the other side were, they discovered that they shared many common values (though disagreeing on how best to achieve them), but more importantly discovered that once dialogue opened up, compromise seemed more reasonable, and indeed attractive. A range of positive outcomes issued from the experiment.

The two sides did not suddenly amalgamate into one, but they did manage to find some surprising points of ideological convergence and each side was able to relax some of the rigidity of its stance and recognise the complexities and ambiguities of the issue, which is after all a very difficult question to be dealt within in the terms of Manichean absolutism. We might say that each side abandoned some of their confirmation bias and consequently were able to develop a more subtle and nuanced understanding of the world around them—without necessarily having to thereby abandon the essence of their particular perspectives. This is a worthy outcome.

> *To exchange one orthodoxy for another is not necessarily an advance. The enemy is the gramophone mind, whether or not one agrees with the record that is being played at the moment.*[44]

The mentality of "schools of thought" deserves some reflection at this point. Schools of thought are dangerous things. They enable us to pigeon-hole one another in categories which at best are simplistic, and at worst which actually impair our freedom of reflection and expression. This is not to say that having such categories is useless: it would be very hard to organise our understanding of this complex world around us without such heuristics.

Nevertheless, schools of thought expose us to the risk of a dangerous mistake: they make us focus heavily on having the "right" beliefs when I suspect it might

---

[43] Bill O'Hanlon. *Do One Thing Different.* (New York: Harper Collins, 2004), 62-63.
[44] George Orwell, *Animal Farm* (New York: Everyman's Library, 1993), 106.

be more helpful for us to be focusing on *how* we go about believing the things that we believe, for example by examining and applying the psychology of the *doing* of belief as I have attempted to undertake in this essay.

If allegiance to any one "system" of thinking or doing—be it a set of assumptions about the gender of dead Heathens or beliefs about the best way to conceptualise modern Heathenry—exposes us to the risk of destructive cognitive biases then perhaps a different kind of philosophy is necessary.

My contention is that we might profit from following Odin's example in hanging from the tree and making the horizon of mystery the benchmark of our knowledge. In other words, orienting ourselves in terms of what we do not know rather than attempting to erect precarious temples around what we think we do know.

Odin and Semi-Permeability

Odin's status as a liminal figure is unquestionable—the formative myth of his hanging on the tree alone attests to this. He is a god of magic, shamanism, journeying, and death, a veritable hedge-rider.

A range of myths also present him as being very psychologically astute. I think it safe to say that Odin has little patience for cognitive failures such as confirmation bias, theory countertransference, and group polarisation. Each of these errors sacrifices honesty and curiosity in favour of emotional comfort. There is little that is Odinic about such an exchange.

Given that any theory, system, or pattern of belief can render us vulnerable to cognitive bias, it is necessary to go beyond such things. Just as Odin transcends all conventional kinds of knowing in his ordeal on the tree, modern Heathens would profit from attempting to cultivate circumspection about what we think we know. Modern psychology has very neatly dissected the various ways in which our thinking can run astray, but it will take courage, reflection, honesty, and discipline for that knowledge to be usefully applied.

I believe that Odin's liminal nature provides a very useful clue and aid in that task, and to that end I would like to offer a tool for understanding Heathenry which I have chosen to term *semi-permeability*.

Semi-permeability is a property some surfaces have which allow them to permit liquid to flow through them *without* losing their structural integrity. If we consider Heathenry to be bounded by a semi-permeable membrane then we are afforded a number of very helpful advantages over the more rigid, dualistic accounts that seem to be popular in some quarters.

A semi-permeable Heathenry is able to sustain a strong sense of specificity in terms of history and culture, however it is not so stuck in abstraction that it therefore ignores that aspect of the Germanic heritage which emphasises the importance of inter-connection. If the hearth is an important image, so too is the hedge and its rider, and the Allfather is himself a rim walker.

For those inside or outside the hedge, that strict boundary seems absolute and non-negotiable. From the point of view of one who rides the hedges—who walks liminality as Odin does—the division is merely the marker for the turning point in a watershed. In other words, the view from the hedge itself reveals that all such divisions conceal the complex interrelations that bind the worlds together.

This point of view exposes a common and easily unnoticed cognitive error—the confusion of purity with specificity. Some Heathens seem to believe that in order to preserve and deepen the specificity of their heritage they must huddle inside the hedge and dream up a world of spooks and villains outside its boundaries. This seems to be what purity amounts to.

Yet our ancestors lived both inside and outside the hedge, and some even rode it. Purity seems to be an (ironically foreign) value projected onto Germanic cultural history. If we grasp the notion of semi-permeability then we realise that what we Heathens are actually grasping for is a sense of specificity (and therefore sacredness); and that this specificity is grounded in our being in a world, in our need to have relationships across all sorts of real-yet-ephemeral hedges. Both are necessary if we are going to succeed in reconstructing the ancestral consciousness.

Certainly there is plenty of archaeological evidence—that one is only able to notice once the blinders of purity-inspired confirmation bias have been put aside—that suggests that the Germanic peoples were very much able to maintain cultural integrity and specificity but also intimate relationships with ecosystems, spirits, differing opinions within Heathenry, and also with other peoples.[45]

---

45 For an example, see: Science Daily. "New Research Refutes Myth of Pure Scandinavian Race." *Science Daily*. (http://www.sciencedaily.com/releases/2008/06/080609172919.htm [accessed 21 December, 2009]); Johanna Blomqvist. "Vikings Did Not Dress the Way We Thought." *Uppsala University*. (http://www.uu.se/news/news_item.php?id=73&typ=pm [accessed 10 January, 2010]); Auslan Cramb. "Treasure Hunter Found 1m Haul on First Outing." *Telegraph*.

Indeed, it seems to me that they wove their sense of specificity precisely from embracing an understanding of the complex causal web of the world (which leave their traces in the layers of the past, or *ørlög*), rather than splitting the world into rigid and hermetically sealed compartments.[46]

The survey of the various controversies and debates that have been presented in this essay is an invitation to the reader to reflect on the possibility that carving the world into rigid divisions is a quick road to crippling cognitive biases—and vice versa. This is part and parcel of Gimbutas' absolutist caricatures of pre-Indo-Europeans and Indo-Europeans (which in turn rest on gross clichés of female and male identity); it is part and parcel of the high rate of error that has been uncovered in 20th century interpretation of Northern European grave goods (which is again shaped by archaeologists' gender-related theory countertransference); it runs to the heart of the simplistic grasp that many Heathens and academics hold on the relationships between Æsir and Jotnar; and it animates the pedestrian agenda of the Euhemerists.

Fox and Hedgehog

Isaiah Berlin's essay on Tolstoy, *The Hedgehog and the Fox*, famously discusses the mysterious declaration of the ancient Greek poet Arcilochus that "the fox knows many things, but the hedgehog knows one big thing."[47] This insight provides a useful shorthand for orienting ourselves toward the question of cognitive bias in Heathenry.

The hedgehog is a creature with low horizons. When threatened, it hunkers down beneath its spiny armour to defend its sense of orthodoxy. It is poorly suited to coping with change. Its stratagems work insofar as it remains safe beneath its spiny armour. However it is also imprisoned in that safety, its field of vision narrow and myopic.

The fox does not confuse its own ideas for reality, but rather flits from point of reference to point of reference. It is an expert in allowing things to be what they are and speak for themselves. It cannot make the kinds of sweeping claims to

---

(http://www.telegraph.co.uk/news/newstopics/politics/scotland/650175 [accessed 10 November, 2009]); Peter Wells. *Barbarians to Angels: The Dark Ages Reconsidered.* (New York: W.W. Norton & Company, 2008), 37.

46 Linzie's exploration of the metaphor of "Round River" in relation to wyrd bears particular relevance to this notion; see Bil Linzie, *Drinking from the Well of Mimir*.

47 Isaiah Berlin. *The Hedgehog and the Fox*. (Oxford: The Isaiah Berlin Virtual Library, undated), (http://berlin.wolf.ox.ac.uk/published_works/rt/HF.pdf [accessed 22 December, 2009]), 1.

truth that the hedgehog can, but then again this also liberates it of much of the risk of getting things horribly wrong. If the fox cannot entirely make sense of its multiplicity of experiences, it is at least relatively safe from the risks presented by confirmation bias and other cognitive errors.

When we get stuck on one big idea and rigidly impose it upon our understanding, danger ensues; conversely, an excess of multiplicity puts us at risk of confusion and circular pursuits. Berlin celebrates Tolstoy as a thinker who is capable of entertaining the tendencies of both fox and hedgehog.[48] The stolid, sincere, and redoubtable hedgehog qualities, combined with the playful, inquisitive, and ruthlessly empirical fox qualities, make for a formidable mind indeed.

To date it seems to me that contemporary Heathenry, perhaps in reaction to the more fox-like tendencies of broader neo-paganism, has tended towards the fearful security of the hedgehog, a conservatism that smacks to me of weakness. However, rather than suggest that Heathens swap their hedgehog record for a fox record, I would like to suggest playing both on the gramophone at the same time.

This seems to me like just the sort of thing that Odin, that hoary liminal god, would approve of heartily, and might perhaps be a useful step towards doing away with the gramophone mind altogether. In its place we might find ourselves taking up the banner of our personal agency, responsibility, and the endless graduated shades of making and revising uncertain judgements. This is a far cry from lazily resting on the laurels of rust-encrusted confirmation biases.

Reverence

In this vein, I contend that an essential component of Heathenry is a reverential attitude. One must have reverence for the life that moves through all things: the generosity of the land spirits, the history of one's family, the stories that bind beings to one another, the secret and unknowable orderings of wyrd and *ørlög* and *runa* (which, after all, means mystery).[49]

Reverence is impossible so long as we attempt to force the world to fit into the narrow confines of our own dogma, so long as we insist on believing that the only reality is the one we see through the narrow visor of our intellectual armour. Reverence requires something different: curiosity, vulnerability, a sense of humour, a recognition of the limits of our understanding. In short, it seems to require something like a semi-permeable Heathenry. How can we entertain a

---

48 Ibid., 3.
49 Sweyn Plowright. *The Rune Primer*. (Sydney: Rune-Net Press, 2006), 3.

sense of awe—the root of reverence—without such attitudes?

It is difficult to hold onto our reverence in this post-industrial age. Technocratic capitalism has bent the Enlightenment ideals into twisted shapes, and the twin laws of disposability and amnesia make reverence a precious jewel, but often one as elusive as the Grail.

> *I would rather have a mind opened by wonder than one closed by belief.*[50]

Perhaps a clue as to why we as Heathens are so vulnerable to crypto-Christian dualisms lies in the title of a song by the black metal band Emperor: "The Loss and Curse of Reverence."[51]

Reverence represents a loss and a curse to those of us who feel its distant call through the haze of modernity.[52] The sense of loss arises from the grievous wound of our being uprooted from history, spirituality, nature, heritage, and so forth. The loss is overwhelming and irredeemable, for there is no going back. The only way clear is through, and this too represents a most uncertain outcome.

Yet once one has been touched by a sense of reverence it is like the thorn that pierces Briar Roses' sleep-soaked prison. The long slow stumbling journey back to one's spiritual heartland begins, and the keen loss of the rootedness that the Heathens of old (and many other peoples) took for granted is our callous shadow. The loss that goes with reverence is brutal and relentless, and it is no surprise that many Heathens seem to be drawn to the macabre in their musical and artistic tastes. We are mourners for the very current that we seek to reincarnate.

This is where the curse of reverence is activated: once it has touched our lives, we cannot simply close up and dissolve into amnesia and somnambulism again, at least not permanently. The curse is a hard taskmaster—the sense of being integrated into the sacred that reverence bestows also threatens to alienate one from the shallow consensus world into which one is thrown. When we grasp the vast majesty of the World Tree in all of its interconnected glory we simultaneously become isolated outcasts in the world of popularly consented beliefs. I suspect that this sense of isolation is what can make us vulnerable to slipping back into dualistic thinking—it is hard to bring oneself full circle, from

---

50 Sign at *Socrates' Table Café*, Nowra, New South Wales, Australia, circa November 2008.
51 Emperor, *Anthems to the Welkin at Dusk*. (audio CD, Candlelight Records, 1997).
52 I feel I should note that I am not nearly as absolute a critic of modernity as some Heathens seem to be, but I certainly entertain no illusions about its failures.

rebelling against modern consciousness to residing in a reverential pre-modern mindset alongside a modern world.

The deeply personal nature of Heathenry necessarily impels us to seek out others who also know the secret of the loss and curse of reverence. We must build a welcome home for ourselves, and it must have strong foundations: I believe that Heathenry as a social or cultural phenomenon will never provide a good house for reverence so long as it remains unconscious of the dangers of dualistic thinking and mole-like self-reference. To truly manifest our love of the roots of Europe we must, I suspect, harden ourselves and put aside such indulgences.

Final Thoughts

> *Theoretical loyalty provides clear direction but is inherently limiting; theoretical anarchy enables flexibility but also inserts uncertainty…there are no fixed and correct ideas or methods… and therefore no inherently right ways…The only caveat is that any selected idea must produce benefit.*[53]

This discussion on the fashion in which cognitive biases impact upon the project of modern Heathenry has exposed a range of pitfalls, but also enabled the sketching of some possibly more fruitful directions for further exploration as we seek to set deep roots for the reconstruction of the old ways of the North.

I have attempted to show how concepts in modern psychology can assist us in following Odin's shamanic or magical example – his willing embrace of mystery. In the process we may find that some of the "obvious" truths we might be tempted to hold as Heathens might actually be quite shallow. This is a good outcome: the more we *sell our cleverness and buy bewilderment*, to paraphrase the great Sufi poet Rumi, the richer we are likely to become. In that spirit I freely acknowledge my own vulnerability to confirmation bias and its cousins. Neither my perspective nor any other can ever be definitive.

> *Could Heathenism best be defined as…listening and sheltering, as open-handedness through strength? In trusting what we cannot know, in abandoning our arrogant, disembodied addiction to the armour of tight-fisted control? Does this mean that we must abandon the right to our own rigidity? Is a Heathen better served by a mind like the light on the ocean at dawn than*

---

53 Barry Duncan, Scott Miller and Jacqueline Sparks. *The Heroic Client.* (San Francisco: Jossey-Bass, 2004), 122.

by a mind like a prison wall at midnight?[54]

It seems reasonable to contend that we would profit from following Odin's example in hanging from the tree, in making the horizon of mystery the benchmark of our knowledge. In other words, orienting ourselves in terms of what we do not know rather than attempting to erect precarious temples around what we think we do know. The courage of uncertainty is Viking courage—it is the intellectual version of coursing over the back of the North Sea, the rising sun behind us. We would well honour the ancestral traditions of Europe by embracing the limits of our understanding rather than fleeing to rigidity and dogma.

One of the great strengths of Heathenry is its polytheism. I hold the perhaps Quixotic hope that as a cultural movement Heathenry will cultivate a polytheism of beliefs and ideas in reverential emulation of the example set by our deities, rather than petrify into abstract dualisms and ideological caricatures as both our more recent Christian forebears and some of our own number have seemed all too willing to do.

---

54 Harigast. "Listening and Sheltering: Grimms' 'The Owl.'" *Hex* 5 (2009), 39.

When the Gods Speak Back:
A Heathen Perspective on Gardening

Loddfafner

Gardening is a Heathen form of prayer. It directly involves the gardener with the cycles of the seasons. Although one might adapt some ancient phallic fertility rite invoking Freyr for success in growing vegetables and flowers, here I am only considering the ordinary tasks of gardening as themselves the ritual.

Gardening, like Heathenry, is homage to our ancestors who needed to grow, hunt, or gather as a necessity for raw survival. Both are forms of resistance to the atrophying of our instincts in conditions of modernity. I assume here, though without certainty, that instinctive responses to the seasons are imprinted in us through generations of surviving in a temperate climate. I cannot easily follow the ways of my agricultural ancestors, nor would it be the same given that I can go shopping in a supermarket if my crops fail. I can at least honor them. I justify the effort as building the skills to survive in case of disaster although most of my vegetables last year were sacrificed to a groundhog. I am no expert, but each year I learn something more, and if it ever becomes a necessity I will know what to do.

In a scientific age I can naturally attribute any success not to the Gods but to the result of my own efforts and of following the directions that agricultural extension agencies compiled from well-designed research. The routines of gardening, however, keep me in contact with the soil on a gut level. Weeding might not be absolutely necessary but it is an occasion to dig my fingers into the earth and feel its texture and wetness. I have an excuse to immerse myself among the insects and keep an eye out for butterflies and praying mantises.

The kitchen scraps that go into the compost are a sacrifice, though the effort to dig them into the earth feels more like one. I can buy bags of compost in a garden center that will do the job, but the ritual of saving coffee grounds and broccoli stems keeps up my connection with the soil. In blots, I have sacrificed good tomatoes to the Gods in gratitude for the harvest, but in returning those tomatoes to the earth, nourishing it along with those drops of mead from the drinking horn, I have only engaged in a glorified form of composting.

Involvement with the seasons goes beyond the basics of waiting for the ground to thaw, keeping track of what to plant early and what must wait for the date of last frost, what thrives in summer heat and what will not get going until the chilliness of Autumn. I plant so each seasonal moment leads seamlessly to the next. Crocuses and hellebores bloom before winter is over. The early, middle, and late tulips give way to German irises by the end of May, and then the foxgloves take over. Midsummer is a challenge as there is little I can count on except daylilies. By August and September, the flowers that attract butterflies proliferate. The zinnias grow where I planted the seeds, and the daisies wherever they felt like planting themselves. The butterflies are as much a part of the garden as anything I plant. Actually, I encourage them by planting the food sources for their caterpillars. Extra parsley and fennel is a sacrifice for the black swallowtails.

I have neither the skills nor the motivation to create an orderly landscape following conventions. On a large scale, perfect order evokes state control of populations and so does not appeal to my Heathen instincts. Think of the gardens Le Nôtre built for Louis XVI in Versailles. On a smaller scale, the plantings around banks, malls, and suburban homes evoke a denial of nature.

Michael Pollan's *Botany of Desire* is a model for weaving philosophy with gardening. He considers gardens, the plants within them, and how people use them in terms of balancing the Apollonian and the Dionysian.[1] If that is too Mediterranean a reference for a Norse Heathen, despite Nietzsche, look instead to the collision of ice with fire in the *Völuspá* out of which the world itself was created. The tension between order and chaos is what makes a garden work. A neat square could contain a cacophony of colors. A rhythmic archipelago of repeated elements such as irises could provide a sense of backbone.

I plant carelessly and plant a range of flowers. I do plan particular effects, and particular juxtapositions of form, color, and texture, but rarely do they come through. I can never be sure which will benefit from the season and which will never take off. One flower is eaten by bugs, another wilts in the summer heat or rots during a long rainy period. That same cool wet spell will let nasturtiums run rampant in place of the dianthus that died down.

Dionysian gardening leaves room for serendipitous and powerful combinations of color and texture. Round nasturtium leaves climb through the vertical spikes of tall rushes that grew as a weed. Blue spikes of sage appear against a cloud of white phlox. When these effects work well, I leave them free while a more Apollonian gardener would pull the nasturtiums off the rushes or yank up the unplanned foxgloves.

---

[1] Michael Pollan. *The Botany of Desire*. (New York: Random House, 2001).

When the gardener, like a good scientist, is open to the unexpected, the beauty of the garden can be that of the wilderness more than that of artwork. In Chapter 6 of Darwin's *Origin of Species* where he described what kinds of evidence could pose major problems for his theory of modification of species through natural selection, Darwin included instances of natural beauty:

> Some naturalists...believe that very many structures have been created for beauty in the eyes of man...This doctrine, if true, would be absolutely fatal to my theory.[2]

One might seize on gratuitous beauty seemingly intended for a human audience as some refutation of evolution, but, as our own creation story is too magnificently absurd to mistake for literal truth, Heathens need not go so far. Those accidental moments of unexpected aesthetic and spiritual triumph that a casual approach to gardening enables might have another theological interpretation—after all those sacrifices, after all that work, the Gods finally speak back.

---

[2] Charles Darwin. *On the Origin of Species: A Facsimile of the First Edition.* (Cambridge, MA: Harvard University Press, 1964), 199.

Die heilige Stunde [The Holy Hour], by Ludwig Fahrenkrog (1918).

Descendants of the Sun[1]

Xenia Bakran-Sunic

Upon the hill, proud men,
Flaming with the pristine spark of life,
Descendants of the sun,
Emerging afresh through the everlasting streaming
Of mauve light aeons of time,
Gathered again in the irised spring twilight
In the comeliness of the sun's garden,
Where golden charms revive the forlorn sun gleam
In the depths of their beautiful eyes,
That once was lost on the altar of their past fallen life,
Their faces smiling to their women who walk barefoot
Amongst the newly flowered softness
Of the sacred blue-purpleness of Iris's paths,
That the New Moon now enchants
Upon the arising mystery
Of their ashen faces.
And so the once hostile sun
Becomes friendly to his returned worshipers,
At the unvanquished cycle of time.

---

1 Written January 2007 in Croatia, this poem was originally published in Xenia Bakran-Sunic's *The Old Life is Dead...: Poems in English and in French* (Bloomington, Indiana: AuthorHouse, 2008), 16.

Twisted Tools by Sean Thayer (aka Gandvaldr Bláskikkja), 2007.

Magic Plants Used Symbolically in Germanic Heathen Hexology

Hunter Yoder

I am frequently asked about the relationship between Hexology[1] and the plants, or *die Blantz*, in Pennsylvania *Deitsch*. My approach to *die Blantz* and their magic is similar to my approach to the Runes, a learning experience. After spending time with herbalists and entheologists,[2] and a bit here and there with Hoodoo[3] root doctors, the plants can be broken down in the following ways: herbal remedies, hallucinogens, and powerful intentional agents. The latter is the subject of this article.

My introduction to *Deitsch* herbalism occurred around 1968 when I was apprenticed to a certain Bumbaugh, a name that even today makes the Christian New Age *Brauchers*[4] cringe. He was a crusty old guy with a penchant for making amorous overtures to the ladies who came into his establishment. Bumbaugh ran and lived in a kind of all-purpose country store that was as dark and crusty as he was. Antiques, old books, herbs, and the occasional animal pelt were his stock in trade. All this thinly veiled what he really was and really knew. Bumbaugh knew *die Blantz*.

One day my mother stopped in to check out his antiques and was propositioned by ole Bumbaugh in return for a good deal. She parlayed my apprenticeship with the old goat instead. My mother was well known amongst the younger witches in Kutztown, Berks County, Pennsylvania and acknowledged as one of their own despite the fact that she taught Sunday school at the local Lutheran church. She and Bumbaugh understood each other.

Bumbaugh's primary interest in the *Blantz* was commercial and he started me out with collecting Ginseng and Goldenseal in various remote areas in Berks County to sell in his store. Despite his business approach, he had knowledge regarding the *Deitsch* version of witchcraft known as *Braucherei*, a Christianized form of the original *Hexerei*.[5] His nickname, Mountain Bummy, was a reference to a

---

1 Hexology refers specifically to the practice of creating Hex signs.
2 An entheologist is one who studies entheogens—psychoactive substances used in a religious or magical context.
3 Hoodoo is a form of folk magic that synthesizes a wide variety of traditions.
4 A *Braucher* is a practitioner of *Braucherei*, a somewhat Christianized system of *Deitsch* healing practices.
5 *Hexerei* refers to the collected practices of Germanic witchcraft particular to the

Illustration 1: Datura stramonium

most well-known *Braucher* named Mountain Mary of Oley Valley, an especially haunted region in Berks County. This was the area my ancestors came to from the Alsace-Lorraine region of Europe.

Ginseng especially caught my attention with its secretive ways. We found it in the nearby Blue Mountains. Its root is in the form of a man and it has a wildness that is commercially far more desirable than any cultivated variety. I also read about it in the early editions of Foxfire[6] and was determined to cultivate it myself. Plants usually have their own ideas and this was my first test of wills with non-human consciousness.

As I was walking the wood with Bumbaugh and opening to plants as conscious beings, I was also learning from my friends, the Claypoole family of Lenhartsville. The father, Johnny, was the unlikely heir-apparent to the famous Hexologist Johnny Ott, who had, in addition to his well known Hex signs, a hotel/restaurant/bar in Lenhartsville called the Deitsch Eck Hotel. Claypoole was an Irish Catholic from Philadelphia, but Hexology has a way of manifesting itself in unlikely ways and so it was that the torch was handed from one Johnny to another. I went to school with Mark and Kevin Claypoole. The family was large as Irish Catholic families can be. Johnny would put everybody to work for the various festivals. The biggest was the Kutztown Folk Festival, now called the Pennsylvania German Folk Festival. Both Claypoole and Bumbaugh had prime

---

Deitsch people.
6   *Foxfire* is a magazine that covers topics pertaining to the cultural heritage of Southern Appalachia.

Illustration 2: Blue Asherah, 2007

locations at this lucrative venue. Bumbaugh was a well known fixture at the Saturday farmers' markets such as Renninger's and sold his used books, antiques, and herbs there. The festival created a special exhibit area for him where the inevitable authenticity the ole guy exuded could be captured. Johnny mostly did the summer festivals including the Philly Folk Festival and would go off to these events with his VW Microbus crammed with psychedelic Hexes.

The third component here in my formation, along with plants and Hexes, is my introduction to art. My mother was a painter and I inevitably created most of her stretchers that I made from wood that floated downstream after the Spring floods on the Saucony Creek that flowed though our farm. She took painting lessons in Allentown at the Baum School from a teacher named Martin Zippen—painting landscapes, still lives, portraits, that sort of thing. She took me along and I got a free evaluation from Martin who concluded that I had very little talent. My father viewed my painting career a different way. He gave me a brush, paint, and a forty foot oak ladder and told me to paint the barn.

The Pennsylvania German bank barns are as famous as they are large. A highly evolved functional form of architecture, they featured a bank barn—meaning that you can drive up to the second story via a banked ramp with corrals on either side and doors that rolled open on all sides. The doorways could be large as 12 ft. × 40 ft. in the back. In the front was the extended fore bay which was cantilevered

Illustration 3: Black Henbane

out beyond the basic structure to provide a covered area to park implements and tractor cars, to tie up the animals, shoe horses, and hang the carcasses during butchering. This one also featured an attached milk house and granary. Painting one of these monstrosities was no small feat. But, being continually in the *Scheisse Haus*—so to speak—for one reason or another, usually involving coming home at cock's crow on school nights, there was little room for negotiation. I covered it with Hexes…and so it begins.

If you grow certain plants you realize that they have a will of their own and your idea of gardening might differ from theirs. Your idea of where things should grow will differ as well. Plant energy is a very good one, a positive connection to the living universe which is actually a lattice of interconnected energy fields. Speaking or having a conversation with a particular plant is a bit more specific however. The conversation can occur externally, with the human as nurturer and

Illustration 4: Belladonna

grower, or internally if the plant is ingested. If ingested, the human has relinquished some of his control and the conversation can be a test of wills as the nervous system is directly interfaced with the plant reality. Using a plant recreationally can be like taking one of those vacations where you get lost high in the mountains or desert and face a struggle for your life.

For me, of all the plants that have been used as herbal remedies, as entheogens, or for intentions,[7] the family Solanaceae stands out with *Datura*, Belladonna and Henbane. These three plants talk the loudest and are the most willful. Some times, depending on the individual 'user,' the three uses are not very separate, and can all blur together. My experiences with *Datura*, Belladonna and Henbane have been externally as a grower/nurturer; their unusual behavior, historical usage in witchcraft and, most importantly, their geometry has led me to use them in Hexology. Their usage in *Hexerei* or Germanic witchcraft is direct. The casting of spells via Henbane seeds or the mere possession of them was enough to get burned at the stake in medieval Germany where more witches perished than anywhere else. Always with a feminine persona, these three have been used tribally everywhere on the planet for shamanic rituals and still are. Growing

---

7 Used in a magical context, intentions are the objects which spells—spoken or, in this case, painted—are directed towards.

Illustration 5: Black Sun Hex, 2008

them is always a weird experience. No pansies, daisies or lilies are these.

The invoking of *die Blantz* has been with man since our beginnings. It is a connection of consciousnesses that many of us have lost over millennia. Plants tend to take on a feminine nature, and as such are physical manifestations of the goddesses. In the ancient cultures of the Eastern Mediterranean, Asherah was a goddess portrayed as a tree, usually an Almond. We see her frequently surrounded by rampant caprids which she feeds with her boughs. Eventually this imagery of goddess was stylized into a tree motif which eventually took the form of the Menorah. As a fertility goddess, an Asherah was frequently present in a stand of young trees, a grove. This took on a special meaning for me growing up in Berks County. In my travels "off road" I would come across such a grove, just off the flood plain on some nice bottom land that went wild. Under the trees in the grove, there was no underbrush, very clear and the rich soil was impressed with thousands of whitetail deer footprints. Obviously from the bark rubbings and such signs of activity, this was where they congregated for mating.

Pennsylvania *Deitsch* lore speaks of The Elder, *Sambucus canadensis*, or as they say, *Hollerbier* after the goddess Frau Holle. The bush-like tree is planted behind the house as a guardian, for she is a goddess of home and hearth as well as the goddess of the underworld. She is depicted as an old hag and her presence protects the house. She does this by grounding out negative energy and directing it underground. She prefers wet rich habitats and her roots reach down into the water table. Stone farmhouses in southeast Pennsylvania were always built on lower ground just off the flood plain locations so that the hand-dug wells were not such an ordeal to create, and were perfect for this guardian.

Male energies exist in magic plants as well. However, maleness in a plant spirit is not quite the same as a male spirit of an animal. Common Mullein or *Verbascum thapsus* with his erect candle like flowering stalks is masculine in the sense that a lightning rod is masculine. Again, in *Deitsch* lore, the candle of a common Mullein is carried in the back pocket not to conduct but to prevent accidental lightning strikes.

Another, not native to Pennsylvania but an interesting male energy, is the Huachuma, or San Pedro cactus, *Echinopsis pachanoi*—formerly *Trichocereus pachanoi*—that is employed in High Andean Shamanism. This one is a tall erect cactus that is masculine in the sense of an old wise Grandfather. It is the *cactus de cuatro vientos*, the sacred cactus of the four winds, and it grows amazingly well in the *Zaubereigartens*[8] of southeast Pennsylvania along with other South American power plants. If you listen you will hear plants talk. One in particular that speaks loudly and clearly, and can be extremely demanding, is Valerian, or *Valeriana officinalis*. While buying herb seedlings at a farmers market, a robust Valerian plant instructed me, "pick me up and take me home!" So I did; and she has multiplied one hundred fold for me. The children of this plant have not lost the willfulness of the 'mother.' More recently, one became unhappy that it was not first on the list to be watered and demanded attention. In fact, she screamed for attention…and got it. Plant spirit is often surprising. This particular willful prima donna is used often as a sedative and to ease nervousness and stress.

Plant spirits, facile as they are, also possess the ability to change sex. *Arisaema triphyllum,* or Jack in the Pulpit, is a very strange plant that I met very early on in childhood. Once wandering into a part of the woods I had never been to before, I encountered "Jack" who promptly spoke to me and told me to "get out!" These

---

8 *Zaubereigarten* is German for "magic garden."

Illustration 6: Geilskimmel Fertility Hex, 2008

come either male or female, but—if in the close proximity of another of the same sex—can change the following year to the opposite gender to ensure success in fertilization. They do not have bulbs but corms, and the leaves are trifoliate. This makes them useful in Hexology as we use three because—as taught from antiquity—"three's the charm."

Most recently, I encountered "Jack" on the *Hexenkopf*, a strange piece of rock outcropping—or the technical term is a mountain pillar—in Northampton County, Pennsylvania where my tribe, *der Stamm*, was holding a Walpurgisnacht ritual. This was historically a place where "Hexes" or witches would congregate in Colonial times in Pennsylvania. Not a part of the Appalachian Mountains which are nearby, it is a distortion in the time/space continuum. On this occasion, after shepherding all but one of the tribe off the Hexenkopf and back to the safety of their cars, I returned for Patricia Hall, who had stayed behind to listen to the place. The walk back up off the road is a relatively short one, and one that I had made several times that day without incident since I was really the only one to know the way. Unexpectedly, as I was returning for her, I became lost and knew that the place was playing tricks on me. It has the strange effect that nobody can hear your calls even if they are nearby. Such was the case with Patricia, who even saw me pass by but thought it was someone else and so did not call out to me. Knowing the *Hexenkopf* and its ways, I used my mind and circled back onto her location at the rock altar. Upon our retreat from the mountain we encountered, "Jack". I was unhappy with the mountain for trying to take her from me, so I pulled Jack, a part of its consciousness, out of the ground to take home. Jack screamed and I involuntarily let go at first, but succeeded and stuck him in my pocket. Later we planted him in one of the gardens we keep.

The turning point in my Hexology was my reintroduction to *Datura stramonium*. This occurred in, of all places, Brooklyn, New York. I knew her from my childhood. It is interesting that, to children, the names of plants are not important. Playing amongst them is the thing. This lady is infamous but hugely important in shamanism, and I was determined to find her again. As I wrote in my blog, *Frank Blank in Brooklyn*:

> Red Hook, NYC's version of a Stalinist-Leninist State, or perhaps NYC's version of Mao's "Great Leap Forward." A grim reminder of what happens when Big Brother controls all aspects of its citizens lives. An example of what billions and billions of dollars achieves when flushed down the toilet, right you got it…a clogged sewage system. From the Projects to the Red Hook recreation area, to the razor wired pedestrian bridge over the BQE into the public school which sure looks like prison. You paid for it I paid for it, we all did…it might as well be a federal penitentiary, you get the unique view of the world through a high security fence. The occupants are…pretty vacant…all employed by the state…wards of the state, permanently damaged and in the business of self replication in a backdrop of a commercial warehouse zone with heavy trucks filled with hard toxic sewage, recycled paper and a pervasive odor of smoked fish—a known carcinogen in the air. Even in the new Brooklyn's spectacular real estate development miracle you can still get down to basics in a porto john in Red Hook, where the homeless still can chill and shoot up in peace…my kinda place. Be careful though, Red Hook is the most police enforced zone in the 76th precinct's jurisdiction. They fund their personal retirements on the summons written here. Oh yeah this is where you go to take your drivers road test in Brooklyn. So amongst the garbage and

Magic Plants Used Symbolically in Germanic Heathen Hexology

Illustration 7: Datura Coitus with Oppositional Pairings, 2008

deserted lots and places the park employees forgot to sanitize I found an old friend from my childhood...*Datura stramonium* growing free and unknown to this mindless crowd. God bless the United State of my mind."

Her smell was her signature, not a rancid or funeral parlor smell as described in books, but an undeniable presence. I dug her up and took her home to my garden...what a mistake. I grew her successfully and indulged a bit in smoking her leaf with my Rabbi friend who lived next door. We both had unfortunate consequences with this adventure, so the following year I was determined not to grow her again. This plant likes me and she came back on her own without me planting seeds and she has never left! In fact she has worked her way into my heart and into my art. Her five pointed pinwheel flower is a no-brainer for the

Magic Plants Used Symbolically in Germanic Heathen Hexology

Illustration 8: Black Sun Black Henbane, 2009

center of a *Hexafoos*.[9] In the *Deitsch* dialect she is called *Geilskimmel*, which is a curious reference to horses. From my childhood on the farm, I remember that a horse could become foundered if it ingested the *Datura*, called "Jimson weed." Her willfulness can only be experienced if you try to grow her. She will grow when and where she chooses. A force of this nature is useful in Hexology.

I have used her so often that she has been stylized into a symbol. As such, I have integrated her into other more familiar aspects of Hexology, especially the raindrops. Rain drops are used traditionally as just that, both physically as water for the plants, the crop on the farm, and spiritually as a manifestation from above, or in the *Braucherei*—or Christian—context as a spiritual cleansing. I prefer to use droplets in the context of *Hexerei* as sperm and blood. Coupled with the

---

9 *Hexafoos* (pl. Hexafoosen) is a *Deitsch* term meaning, "witch's feet," referring to the painted Hex signs.

Illustration 9: Barricks Kaundi Niger Bilsenkraut Hex, 2009

Geilskimmel, I have created, in effect, the beginnings of a Bindrune with the combination of nature spirit and traditional Hexology. The third element is the Rune, or Bindrune, in the center of the Hex to complete and seal the intent. *Ingwaz*[10] works well with Lady Datura.

Once *Datura stramonium* and I established our relationship, I was determined to find other plants specific to *Hexerei*. The Black Henbane, *Hyoscyamus niger*, also known as *Niger Bilsenkraut* became immediately apparent and I purchased the seeds from a French Canadian witch and grew her. True to form, she was very particular and would germinate but not grow to fruition as normal plants would. This one is trickier than—and just as willful as—her sister *Datura*. The flowers are striking. She has the usual inverted pentagram shaped flower configuration with a spooky dark veining on the petals, which is unique among

---

10 *Ingwaz* is a Rune in the Elder Futhark, with the phonetic value of *-ng*. Its name is connected to Yngvi, an epithet of the Norse God Freyr.

all flowers to my current knowledge. We experienced success at last with this one at the Downingtown, Pennsylvania *Zaubereigarten*, which is Patricia Hall's place, and has that gingerbread cottage in the middle of the Black Forest feel to it. So it was no big surprise the *Niger Bilsenkraut* would flourish there. What I could not grow, Patricia did. It liked her first, Hex that she is, and me next, male that I am. And so it goes with these deadly ladies.

This same season, the *Atropa belladonna* seeds, earlier planted, flourished along with the *Datura stramonium* under a bed of 12 ft. Sunflowers. This Sunflower variety has significance to the *Deitsch* culture via the Chihuahua desert in Northern Mexico. The Mexican government invited Canadian Mennonites to come to Mexico and settle a desolate, dead section in the state of Chihuahua, which was inhabited by the Tarahumara—an indigenous tribe whose ceremonial usage of a small native cactus, peyote, was made famous by the French author Antonin Artaud's book, *The Peyote Dance*. The Mennonites transformed the Chihuahuan Desert they settled upon into a garden and exchanged seeds with the Tarahumara. These were the snow white seeded Sunflowers under which the much darker Belladonna prospered.

Belladonna flowers also appear as an inverted pentagram along with *Datura stramonium* and Black Henbane. So it is easy to see how these guys have been viewed as agents of the Devil in the monotheistic religions. *Dämmerschlaf*, or Twilight Sleep, was a well known combination of the Belladonna and the Opium Poppy; the effect was a dream-like waking state. This was prescribed by doctors during child birthing to deaden pain in Victorian England. The tropane alkaloid scopolamine can be found in the honey of bees when they drink from the flower. Even the sting from a bee who has ingested the flower's nectar, can have a hallucinatory effect. Our experiences growing her have been a mixture of luck with an early success with her this season, and being tricked by her look-alikes, namely Pokeberry and *Nicotiana rustica*. Just when we thought our consciousness had been lifted and the blinders pulled from our eyes with this one, she reverted to confusing us. So it's been joy mixed with confusion, although we have enjoyed a very good season with her this year.

These pentagrams, or star-like images, are essentially feminine in nature. Feminine energy is an endless resource and only requires a directional impulse and a coupling. The more intense the coupling, the better the power the Hex has. Usage of plants, special plants in a stylized manner, is just another way the Hexologist can tap into the universe of feminine energy. And so I use *Datura stramonium*, Black Henbane, and Belladonna. The willfulness of these plants can be used not by imposing the magician's will but by allowing their unpredictable nature to equal out the discordant psychic energies in a creative,

Illustration 10: Belladonna Hex, 2009

natural way. This will always work in a positive way. The natural universe is always seeking the most direct route to resolving dynamic energy inequalities. As a Hexologist, I prefer to work with nature and let it decide. My job is only to pose the question, not impose my will. If the question is a good one, there will be an answer. The need will activate your subconscious mind and what is sought is usually right in front of your eyes. Is it magic? It's Hexology.

To Vinland

Steven "Piparskeggr" Robinson

Foamy necked waves break o'er the shoal
Racing to wash granite toothed beach
Greenish sea moss garlands the rocks
Dark, wet and grey set in the sand

The land ever waits patient and hard
Always unchanged, uncaring, still
Beckoning those who hear the call
Find me, find me, I lie in wait

Oaken sea steed dances in mist
Crossing whale way, gull road taken
Into sunset, onward to West
Driven to prove tales of new land

Ship's crew sings out words to the sky
Odin, Ægir, Thor speed our way
Trust in the Gods and strength of back
Steersman holds board, sets a true course

Long are the nights, longer the days
Grey backed swells, endlessly same
Evening stars bright, lead ever on
Darkened sky sheep, cloud gift fills kegs

Noise comes to ear, watcher hears roar
Breakers tumbling, whispering birds
Fading mist lifts, sight to behold
Lowslung land dark, o'ertopped with green

Beyond the beach, river's mouth gapes
Calling the crew, travel this way
Longship slips in, trout home to wend
Pull to the bank, landsmen again

Uneasy heads, fitfully rest
Dreaming a dream, unproven land
Unproven folk, unproven wealth
Unproven Gods, unproven Fate

Wake to the dawn, Sun smiling warm
Heavy branched trees, round fragrant lea
Firs like at home and grasses too
Eagle's shrill cry splits morning calm

Sights to behold, richness of beasts
Branch antlered stag, bushy tailed squirrel
Trees of strange hue, flowers not known
Wild grapes found, Vinland is named

Old crewman dies, tree falls awry
Grave hole is dug, then mound is raised
Kin bones in earth, strange place no more
Witnessed by death, Land Bond is made

Timber and fur, fruit, fish, and drink
Ship is laden, cargo for home
East points the prow, foam trail behind
Trackless travel, wooden hull glides

Tales of new land, rumor no more
Place now to go, homesteads to build
Wealth to be had, cargoes to gain
Hofs to hallow, children to bear

Long the years pass, many ships sail
From many lands, head to the West
Making a Home for Kin and Kith
Seeking ever, frontiers to tread

Foamy necked waves break o'er the shoal
Racing to wash granite toothed beach
Greenish sea moss, garlands the rocks
Dark, wet and grey, set in the sand

The land ever waits, patient and hard
Always unchanged, uncaring, still
Beckoning those, who hear the call
Find me, find me, I lie in wait

The Ásatrú Folk Assembly

Ásatrú is about roots.

It's about connections.

It's about coming home.

www.runestone.org

Thoughts on Poetry

Steven "Piparskeggr" Robinson

Starting Point

The long trail ends, homestead's in sight,
Hunter smiles, journey is done.
Strides 'neath the trees, enters his yard,
Lengthens his pace, comes to his house.

Puts wealth of hunt in cooling hut;
The huntsman grey then enters door.
Puts up his bow upon its pegs,
Removes his cloak and other gear.

Embrace for wife and scritch for cat,
Hot water bath and toothsome meal;
A mug of mead and yawning stretch,
Sits at his desk, takes up the pen.

Within the Northern Folkways (Norse, Germanic, Celtic, Baltic, Slavic and others) storytelling became a high art. Long, cold winter nights, an appreciation of the heroic, wanting to explain the world, tales of Gods and Monsters—all these and more were inspirations to folk who could put words to thoughts in a coherent, entertaining and enlightening manner. Poetry and song...crafts so powerful that a master of them, Skald, Bard, *Minnesinger*, *Trouvère*[1] and the like, would be afforded special status, able to travel freely, welcome at any hall or home...

An important part of my outlook on the world is the idea that everything has Poetic Significance: happenings, large or small; relationships, personal or impersonal; feelings, imagined or concrete...described in words, spare and lean, or grandiose and sweeping. Almost anything can spark a thought, which leads to verse, though a little thing may inspire just a few lines and a big one an epic of Homeric proportions. Though, the converse can happen, too.

---

1 Skald, Bardd, *Minnesinger* and *Trouvère* are the respective Scandinavian, Welsh, German and French terms for poets and troubadours, with the first two having been adapted into the English vocabulary.

Poetry is, to me, like writing a personal mythology, a method by which one tries to explain the surrounding world and its phenomena (natural/realistic and supernatural/mystic).

Poetry is also a dialect of its own, no matter the language used. Poetry has its own structure, word usage, stilted stylings of non-grammar, intuitive declamation rather than reasoned rhetoric…

Poetry is something anyone can write, just as is prose. I do admit that not every effort is good; some is downright horrible in fact. *But*, the important thing is to write, get the story down. Write, write and write, this is how the effort gets better.

I've long thought that a Skald is of little worth without the Folk. Apart from them, his life means no more than someone who mumbles to himself. It is for their ears, minds and hearts that a Skald spends his voice, words and inspiration.

It's a wonderful exercise to write stunning words of prose or poetry, but of little use, I think, if one writes for himself. Writing for one's self is sometimes a useful practice exercise; offering your words only to the Holy Ones is well and good, a good act of Worthship,[2] but best, and most worthy, is being of and for the Folk.

To The Folk

I write my words, I hum my tunes
I bring it all, into one shape
My staves fly out, unto the world
What gives them Worth? 'Tis those who hear.

To be a Skald, is wonderful
To feel the kick, of Odin's Mead
To have a bit, of Bragi's Wit
To know the words, of Saga's Hoard

But without Folk, whose eyes and ears
Do see and hear, my efforts bold
I shout at self, 'tis pitiful
No man should be, without others

---

[2] An Early Modern English (*worðscip* in Old English) term from which the Modern English *worship* is derived.

Thoughts on Poetry

> For Skald is of his Folk and Kin
> His words and deeds, their words and deeds
> His hopes and dreams, their hopes and dreams
> All come to make, his drink from Well
>
> For Gods and Man, are halves of Whole
> And Skald and Folk, are likewise thus
> We give to each, a Gift of Mægn
> Our Orlays swirl, within the Well

Another thing I've thought about is a set of Laws for Skalds, a personal exercise, but one I trust will spark thought. It springs from my meditations upon poetry and its basis, in structure and culture.

Ye Piparbók - Skald Law (a beginning)

> The Skald must have ~
> A large word-hoard;
> A strong grasp of kenning, imagery and rhyme;
> A good idea of accepted poetic form;
> A fair knowledge of History, Lore, Custom and Thew.
>
> The Skald in practice ~
> Gains these from reading and listening,
> Hones these by writing and talking,
> Strengthens these by reciting and singing.
>
> The Skald must also be ~
> Bold at heart,
> Quick in wit,
> Confident in manner,
> Proud of his work,
> Humble in accepting praise.
>
> The Skald must also have ~
> Fondness for the Folk,
> Respect for their ways,
> Gratitude for their stories,
> Regard for their lives.

Never apologize to the Folk for a failed effort. However, do acknowledge that it was not what it needed to be. Listen to what they say and rewrite or discard poems or songs as necessary. But, always maintain your air of confidence. Little setbacks are learning experiences.

If you have to explain something in a poem, you have failed in preparing properly. Know the Folk and tailor your words to them. Your poems and songs should evoke, invoke and provoke within Meaning to them, without a word list appended.

Lastly, a Skald need not be iron-bound to any set poetic form. If trying to be true to form interferes with the Words and the way the Inspiration Flows, go with the Words. The Words are our connection between inspiration and audience, they are our conversation.

Stop reading this (for now). Go Write Something Of Your Own!!!

In Frith under Troth, may the Holy Æsir and Vanir see you well!

>   Our forebears hands, reach out to us
>   And give the Horn, into our grasp.
>   They look upon, our efforts Trú
>   With knowing nod, and easy grin.[3]

---

3 Stefn Ullarsson Piparskeggr. *Piparskeggrsmal*. (USA: Catamount Grange Wordsmithy, 2006), Stave 5.

The Feminine in the Post-Modern Age: How Feminism Negates Folkways

By Juleigh Howard Hobson

Women, I allow, may have different duties to fulfill; but they are HUMAN duties, and the principles that should regulate the discharge of them, I sturdily maintain, must be the same. To become respectable, the exercise of their understanding is necessary, there is no other foundation for independence of character; I mean explicitly to say that they must only bow to the authority of reason, instead of being the modest slaves of opinion.[1]

—Mary Wollstonecraft Godwin

The sacred is the unconditional respect for something.[2]

—Alain de Benoist

"Cabbage, like a good wife, is often taken for granted."[3] Your reaction to that statement will show you either just how far both a staple European foodstuff and a staple European occupation have fallen in your estimation, or how much you are in tune with the ancient folk-soul. Cabbage is unpopular these days, considered a vile and stinky vegetable, abandoned to short stories about the lives of the poor and a half-hearted appearance on less and less tables every March. Good wives, too, are unpopular. Taking either as the prop upon which life itself is sustained is unthinkable these days for most people. What a shame. At least the dependable cabbage has been replaced by various vegetables of equal or superior taste and nutrition…

Despite the long-term damage inflicted on the Northern European peoples by the scourge of Christianity, it is feminism (not femininity, not strong womanhood, but feminism) which has done the most deep-seated harm to our folk. I say this, because while Christianity converted the veneer of our folk, we must always keep in mind that the Christ of our folk is typically pictured as being blue-eyed, light brown-haired and pale-skinned. Our ancestors were Christians, or so they thought, but the God they followed was not the wooly-haired fellow from the

---

1 Mary Wollstonecraft-Godwin. *A Vindication of the Rights of Women*, 2nd ed. (London: Joseph Johnson, 1792), 50.
2 Alain de Benoist. *On Being A Pagan*. (Atlanta: Ultra, 2004), 18.
3 Folk saying.

South; our ancestors, who were the Northern people that were converted to Christianity, were following what you might call a Christian overlay of their own *trú* religion…an overlay that did not fully obscure (it actually tended to preserve) almost all of the ancient beliefs. Yes, these beliefs were sometimes, and to different degrees, distorted; yes, these beliefs were sometimes permuted…but, to this day, they were never purged. Never quite.

> Everywhere Christianity has gone it has had to subsume the worship of native divinities…Actually the lore, myths, rituals and beliefs of the church often accommodated themselves to heathen practices. Examples of this are found in everything from the adoptions of the pagan calendar of festivals to popular things such as the Christmas tree, Santa Claus and the Easter Bunny. Indeed, heathen forms and practices survived in syncretization with Christian customs both positive and negative.[4]

As a folk we were able to continue to exist within the confines of a stranger faith —the green man peered from the churches as our gods went under different names, meanwhile the old foods, the old tales, the old ways remained. As a folk we could, and can, withstand Christianity. The fact that you are reading this sort of essay in this sort of journal is ample proof of that, but as a folk we cannot withstand the onslaught of diminishment from within.

As a folk, we are situated in Midgard—in bodies, in families. We need families, and all that a traditional family life encompasses, to continue, or re-continue, our path. When the basic units of the family are blasted apart…then everything we are, as a folk, means nothing.

> The family is the pillar of Asatru. By tradition, people have been devoted to family, and rightly so, for the family is the basis of all enduring social achievements.[5]

As regrettable as the Christian conversion was, and while the roles of men and women were disrupted at this point, importantly, the family unit continued. Thus the core of the folkways survived to be handed down with the recipes, the traditions, the parents passing them to the children one generation after another.

---

4 Edred. *Witchdom of the True: A Study of the Vanit-Troth and the Practice of Seidr.* (Smithville: Runa-Raven, 1996), 16.
5 The Indiana Asatru Council. "What is Asatru." *Idunna* 24, no. 5 (September 1994): 34.

> Traditionally it is a woman's role to feed the race and it is a role that gives most of them a real joy. But equally important is their attitude towards life, a love of the soil and of nature's work, their songs and dances, their fairy tales related to the children, their anecdotes, proverbs and riddles, their famous spinning evenings where work and fun are so intermingled that the spinning and weaving takes on a festive air, their embroidery and carpet weaving, the making of the peasant costumes, the painting on pottery and even the painstaking carvings on their wooden household utensils. All this gives them no time to feel bored. They are busy and happy.
>
> It is a tradition from olden times in Romania to look with reverence not only upon God, but also upon the earthly good he gave us, like bread, water and the fruits of the fields. And this respect applies also to cooking. It is considered a sin to change in any way the patriarchal dishes and drinks which their beloved ancestors have created and passed on to them.[6]

A millennium is a long time, and still we remember so much of who we were and what we did as a folk.

Break this line and you break the back of the folk, one and all. Take the links from a chain and there is no chain left—only disarticulate pieces. For being such a "modern" invention, feminism has wrecked havoc nearly beyond salvage, for the damage it does is irreparable destruction. Far more damage than Christianity —which did harm enough to women by devaluing and oppressing them…but, at least it left them where it found them: still in existence as the heart of the family, with their valuable customs and folkways (if not their native religion) gathered around them.

Common sense dictates that the lesser of two evils is better than the greater. Our folk are better served by a devout Christian woman in braids and long skirts who has eighteen home-schooled, European-descended children than by some Mjollnir-wearing SCA[7] "battle Valkyrie" feminist who has not provided a single child for the folk's future. With the eighteen children, no matter how repulsive their present Christian faith may be, there can be real hope that their descendants will return to the *trú* ways. With no child, however, there is no hope to be had.

---

6 Anisoara Stan. *The Romanian Cookbook*. (Secausus: Castle Books, 1951), xii.
7 The Society for Creative Anachronism (SCA) is an international historical recreation society that focuses on the Middle Ages.

Feminism negates the value of, and therefore repudiates the existence of, the good wives of our folk and replaces the important role of the feminine with nothing at all.

It never intended to replace it with anything. Feminism does not exist for the good of good wives. Feminism exists to feed and support two main agencies of modern social construct. These agencies are capitalism "with its transformative process of turning the sacred into the profane, and the worship of crass materialism"[8] and cultural Marxism.

> Marxism and Feminism are one, and that one is Marxism.[9]

> Writing in the Winter 1996 issue of the Marxist journal *Dissent*, Michael Walzer enumerated some of the cultural victories won by the left since the 1960s: "The visible impact of feminism... The transformation of family life," including "rising divorce rates, changing sexual mores, new household arrangements—and, again, the portrayal of all this in the media. The progress of secularization; the fading of religion in general..."[10]

Cultural Marxism thrives on false equality and the break up of family, folk and faith. Mom working for wages as well as Dad means that no one is working for the folk at all and, who needs Mom *and* Dad if they both do the same thing (work for wages)? Who needs marriage? Who needs, for that matter, children? Single people are greater consumers of so many more service industries than even dual wage families are...

> According to the Frankfurt School ideology, Europeans who identify with family, nation or race suffer from a psychiatric disorder. In the ideal Frankfurt School world, Western nations would become therapeutic states. They would be dedicated to rooting out the remnants of adherence to traditional cultural forms of family, nation, religion and race in their citizens...In

---

8 David J. Stennet, foreward to Tomislav Sunic. *Against Democracy and Equality.* (Newport Beach: Noontide Press, 2004), xv.
9 Heidi Hartmann. "The Unhappy Marriage of Marxism and Feminism: Towards a More Progressive Union." from Lydia Sargend, ed. *Women and Revolution: A Discussion of the Unhappy Marriage of Marxism and Feminism.* (Cambridge: South End Press, 1999), 2.
10 William Norman Grigg. "Toward the Total State." *The New American.* 15, no. 14 (1999): 8.

> this upside down world, families that are proud of their ancestors, concerned with moving up socially or even having biological heirs are viewed as pathological. In fact, one might conclude that the real agenda of *The Authoritarian Personality* [a major work of the Frankfurt School intended for an American audience] is to pathologize adaptive behavior in general. Those who value highly committed marriages and cohesive families, who are upwardly mobile and seek material resources, who are proud of their families and identify with their parents, who have high self-concepts, who believe that [religion] is a positive moral force, and a spiritual consolation, who strongly identify as males or females—but not both!—and who are socially successful and wish to emulate paragons of social success (e.g. American [or cultural] heroes) are viewed as having a psychiatric disorder... Good parenting, upward social mobility, pride in family, religion, nation and race were all suspect. Many of the central attitudes of the 1960's counter cultural revolution find expression in *The Authoritarian Personality*, including idealizing rebellion against parents, uncommitted sexual relationships, and scorn for upward social mobility, social status, family pride, [religion] and patriotism.[11]

Without family, without faith, the whole issue of us as a folk becomes a non-issue. We exist as a folk with a folkway because we continue our lines down through time—we exist because we wanted to exist in the past, and we can only exist in the future if we want to. Having no families means having no future, means having only a very materialistic here and now, with nothing else at all.

> Viewed at its most abstract level, the fundamental agenda of the Frankfurt School [and therefore feminism itself] is to influence European peoples to view concern about their own demographic and cultural eclipse as irrational and as an indication of psychopathology. People who do not identify with the basic social categories of family, religion, nation or race would not be concerned with their demise.[12]

We do not need the "help" that feminism seems to give to the women of revealed religions—we never have. Let's face it, our ancestors were neither women haters

---

11 Kevin MacDonald, forward to Tomislav Sunic. *Homo Americanus: Child of the Postmodern Age*. (Charleston: Book Surge, 2007), xix.
12 Ibid., xxi.

nor men haters—they were folk who recognized the divine in the winter woods and the summer sun, who took part in Krampus events and Mothers Nights, who revered Freya and Frey, who found wisdom in the Norns as in Odin. The Valkyries are not the Einherjar, yet even today, in the midst of mostly unchallenged feminism and all that this movement has influenced, does any one of us think one better than the other? We would not, because they are not.

Our folk's feminine heritage is a strong and valid one; it is a heritage of balanced power, respect, honor and action. The feminists today chortle with self-satisfied glee about getting women the right to vote, but...all the feminist movement ever did was to return to our folk what we already had before. This is why free-thinking, unoppressed, strong women are so natural to us!

> Though the revolutionary women's movement has done some great things to reestablish our valued status, we still have a long way to go before regaining the stature we held in the prime of our folk history.[13]

The stature we held in the prime of our folk history was not one of women versus men, like it is now. It was a stature based on mutual respect, on equivalency of value. Our ancestors—female and male—were equal in all dealings from the moment they matured to womanhood and manhood. And their equal footing was not based on women behaving like ersatz men—which, when you look at it, is not equality at all but a pathetic mimicry.

> The Judeo-Christian-Islamic [as well as Femino/Marxist] idea of just one life, after which you either go to heaven or to hell gives the impression that time is running out. Some even think 'you have to get everything out of this life, because when you're gone, you're gone, so grab all the gusto that you can'. This has given the Modern Western woman the idea that she is not getting everything she should, and therefore the man's world looks doubly attractive, because she is just passing through and will never come back. So, living a man's life is very, very attractive. She doesn't want to stay home all the time and not see anything, not meet anybody, go through the boredom of raising a family, taking care of the children. She wants to be out with life, functioning in a man's world because she is told that she missing something.[14]

---

13 Mark Puryear. *The Nature of Asatru.* (Lincoln: iUniverse, 2006), 131.
14 Satguru Sivaya Subramuniyaswami. *Living With Siva: Hinduism's Contemporary*

No wonder modern women leap headlong into the feminist notion that equality means women being equal to men (men being the default normative against which women's value is weighed) instead of seeing equality as our ancestors did: each gender equally balanced to the other, with female gender having no need to try and become like the male.

Our equal gender footing in Midgard was based on the healthy respect of each for each. Respect for the warrior, respect for the weaver, respect for the father, respect for the mother. Respect for those who bear the arms and those who bear the keys. Raising/nurturing the family properly and protecting/providing for the family properly are of crucial and very equal importance to a healthy civilization, a strong folk, a spiritually vital folkway.

> Idun holds the seeds of new life which must be awakened each spring to release Midgard from the world of winter and death ruled by etins. Her might keeps the forces of chaos and uncertainty at bay every bit as much as Thor does.[15]

We must bring every facet of our daily lives in line with our spirituality. We are a folk spirituality—a hearth religion. Every home is holy. Each act of home making has a spiritual as well as practical purpose. Every member of a home has a distinct and distinctive part in the running of it. Like the roles of *gyðja* and *goði* in a kindred, the roles of man and woman—mother and father—husband and wife are each distinct, distinctive and important. Neither is transferable; neither is superior. As our Vedic cousins note:

> From the point of view of the Second World, or astral plane, the home is the family temple [like the heathen hearth and hof] and the wife and mother is in charge of the spiritual environment. The husband can come into the sanctum sanctorum, but should not bring the world into it. He will naturally find a refuge in the home if she is doing her duty…He needs that inner balance in his life…If a woman is working [for wages outside the home] she cannot provide this balance. She has to start thinking and acting like a man. She has to become a little tougher, create a protective shell around her emotions. Then the home loses its balance of the masculine and feminine forces…[16]

Culture, 2nd ed. (Kapaa: Himalayan Academy, 2001), 254.
15 Alice Karlsdottir. "Idun." *Runa Magazine* 18 (No date listed), 24.
16 Subramuniyaswami, 253.

The importance of the family, with the sacred feminine roles of mother and wife, carefully installed in the heart of it, cannot be overstated. Even today, in one of the most liberal progressive weeklies out there, *The Willamette Weekly*, where you can get phone numbers for single women chat lines, get directions to erotic balls, obtain information on herpes support groups and find out how to adopt away your unwanted baby ("living expenses paid"), the truth about what is best for families still shows itself. Under the "Adoption" heading of the October 14, 2009 classified ads, an ad looking for "a precious first baby" appeared.[17] The prospective adoptive mother listed herself as a college professor and journalist—reading between the lines you can get a sense of a woman whose biological clock stopped ticking either due to a youth spent working to be the best man-like woman she could be, or due to years of birth controlling hormones designed to make her body as unwomanly and unnatural as medically possible (so she could be the best man-like woman she could be without all those nasty female side effects!). The ad states this at its conclusion: "will stay at home mom." A simple eloquent five word statement, intended to persuade, designed to show what a good mother this woman would be, how she will do the best, be the best, give the baby she wants the best that can be given. How up-to-date she is. How utterly feminine her impulse.

> Biology, culture and spirituality are all intimately connected, and any attempt to separate them is doomed to frustration.[18]

To make a difference, we must be different. We are the deed that says: "I know my value as a human, as a parent, as a spirit, as a heathen—and thus I know everyone else's value as well. I am the deed, I am the decider. I know that my folk is wise, my folkways valuable, my time here of worth. I know that my decisions will not be the same as decisions made by those of strange faiths. I am the deed that breaks with these foreign ways. I am the deed of coming home, of acknowledging what is right and, of fixing what is wrong. No matter how difficult, no matter how it looks to a non-folkish mainstream set up to judge and thus keep me from upsetting the status quo, no matter what."

> If we believe in reincarnation through family lines, who are these children we are abandoning to daycare in order for their mothers to leave the house?[19]

---

17 Classified ad under the column, "Adoption," from the 14 October 2009 issue of *The Willamette Week*.

18 Stephen McNallen. *The Hoosier Heathen Hoedown Hawg Roast: A Wotan's Watchtower Publication* 1 (2006), 3.

19 Dave Hobson; from a private speech given by RavensHalla Arts Publishing, Portland,

As heathens, we need our families to be strong. We need our men to be successful as fathers and husbands, we need our women to be successful as mothers and wives. We need our children brought up at home, with values and spirituality that reflect our age-old folk ways, with nourishing—properly made—food, with love, with trust, and with people who know and respect them both for who they are now, the ancestors they once were and the future folk they will be again.

> We who seek the revival of our native faith and a resurgence of our people owe it to ourselves, to our ancestors and to our descendants to explore every possibility.[20]

As hard as you think it might be, there is no room for lack of conviction in the bringing up of the next generation. Having a traditional, one income family, with feminine and masculine roles naturally delineated is still viable. It can be done, and is being done, by heathen families (as well as other families) who have chosen to follow their spiritual heart rather than be led around by their economic noses.

> Respect for our forefolk [and thus our folkway] may be expressed in a variety of ways. Especially in the way we live our everyday lives.[21]

The writer of this essay is a stay at home mother of three, who home-schools, has home-birthed, and cooks three meals a day—sometimes more if there's a holy event coming. The old folk wisdoms come into play every minute, and the commonplaces are made sacred by the fact that everything we do is done for the good of our family, of the folk, and for the future as well as the present. Our home, like so many homes where a mother is the feminine core and a father is the masculine guardian, is at once happy and holy, chaotic and charmed, timeless and very much part of a long chain of once-upons and here-and-nows.

The past and the future meet constantly, in each of us. Remember who you were and who you are going to be.

Mothers Night, 2009.

[20] Stephen McNallen. "Comments on Carl Jung's 'Wotan.'" Introduction to Dr. Carl Jung's *Wotan*, Private paper distributed during a lecture at the AFA Winter Nights, 2007.

[21] James Allen Chisholm. *The True Hearth: A Practical Guide to Traditional Householding*. 2nd improved edition, (Smithville: Runa-Raven, 1994), 4.

If you would like to ask questions, or obtain recommendations about resource books pertaining to various aspects of traditional householding, feel free to email the author at: juleigh@ourfolkway.org

Heathen Householding Creed

(Inspired by the Homemakers Creed of the Home Legion, 1944)

- I believe in the feminine heart of the home.
- I believe householding is an irreplaceably valuable role.
- I believe householding requires various skills, noble arts and knowledgeable ways.
- I believe a trú folk are known by their homes.
- I believe every hearth and home reflects the soul of the feminine.
- I believe home particularly encompasses ᛭ᚠ᛬ᚹ᛬ᛋ᛬ᛏ᛬ᚱ᛬
- I believe a homemaker must adhere to the highest standards of faith, folk and family.
- I believe that no aspect of householding is too lowly; life has many facets —dark as well as light, enjoyable as well as tedious—for all.
- I believe that householding done well adds to the good *ørlög* of the folk.
- I believe homemaking is one of the most important jobs on Midgard and has an influence on the folk both now and forever.
- I do not put faith in foreign religions or feminist agendas; I know what is right and *trú* for my family, my folk and my wyrd.

Say Hello Nicely, by *Carl Larsson.*

WolfTyr Productions

ROBERT N. TAYLOR
'Pathway to the Gods'
A book concerning the Odinist movement. Essays. Art. Poetry. Mr. Taylor is Half of the US Neo-Folk group 'Changes'. He lives what he espouses in Writing and Music.
Due out : Summer/Autumn 2010

WOTANORDEN
'The Hands of Fate' CD
The 3rd full length album from these Vinlandic barbarians! Pagan Folk/Black metal with a mixture of singing and growling vocals!
Due out : Summer/Autumn 2010

PO BOX 682
Holbrook, NY 11741
USA/VINLAND

E-Mail:
wolftyrprod@gmail.com

LORD WIND
'Atlantean Monument' CD
-OUT NOW-
Polish Epic Neo Classical music with a Pagan war-spirit. From the same mind that brings you GRAVELAND! This is a re-release of the 4th album from 2006.
OUT NOW!

Visit our store for Clothing, Books and Music pertaining to Paganism, Esotericism and the Obscure.

Items from: Alain de Benoist, J. Coulter, K. Pastenaci, M. Moynihan Burzum, Eona, Dead Ravens Choir, Halgadom, Fjörd, Kroda, Piarevaracien, Hel, Perunwit, Temnozor, Uruk-Hai

New Lord Wind CD later this year on WolfTyr!

www.wolftyr.com

Sommer

by Juleigh Howard-Hobson

These fields we till, our fathers knew
This sun the sun they saw
The land wights whisper in our ears:
The wild-hunter's home; we thaw.

Cakes and ale are farrowed here—
To Thor—to Frey—to wight—
We feed the land our fathers fed
As summer brings the light.

Hermod Before Hella, by J.C. Dollman (1909).

Wandering The Nine Worlds: Heathenism's Shamanic Origins

Dan Cæppe

Heathen Genesis

*I know that I hung,
on a wind-rocked tree,
nine whole nights,
with a spear wounded,
and to Odin offered,
myself to myself;
on that tree,
of which no one knows
from what root it springs.*

*Bread no one gave me,
nor a horn of drink,
downward I peered,
to runes applied myself,
wailing learnt them,
then fell down thence.*

*Potent songs nine
from the famed son I learned
of Bölthorn, Bestla's sire,
and a draught obtained
of the precious mead,
drawn from Odhrærir.*

*Then I began to bear fruit,
and to know many things,
to grow and well thrive:
word by word
I sought out words,
fact by fact
I sought out facts.*

Above are some of the most well-known verses contained within the *Hávamál*.[1] They are the opening stanzas of *Rúnatáls-tháttr-Óðins*—Odin's Rune Song, and there is, in all probability, no better, nor more authentic an introduction to the concept of Germanic Shamanism, or to use its proper term: *seiðr*.[2] Primarily perceived as a vital contribution to the *mythology* surrounding the *Allvater*[3] of the Æsir, Odin, I have rarely encountered Heathens who grasp the full practical, spiritual significance of these words. Some of the secrets therein will become apparent as we explore what I believe to be the core of all Pagan tradition.

What springs to mind when we think of Heathenism? For those non-Heathens it will usually be the gods, runes, war and the veneration of nature. But even for most Heathens their faith is only further characterised by ritual, divination, ancestry and perhaps magic. The Shamanistic aspect is regularly considered to be an important but periphery practice within the wider tradition; an indispensable supplement to regimented and non-regimented ritual and rune-work. I whole-heartedly challenge the view that Shamanism serves as anything less than the very origin of, not only Heathenism, but of all true religion. There is a huge cultural aspect to Heathenism and all Pagan religions, for faith was not considered an add-on to social and political life—it was an inextricable part of it. Raw, *practical* Heathenry was, however, rooted in Shamanism. There may even be grounds to suspect an age-old conspiracy in the suppression of Shamanistic practice both within Pagan traditions and outside of them.

Understanding the supreme importance of *seiðr* within our tradition is essential. If our ambition is to grow, spiritually, and to enjoy all of the practical benefits that are brought about by this growth, then we must endeavour to *liaise* as closely with the spirit world and with the gods as possible. In addition, there are pragmatic and comforting gains to be had by understanding the relevance of the spirit world. For example, how many times have you been challenged as to why you 'worship' imaginary beings? If not the gods (who are varyingly explained as being famous distant ancestors of the Germanic folk or the personifications of natural phenomena), how about the elves, dwarves, dragons and array of other mythical beings? Their presence within Germanic mythology is undeniable and yet less-easily justified to those people so well-adjusted to a modern, materialistic understanding of atheism, or indeed religion, that they laugh at the very idea. Yet, as we shall see over the course of this presentation, there is much to warrant the prominence of mythology in our faith.

---

1 Benjamin Thorpe. *The Elder Eddas of Saemund Sigfusson Translated from the Original Old Norse Text Into English*. (Alabama: Norroena Society, 1906), 44-45.
2 Sometimes Anglicised as *seidhr, seidh, seidr, seithr,* or *seith*.
3 German translation of *Allfather*, a key synonym for the god Odin.

Acquainting With The Spirits

'Shamanism' is the popular term for the most ancient belief system known to man. The word is derived from the Tungusic *šaman*[4] and its central belief revolves around the existence of a spirit world with which we can learn to interact. Traditionally, only certain members of a tribe would either aspire to become Shamans, or would have the innate aptitude to do so. Through interaction with the spirit world, the Shaman would acquire knowledge relevant to his or her community, or would seek specifically to heal those who are sick. Sometimes harmful entities would be sought out and confronted in order to prevent them from affecting people in this world. Although only a few of the tribe might adopt the role of Shaman, all would have understood the relationship between our immediate, material world and the less apparent spirit world.

Our understanding of the spirit world differs from culture to culture, but it is a universal concept among the world's ancient peoples. Some cultures saw the spirit world as divided between a multitude of realms, whilst some may have dealt with just one all-encompassing realm aside from our Earthly one; but all would have been unanimous in their perception of it as an invisible world that exists and operates concurrently to our own. More accurately, the spirit world, or *worlds*, are not bound by our physical laws and therefore exist within the same space as our Miðgarðr.[5] How this can be possible will be investigated at a later stage.

The relevance of the spirit world to us in our human world is paramount. We are not two disconnected plains of existence inhabited by unrelated beings; we are interlinked and interdependent. Indeed, according to our own Heathen understanding of the nine worlds,[6] parts of us can dwell in multiple worlds simultaneously. But there is a troubling element to our time: at this stage of mankind's development, we are less willing to acknowledge the existence of a spirit world than we have ever been. Critics of the Shamanic belief system would no doubt argue that this development away from belief in spirits has been the natural result of scientific *advancement*—the assertion being that we are a more enlightened species as a result of modernity. Yet, for those of us who

---

4 Mircea Eliade. *Shamanism: Archaic Techniques of Ecstasy*. (USA: Princeton University Press, 2004), 4.
5 Old Norse word meaning "middle enclosure." Can be Anglicised as *Midgard* or, sometimes, *Middle Earth*.
6 According to Heathen tradition, there are nine worlds including our Earthly one: Midgard, Asgard, Vanaheim, Jotunheim, Alfheim, Hel, Nidavellir, Svartalfheim, Niflheim and Muspelheim.

consider belief in the supernatural to be an unavoidable aspect of human nature—an aspect there, not to be overcome, but to actually aid in our advancement as a species—the inevitable result of our detachment from the spirit world is that we have simply become subject to a force that we do not officially recognise. For no matter how ideologically distant we make ourselves from the spirit world, those otherworldly influences will remain ever-intrigued by us.

The concept of a spirit world, or the nine worlds of the Heathen tradition, will be well-known to most readers, but I fear that the full connotations of it, and direct engagement with it, are too often neglected. What is important, at this stage, is that the concept be understood.

Mind Over Matter

Attitudes to death and the afterlife, amongst our Heathen ancestors, are likely to have varied; but one sure commonality was the diminished level of fear and uncertainty. In Brian Bates' dramatic account of Anglo-Saxon Heathenism—*The Way Of Wyrd*, two friendly warriors sword-fight in the great hall whilst their kin observe.[7] When one is slain by the other, for no apparent reason, the central character of the book, Brand—a Christian Missionary—is horrified; yet it is him alone who is horrified. This is neither barbarism nor murder. The slain soldier, it is explained, gladly sacrificed his own life due to the commonly-held spiritual beliefs of the time. There was no great uncertainty in death; a warrior was prepared for it from a young age. Socrates addressed the fear of uncertainty in a most rational way:

> For let me tell you, gentlemen, that to be afraid of death is only another form of thinking that one is wise when one is not; it is to think that one knows what one does not know. No one knows with regard to death whether it is not really the greatest blessing that can happen to a man; but people dread it as though they were certain that it is the greatest evil; and this ignorance, which thinks that it knows what it does not, must surely be ignorance most culpable.[8]

There may well have been a Socratean approach to death by our ancestors, or they may well have anticipated something—a knowing comfort; for their daily lives had been intertwined with the knowledge of a spirit world from birth. But,

---

7 Brian Bates. *The Way Of Wyrd*. (London: Lay House, 2005), 102-104.
8 Plato. *The Last Days Of Socrates*. trans. Hugh Tredennick. (Aylesbury, England: Penguin Books, 1973), 60.

as Socrates suggests—and free from the fear-mongering of dogmatic Abrahamism[9] or rigid materialism—Heathen warriors at least had no good reason to fear what may lay beyond.

My own intuition encourages me to project the same fundamental attitude towards death on to other, non-Heathen cultures. I would ascertain with some confidence (but minimal investigation, admittedly) that all Pagan warrior cultures were equally free from the bonds of uncertainty with regards to their own demise. But more fascinating is the idea that the subjects of human sacrifice may have committed themselves willingly, armed with the knowledge that this Earthly existence is merely one manifestation of their consciousness. Much is made, in popular culture, of the barbarity of those Meso-American civilisations who at one stage or another made regular sacrifices to their gods. The Maya are widely-known to have made offerings of their children and we deplore them for doing so. But scholars and historians may have been too quick in assuming the circumstances under which sacrifices were made. Their immediate relationship with the spirit world could have implanted them with the confidence to willingly commit themselves.

The Wholly Spirit

Much has been written elsewhere about Christianity's adoption of Pagan institutions: Easter, Yule, the use of water, the cross—to name just a few. But one of the lesser known 'loans' is the concept of 'holiness.' As footnoted by Edred Thorsson in his *Futhark: A Handbook Of Rune Magic:*

> It is interesting to note that the Germanic idea of "holy" is identical to that embodied in "holistic;" i.e., the wholeness, completeness, and unity of all realms, leading to well-being. The English words "holy," "hale," and "whole" all derive from the same root: *kailo- (whole, uninjured, of good omen).[10]

In short, whilst Christian perceptions of holiness are dependent primarily upon one's *moral* integrity, the original, Heathen requirement for holiness was that one quite literally be 'whole.' It is funny how such logic—the relationship between such similar words as 'whole,' 'holy' and 'heal'—can be overlooked in the name of Christian subversion. Nevertheless, the Heathen concept of wholeness was concerned with physical and spiritual *balance*. This meant that if one vital part

---

9 Religions who treat Abraham as a Patriarch: Judaism, Christianity and Islam.
10 Edred Thorsson. *Futhark: A Handbook Of Rune Magic*. (San Francisco: Weiser, 1984), 17.

of a person was lacking, there would be an imbalance which would manifest itself as sickness or misfortune. We will now uncover the Shamanic connotations of this.

Earlier, I referenced *The Way Of Wyrd* by Brian Bates, who is most renowned for his work in reconstructing the Shamanic traditions of the Anglo-Saxons. His extensive research has enabled him to compile a body of knowledge which is a reasonable representation of original Germanic attitudes towards the spirit. *The Way Of Wyrd*, a fictional tale rooted in factual evidence, describes the composition of a man as

> Life-force permeates everything. It is the source of all vitality. In a person it is generated in the head, flows like a stream of light into the marrow of the spine and from there into the limbs and crevices of the body.[11]

And...

> Within each person, three forces surge like three streams converging on a whirlpool. These forces are the life-force, soul and shield skin. Life-force I have told you about. The soul is the essence of wyrd, present in everything. It is the very being of which we are formed. The soul is what gives form, direction and pattern to all things, for it forms a shield skin around the life-force, enveloping vitality in a recognisable shape. The form of the shield skin defines the kind of creature we are.[12]

That there are multiple seen and unseen layers to a person is universally-accepted among Shamanic cultures of the world. Details and interpretations may differ but for us—who are primarily concerned with Heathen tradition—we can take the above description as a legitimate description of inter-Germanic belief. All of these 'parts' that play a part in forming us must remain healthy even though only our material form is commonly apparent.

With this in mind, consider what happens when one of these 'parts' is lost. In *The Way Of Wyrd*, the character Brand's soul is stolen by the spirits. Brand, wounded, must then seek to *retrieve* his soul; for if he does not, not only will his physical self perish but his soul will not have the opportunity of dwelling in its rightful place in the after life. Soul retrieval is a fundamental duty of the Shaman

---

11 Bates, *The Way of Wyrd*, 57.
12 Ibid., 108.

because, if a person's soul, or part of it, is lost then that person cannot be considered *whole*. In this way, 'holiness' denotes those people who are spiritually whole.

The soul need not always have been stolen or lost for *wholeness* to be compromised. A common 'superstition' among our ancestors was the claim that someone was 'Elf-shot,'[13] that they had been pierced by elven arrows. This was a figurative term, or depending on one's faith in the existence of a parallel otherworld, a description of what had happened in that otherworld, unbeknown to our Earthly eyes. One who had been Elf-shot would be expected to suffer some kind of physical ailment which *would* have been physically apparent.

In our modern, Western world, our refusal to acknowledge our spiritual element means that we have little hope of maintaining spiritual *wholeness*. Those of us who accept the reality of a spirit world should therefore have concern for the collective health of our kin and species. Spiritual afflictions can not only account for physical sickness but also for ethical shortcomings and forms of depression. Many things can cause this imbalance—most often some form of trauma. The phrase 'to be beside oneself'—with grief, for example, takes on fresh meaning when we entertain the notion of our soul disconnecting from our physical form in order to escape traumatic episodes. Sometimes parts of the soul become so disconnected that they go missing.

Tuning In To World Rhythms

At this point in our exploration of *seiðr* there may remain some doubt about the scientific grounding for the existence of alternate worlds. I would anticipate most of the readers of this journal to be themselves Heathen or some other denomination of Pagan; and as such sympathetic to faith-based consideration of the supernatural. Regardless, I would like to try and approach the concept from somewhat of a scientific direction for a moment. I feel some obligation do so after having earlier made claims about Shamanism being the key to rationalising our belief in 'imaginary beings.'

There is a small gland in the centre of our brain called the pineal gland and, although its functions are still debated, it has attracted popular attention amongst psychiatrists, parapsychologists and meta-physicists. One among them is psychiatrist Dr. Rick Strassman, who has conducted research into the relationship between the pineal gland and the alkaloid naturally produced therein:

---

13 Brian Bates. *The Real Middle Earth: Magic and Mystery in the Dark Ages.* (Chatham, England: Pan Macmillan, 2003), 108.

dimethyltryptamine (DMT). DMT is popularly known as a psychedelic drug, but it would surprise many people to discover that it occurs naturally in our bodies in minuscule amounts. Strassman's experiments have led him to some startling discoveries; namely, as indicated by the title of his book *DMT: The Spirit Molecule*, that DMT and the pineal gland are our window to the supernatural; the spirit world. The consumption of DMT is, however, not essential for the opening of this window and techniques are wide and varied. The results of Strassman's experiments suggest that not only do a minority of people produce sufficient levels of endogenous DMT to experience visions or hallucinations, but that there may be other paths to harnessing naturally-occurring DMT: electro-magnetism, sound waves and repetition of sound or movement. This, then, provides an exciting scientific rationale for why indigenous cultures have made persistent use of drums, chants and dances, as well as plant-based hallucinogens, for longer than documented history can account for. They were all means of activating 'the spirit molecule.'

Several scholars have likened DMT and our pineal gland to a radio or television *receiver*. Dr. Strassman is prominent among them:

> If we accept the "receiver of reality" model for brain function, let's compare it to another receiver with which we're all familiar: the television. By making the analogy of the brain to the TV, it's possible to think of how altered states of consciousness, including psychedelic ones brought about by DMT, relate to the brain as a sophisticated receiver.[14]

To expand the metaphor, the multiple worlds—in the Heathen's case, nine—which simultaneously occupy the same space and time (or *not,* as the case may be) are each like a separate radio transmission. When we tune into a radio station we are not prompting a new transmission; multiple signals are in fact already *out there* waiting to be received. What if the same applies to the multiple spirit worlds? What if these different levels of perception simply need to be tuned into and we, as humans, are evolved to only pick up one transmission—one 'world'—one level of existence?

Science has not discovered every secret that this universe, or even this planet, holds. The field of metaphysics is perhaps one of the most active currently and an increasing number of scientists and scholars are rallying around ideas about parallel dimensions—ideas which vary. One such theory proposes that, because

---

14 Rick Strassman, M.D. *DMT: The Spirit Molecule.* (Rochester, Vermont: Park Street Press, 2001), 311.

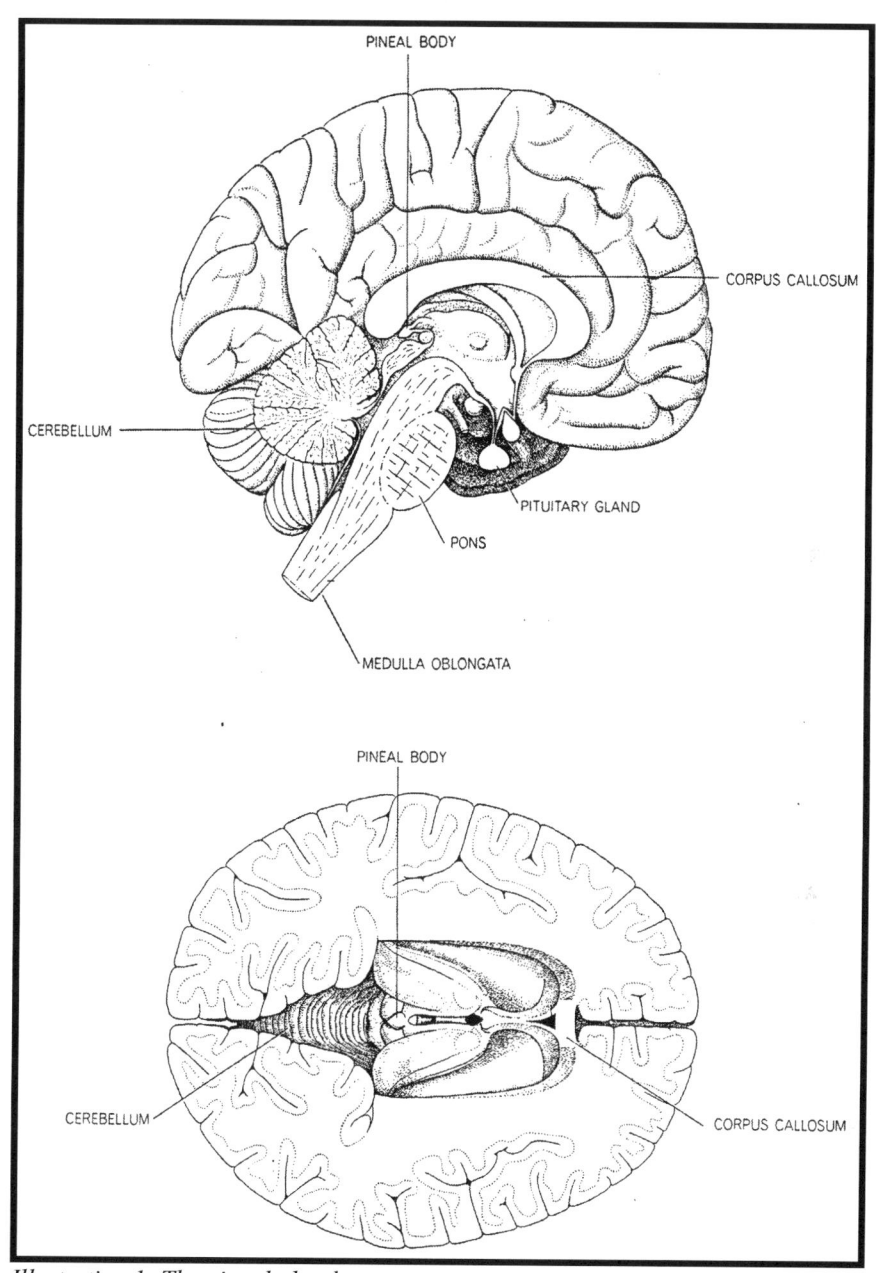

Illustration 1: The pineal gland.

all matter vibrates at a sub-atomic level, everything mundane that we can see is only perceived because its sub-atomic vibration is at a suitable rate for the human senses to comprehend. This is sometimes referred to as the 'Law Of Vibration.'

We cannot see matter vibrating because it happens at such a slow speed. The varying rates at which matter vibrates could also be considered its *frequency*. And so we find ourselves back in line with our 'radio transmission' metaphor—there are several worlds out there but we humans are 'tuned in' to this one. It may be that we can tune in to different 'frequencies' by use of psychedelic drugs, repetitive sound or movement; and it may be that a small minority of us are permanently adapted or *can* temporarily adapt to these spirit frequencies and glimpse worlds which most of us refuse to believe in. Indeed, the rightful role of those fortunate people who are naturally 'tuned in,' among the tribal communities of antiquity, would have been that of *Shaman*. So when these chosen ones sight ghosts they are often at a loss as to how they should react—a gift squandered, perhaps.

This point is a suitable one at which to welcome our most characteristic of treasures—the runes; and to discover their Shamanic relevance. I believe in the holistic nature of the runes; far more than mere language, tool of divination or visual-based magic, the runes aid us in picking up otherworld transmissions. They can establish correct connections—like the tuning display on a radio. This is of enhanced relevance when we look into 'rune streams.' Rune streams are flows of energy which enable us to connect with the spirit worlds; they are terrestrial—on the Earth's surface; Heavenly—within the atmosphere above; and chthonic—subterranean. Rune streams conjure comparisons with the commonly-identified phenomenon of *ley lines*[15] and are surely one and the same thing. Rune streams and ley lines are largely unscientific—meaning that they are mainly substantiated by esoteric practices only. Ley lines are discovered and used by methods of Divination, but also play a significant role in the placement of sacred historical sites. In his book *The Keys To The Temple*, David Furlong surmises that an anomalous number of stone circles, dolmen and churches are found situated along a precise line running from Cornwall to eastern England.

The coalition of rune and rune stream is exemplified well in the practice of *stadhagaldr*. This magical practice consists of striking poses which embody or resemble runes and

> The practice of this magical form is closely connected to the mysteries of the rune streams. The runic postures act as antennas of force by which the vitki may attract, modulate, and reproject rune might for magical purposes.[16]

---

15 The existence of ley lines was first suggested by archaeologist Alfred Watkins, in his book *The Old Straight Track*, (London: Abacus, 1994).
16 Thorsson, *Futhark*, 125.

Again, the metaphor of transmission and antennae appears. *Stadhagaldr* joins our list of techniques for transforming one's mind and body into a receiver for capturing the transmissions of the spirit worlds. When we succeed in doing this we not only gain wisdom from the spirits (divination) but we can project our desires into the spirit worlds and see those desires manifested in our human world—our Midgard. We are both receivers and transmitters, but we must alter our state of consciousness to access those channels of communication. This is Shamanism—this is *seiðr*.

Lessons From Odin's Rune Song

Gaining wisdom from the nine worlds...we are reminded of Odin's time upon that wind-rocked tree. And so we shall let this essay find its way back to *Odin's Rune Song* if it so wishes. If I may, I would like to ask the reader to refer back to stanzas from *Odin's Rune Song* as we investigate the wealth of Shamanic symbolism therein.

In the first of the four quoted verses, we learn immediately that Odin hangs upon a 'wind-rocked tree.' The 'tree of life' features prominently in worldwide religious lore. *Saosis* in Egypt,[17] the Hebrew *Etz Chaim*,[18] *Wacah Chan* to the Mayans[19] and of course, *Yggdrasil* in Norse mythology. This 'world tree,' as it is also commonly known, connects the various worlds or realms. Amazonian Shamans report ascending or descending an enormous tree or ladder when journeying to or within the spirit world. *Yggdrasil* is the wind-rocked tree upon which Odin hung, but the tree's purpose is to symbolise transportation from one world to another:

> The name is a compound of two words—the stem of 'ygg' is a nickname for Odin, meaning 'the awe-inspiring one.' 'Drasill' is a literary word meaning 'horse.' The name identifies the tree as the means of Odin's 'ride' to the spirit world, and his transportation for the quest.[20]

The tree may have been 'wind-rocked' because journeying to the spirit world is not always smooth-sailing.

---

17 Claas Jouco Bleeker. *Hathor and Thoth: Two Key Figures in Ancient Egyptian Religion.* (Belgium: Brill Academic Pub., 1973), 36.
18 עץ חיים, a term found throughout the Old Testament translated as "tree of life."
19 Mary Miller, Karl Teube. *The Gods and Symbols of Ancient Mexico and the Maya.* (London: Thames & Hudson, 1996), 186.
20 Bates, *The Real Middle Earth*, 167.

In the same verse, Odin claims to have hung upon that tree—*Yggdrasil*—for "nine whole nights." Relative to this, stanza three begins with "potent songs nine, from the famed son I learned"—why nine? The significance of the number nine in Heathenism will be instantly apparent to most readers. Close inspection of the intricacies within Heathen mythology will reveal considerable references *to* and mention *of* the number nine—in something as seemingly-trivial as the number of steps taken by Thor after he slays the serpent Jörmungandr, or the number of deities who survive Ragnarök. Is the existence of nine worlds subject to this strange obsession with that particular number or is it the cause of it? My instinct leads me to believe that it is the cause, as the central aim of this essay is to show that the spirit world and all proto-Shamanic tradition served as the origin for all latter peculiarities within Paganism—the mythology, pantheons, ritual and superstition. However, it is worth briefly noting that there are also nine original planets in our solar system. In fact, a ground-breaking essay by Giorgio de Santillana and Hertha von Dechend called *Hamlet's Mill* finds precisely that mythology acts as a time capsule for preserving ancient astronomical knowledge through the mists of time.[21]

What is the importance of Odin having been "with a spear wounded?" Well, it could have referred to the notion that Odin, as a real historical figure, had come near to death in battle and as a result found himself hanging upon that tree of life, in the realm of the dead. Or, more likely, it could signify the *rebirth* of Odin as a Norse Shaman—or Wizard. A universal feature of the Shaman's initiation is that he or she observe or experience their otherworld self die and be reborn, or break into pieces and be rebuilt. This is the symbolic, or spiritually literal, transformation of average human into healer or wise-man and marks the point at which strong relations with the spirits is established. Furthermore, in offering 'myself to myself,' Odin is encountering his otherworld self and pledging his allegiance to a life of knowledge-seeking and work with the spirits.

About the tree —"no one knows from what root it springs" because no one of the nine worlds is objectively superior nor parental. My interpretation—which, I emphasise, is very much personal and dynamic, in accordance with the fluidity of Heathenism—is that this particular line intends to establish an equality between all worlds and entities so that we humans, here in Midgard, learn to assume somewhat of a more humble understanding of existence and our standing within the larger scheme.

---

21 Giorgio de Santillana and Hertha von Dechend. *Hamlet's Mill.* (New Hampshire: David R. Godine, 2007).

In the second stanza of *Odin's Rune Song* the Allfather begins, rather strangely I think, by mentioning his lack of food and drink; a mundane fact that most students of the *Hávamál* would be forgiven for overlooking. But in the context of Odin as Shaman, the statement about lack of food is key advice. The food that we know in our world 'grounds' us—it is of this world and it reminds us that we, as humans, are of this world. So another way that we might tune ourselves into those spirit world frequencies is to fast prior to any 'journey' we plan on undertaking. But whilst food from our world grounds us here, so does food from the spirit worlds ground us there. Shamanic tradition advises us not to eat the food offered to us whilst in altered states of consciousness—exploring the otherworld. This advice will be found in contemporary guides to modern Shamanic practice, but it is advice rooted in the collective experience of spiritual folk throughout history. Numerous fairy tales from Britain document fascinating cases whereby men and women find themselves banqueting in the kingdom of faeries for many years. They might return to their town or family years later, unable to account for the time passed. It sometimes seems as though faeries and elves are driven primarily by an urge to feed us when we visit their world. The lesson to be heeded, by all Shamans and otherworld travelers, is that consumption of otherworldly foods may strengthen our dependence upon worlds that are secondary to us, to a degree where we might fail to depart from that world and return to our own fully intact—fully *whole*.

Learning runes by "wailing" is no doubt a specific reference to *galdr*—the use of sound to represent or 'call' runes. The *galdr* of each rune is generally incomprehensible—it is a sound rather than a word.[22] But each unique sound we create with our tongue, throat, mouth and breath forms a different frequency of vibration. These varying frequencies receive different transmissions and transmit different signals, to and from the spirit world. In this way, Odin was able to connect with and understand the runes.

The remainder of the four quoted stanzas simply details gains and acquisitions made by Odin. Songs are learnt, mead is received, fruit is borne and growth occurs. These are symbols of the spiritual gains, the knowledge and the overall advancement that Odin enjoys through interaction with the nine worlds. But a key aspect of this fortune is clarified in final lines of the fourth verse: Odin "*sought* out words" and he "*sought* out facts." His visit to the spirit world did not bestow upon him unconditional gifts but rather an opportunity and a will to seek these treasures. This is an important distinction because it is the quest for knowledge itself which provides the knowledge sought, and the strengthening of that hunger for knowledge which makes it available. The fruits of the spirit

---

22 Thorsson, *Futhark*, 19-69.

world are abundant, but effort and focus is necessary in finding them. There are other secrets to be found in these verses, and indeed in the rest of *Odin's Rune Song*; but as with all the fruits of the nine worlds, it is better that each curious soul investigate them independently.

Myth Or Fiction?

The mythologies of the Abrahamic religions are usually taken quite literally. Miracles performed by Jesus are treated with no suspicion or disbelief by those adherents to Christianity; nor, indeed, is his very existence. It is beyond the remit of this piece to question the integrity of faiths other than Heathenism, but equally, we would expect the same consideration for our own from others—bar perhaps staunch Atheists. Yet there is little respect: the myths and legends of Northern Europe have been firmly placed in the 'fiction' category by writers, scholars and publishers for so long now that modern Heathens themselves can be forgiven for seeing them in a predominantly creative light. But as we shall now see, there might be more to it than meets the (Earthly) eye.

Battles with dragons, meetings with dwarves, quests to the depths of Hel[23]—the cornerstones of fantasy, surely. The Fantasy and Science-Fiction genres have reached prominence in popular culture but, to be more accurate, have entertained people since the advent of speech. But have such tales always been considered fictional? It is in our story-telling nature to recount the heroic or comedic deeds of our living and deceased associates; think of the most enjoyable conversations you have with family and friends—they usually involve stories. Our modern day-to-day tales are always rooted in physical reality, but the stories of our ancestors employed plenty of creative license. One might explain this by either insulting the intelligence or faith of our Heathen ancestors and concluding that they were so deluded as to believe in the impossible, or by assuming that they simply liked to fabricate grand tales. As a society we have applied the latter explanation to them, retrospectively. Have we jumped the gun in doing so?

The key to understanding why we might have misinterpreted Heathen mythology is in the fact that our modern world-view is in stark contrast to theirs. We cannot apply our scepticism nor materialism to them—we must analyse their stories through *their* eyes. From the Heathen's perspective, there are nine worlds and our human world—Midgard—is only equal among them. This reality is not the only reality and amongst indigenous, Shamanistic folk, it is (and has been for tens of thousands of years) believed that we can communicate with and in some

---

23 Hel is the ruler of the underworld, Helheim—one of the nine worlds. Hel and Helheim are often interchangeable.

Illustration 2: Odin astride Sleipnir from the Tjängvide stone.

cases *travel* to those otherworld realities. These journeys to the spirit worlds, in search of wisdom or to confront dangerous entities, surely account for much of the fantastical legends we dismiss as fiction or embellishment.

One legend which perhaps still enjoys some credibility in terms of its factuality is the great *Beowulf* poem. Seamus Heaney, in the introduction to his translation of *Beowulf*, tells us that the tale is set "in Scandinavia, in a 'once upon a time' that is partly historical." He also refers to its "dream element."[24] Whilst that part of the poem which is deemed "partly historical" does appear to represent mundane occurrences, those other dream-like parts are easily recognisable—one of which occurs when Beowulf seeks out Grendel's Mother:

> After these words, the prince of the Weather-Geats
> was impatient to be away and plunged suddenly:
> without more ado, he dived into the heaving
> depths of the lake. It was the best part of a day
> before he could see the solid bottom.[25]

---

24 Seamus Heaney. *Beowulf*. (London: Faber and Faber, 2000), ix - xiii.
25 Ibid., 49.

The part here of most note is that of the lake and the fact that Beowulf swam downwards for "the best part of a day." Instead of merely painting a vivid picture of a historically-*accurate* Scandinavia populated by historically-*inaccurate* mythical beasts, the poem also exaggerates what we know is biologically possible for humans to achieve: holding one's breath for the best part of a day. But why? Superstition was rife in the dark ages and we would probably look back upon those 'unenlightened' times and conclude that the people mistook shadows, animals and howls in the night for elves, orcs and dragons; or that they tended to embody natural phenomena within imaginary creations. But why would they impose the impossible upon what is otherwise a very grounded, rational story? Beowulf does not fly to Denmark, he sails; he is not immune to wounding, he bleeds. In all dealings with the human world Beowulf is shown to be exceptionally brave and strong, but not *inhuman*—in all dealings, that is, except for those dream-like quests to fight inhuman foes. The symbolism of plunging into an impossibly deep lake to confront a mysterious entity is overtly Shamanistic; water, the gateway to the other world and the long journey a metaphor for the patience and focus essential in such undertakings. In an altered state of consciousness—in one of the nine worlds where we are not bound by the same laws of physics as in this—that is where a man might be able to survive underwater for the best part of a day; and such a world was considered so real by Heathens-of-old that accounts of happenings in that world were as real as great deeds in this mundane one. That Beowulf seeks Grendel's Mother on his own lends further weight to the suggestion of this great deed being a projection of spirit or consciousness as opposed to literal, in the conventional sense of the word.

The Beowulf tale is just one of the more prominent Germanic quest legends, of which hundreds or even thousands have existed. But the common themes that relate many of them are highly indicative of a Shamanic aspect. Rarely do our heroes meet their inhuman foe on an open plain, or outside of their home; and rarely do our heroes undertake their more fantastical quests accompanied by others. The hallmarks of these otherworldly endeavours are often marked by entrance through a cave, tunnel, forest or lake, or by traversing a mountain. In any case, the voyager passes through a type of obstacle to reach a secluded, ominous setting. Such conventions have become so commonplace that even modern, post-Shamanic stories make regular use of them; such as the Heathen*ish* tale of Tolkien's *The Hobbit*:

> The stars were coming out behind him in a pale sky barred with black when the hobbit crept through the enchanted door and stole into the Mountain. It was far easier going than he expected. This was no goblin entrance, or rough wood-elves' cave. It was a

> passage made by dwarves, at the height of their wealth and skill: straight as a ruler, smooth-floored and smooth-sided, going with a gentle never-varying slope direct—to some distant end in the blackness below.[26]

The hobbit, Bilbo Baggins, is here venturing into the dragon Smaug's lair; and whilst Tolkien's works are not intended to be factual in any way, they do often exemplify the type of events and beings which are reminiscent of the spirit world. Tolkien once said "[England] had no stories of its own, not of the quality that I sought, and found in legends of other lands."[27] That he said as much, proceeded to write some mythology for England and then used traditional conventions—such as the above where Bilbo enters Smaug's lair by tunnel—confirms the prominence of such commonalities within early Heathen mythology.

Rather than insist upon the Shamanic interpretation of Heathen mythology, I'll say only that it is difficult to argue against the potential for finding obvious Shamanistic tendencies within much of it. Most Heathens will no doubt already be wary of the lessons and symbolism within mythology, but I hope the majority are not overly-anxious to dismiss all as fictional or purely-metaphorical.

Forbidden Fruit

We have so far delved, with reasonable depth, into the meaning, practice, theory, symbolism and importance of Shamanism's Germanic equivalent—*seiðr*. What appears to be most worrying is the decline of such practices within our modern world. In introducing this essay I mentioned the possibility of an age-old conspiracy in the suppression of Shamanistic practice. The full truth behind such an accusation would necessitate an incredibly in-depth study into the integrity of post-Shamanic Abrahamic religions and control system. We do not have the time, nor perhaps the required focus here, but we can raise some questions.

Amazonian tribes, such as those who use a psychoactive substance called ayahuasca, promote ritual consumption of this DMT-containing drug. Ayahuasca puts subjects into direct contact with the spirits and as a result, members of the tribe may seek answers, cures and solutions, or simply grow spiritually and morally. This is a living example of how Shamanic tribes encourage direct contact with the spirit world for all people. And whilst the

---

26 J.R.R. Tolkien. *The Hobbit*. (London: Harper Collins, 1997), 200.
27 Tolkien-online.com. http://www.tolkien-online.com/tolkien-and-mythology.html (accessed: January 10, 2010).

Shaman, in contrast with the non-Shaman, might conduct more frequent and vital spirit work, all members of the community were expected to understand and nurture their own personal link to the spirits. Compare this approach with that of the world's more dominant, newer religions: Judeo-Christianity and Islam. Rabbis, Priests and Imams grasped all authority over the direct contact with God. They assumed the role of mediator and those subjects recounting premonitions or significant paranormal sightings were in severe danger of being tried for witchcraft, even if they were themselves committed Christians. The people were permitted to pray, but should their prayers bring results too effective—in other words, should their direct contact with God be too strong—they would be held under suspicion. The Priests of the Abrahamic religions alone enjoyed that privilege. Why should they? Why would they seek to?

The obvious, and most probable answer to this is: the age-old search for ever-greater power and authority. The centralisation of spirituality is what separates the newer, monotheistic religions from the indigenous Pagan and nature-based ones and it is for this reason I prefer to call Heathenism a 'faith' or 'tradition' rather than a 'religion.' Indeed, the fact that the Abrahamic religions are monotheistic itself demonstrates the centralisation of spiritual authority into the hands of one God, rather than many gods who might offer alternative solutions to our Earthly plights. The centralisation of religious power into the hands of Priests and, worse yet, the Vatican or Monarchy reflects the omnipotence of one unquestionable God. If we source answers to our spiritual needs from a mediator-Priest, rather than by our own channels which require no middle-man, then we are susceptible to the authoritarian whims of Church or government. Could this explain the Biblical tree of knowledge, whose fruit mankind was forbidden to eat—the serpent representing spirit and rebirth as it so often has throughout history? It may, or the fruit might only be forbidden for the same reasons that Odin did not eat when hung upon that wind-rocked tree. Either way, a mystery worthy of meditation.

But is the Church spiritual at all? Was it ever? Or was it co-opted at some point in history (perhaps the very beginning) by materialists-in-disguise? The majority of Christianity's subjects have no-doubt been sincere in their faith, but one must wonder why any genuine, free religious authority would not embolden its flock to establish personal connections with the Holy Spirit in any harmless way possible; perhaps because they were always only meant to *be* the 'flock' and never truly free. It is almost as if at this stage in the story of mankind most of us decided to *outsource* our spiritual growth for the sake of ease and for the promise of security. Strong parallels can be drawn between the issues of spiritual independence and those of political independence (liberty) and the two are heavily intertwined.

More current incarnations of this suppression of direct contact take the form of social ostracisation rather than overt authoritarianism. We are free to practice *seiðr*, Shamanism, or any form of direct interaction with the spirit world, but the moment we talk freely about it we risk the scorn of mainstream society—a society who have been taught that science already has all the answers, that it is safer to close your mind than leave it open and risk facing great responsibilities and uncomfortable truths. Pagan traditions are today still less acceptable within the mainstream than the dominant religions, quite expectedly; but even within Pagan tradition the more obviously supernatural aspects are treated with some scepticism. For example—tell someone you practice Heathenry out of respect for your forefathers or because you love nature and your sanity will scarcely be called into question. However, explain to that same person that you practice Heathenry in order to communicate with the spirits and to prevent malevolent entities from harming you and you will likely be met with confounded stares and broken bridges. We live in a dispirited, post-spiritual world that not even cultural Heathenism can heal. *Practical* Heathenism, I suggest, is no better implemented than by rediscovering Germanic Shamanism.

If this is true—that direct spiritual contact has been deliberately hindered, then any increase in the practice of *seiðr*, or understanding of the Shamanic element to all of Heathenism is surely long overdue.

Reconciliation

This argument for Shamanism is not intended to diminish the value of other practices within Heathen tradition; it is simply an attempt to firmly establish the all-pervasive nature of *seiðr*. Perhaps we as a folk have been slowly conditioned to neglect spiritual work in favour of more cultural, regimented Heathenry; or perhaps the issue is simpler—we have been conditioned to favour materialism over any genuine faith whatsoever. Whatever the cause of the direction the World has taken, we here are familiar with the solution—the solution not only to societal shortcomings, but to our everyday problems and questions. That solution is to develop our relationship with the natural and supernatural worlds around us. Our actions here in Midgard impact upon all living things here in this familiar world, but they also affect those unfamiliar spirits who inhabit the other eight worlds: Asgard, Vanaheim, Jotunheim, Alfheim, Helheim, Nidavellir, Svartalfheim, Niflheim and Muspelheim. In turn, occurrences in those worlds may have the potential to affect us—this is the wisdom of the ancients. We can honour nature, gods and the seasons; we can applaud honour; we can work with runes and we can know mythology inside and out; but these things do not cut to the spiritual origins of Heathenism.

Archaeological evidence suggests that in the development of human spirituality Shamanism came first. We can see this not only in those indigenous tribes that remain but also in how ancient cave-art represents the world-view of the artists responsible. In addition to this, it seems logical that the various Pagan traditions of the world were simply the result of culture building up around an essentially Shamanistic belief system. If we look at the varying forms of Paganism worldwide, we will find differences and similarities. Variation is most prominent in terms of the culture, the mythology and the festivities (which were expressions of how each folk approached their spirituality); and commonalities are most recognisable in the *non*-cultural aspects of each group: the relationship with a spirit world. And surely, wherever the same belief crops up again and again throughout time and space, it is a likely candidate for a greater truth.

EXPERIMENTAL NEOFOLK
RHYTHMIC INDUSTRIAL NEOCLASSICAL
DARK AMBIENT METAL
INDUSTRIAL NOISE & POWER ELECTRONICS
DARK AMBIENT METAL INDUSTRIAL NEOFOLK
NOISE & POWER ELECTRONICS EXPERIMENTAL RHYTHMIC INDUSTRIAL NEOCLASSICAL
DARK AMBIENT METAL INDUSTRIAL NEOFOLK
NOISE & POWER ELECTRONICS EXPERIMENTAL RHYTHMIC INDUSTRIAL NEOCLASSICAL
heathen harvest
ILLUMINATING THE POST-INDUSTRIAL UNDERGROUND
www.heathenharvest.com

Baldr, by Elmer Boyd Smith (1902).

Baldr's Temple

by Troy Wisehart

A temple we have built for Baldr god of light
the altar therein is Helgrindr hight
Where in lies Baldr's altar, the floor is wrought of stone
but inlaid in the rock is a helm of awe of bone
Burning are the recels, pounding is the beat
Looks down upon us Alfather from his high seat
Blot upon that altar singing three times eight
sing runes 'til wide open swings the darkened gate
Frigga too is weeping hot wet tears of joy
her children's children's children welcome her dear boy
Up from Hel now chant we Odin's golden son
Walks he here among us Hella's guest is come
Soon now is the time when in grass the gods find gold
and sing the mighty runes the powers from of old

Intolerance and Religion

by Alain de Benoist[1]

In his book entitled *Qu'est-ce qu'une vie réussie?*, Luc Ferry writes: "To those who lament the withdrawal of religions from the forefront of life, one must again state how, under their traditional forms at least, they continue as ever to be the source of almost all the wars and conflicts which bloody this planet."[2] It comes as a surprise to hear such remarks from the mouth of the Minister of National Education for at least two reasons. The first relates to the fact that the vast majority of wars since the two World Wars which have occurred during the 20th century have not had religious causes. The second reason relates to the fact that Luc Ferry evidently encompasses under this generic term "religions" beliefs which are very different in nature, as we shall see.

Indeed, what is most striking, when studying Europe's ancient religions—the pagan ones—is precisely the fact that they do not know any form of intolerance which is, properly speaking, religious in nature. These are polytheistic religions to which peoples adhere without thinking for one instant that they must criticize other peoples' needs to sacrifice to other deities. These religions are strangers to fanaticism. They know neither religious persecution, crusades against "infidels" or "non-believers," nor war in the name of God. More orthopractic in nature than orthodox, they equally know nothing about notions of dogma, schism or heresy.

The Roman Empire always respected local beliefs, just as they respected the legal customs of the people they had conquered. If the Empire had not regarded the Druids favorably, during the Roman Conquest, and later the Christians, it was strictly for political reasons: the first group were condemned for their galvanization of the Gallic resistance, the second for being bad citizens. As for the Greeks, they went as far as to support a cult of the "unknown god." This same tolerance is also found in religions of universal scope, such as the Asian religions. Throughout its history, Buddhism has never been a missionary religion. Equally, traditional Hinduism has never been known to be a proselytizing religion. Professing that God is present in all forms in the universe, Hinduism makes tolerance towards the Other a duty, and not a concession. The Japanese have also never sought to export Shintoism, no more than Athens felt

---

1 Translated by Jennifer Roberge-Toll. Footnotes and parenthetical notes in this paper, unless designated, are those of the author.
2 Luc Ferry. *Qu'est-ce qu'une vie réussie?* [What is a Successful Life?] (Paris: Grasset, 2002).

impelled to impose the cult of Athena onto Sparta.

Religious intolerance, generator of wars waged in the name of faith, does not appear in the history of humanity other than in a precise context, one made possible with the birth of monotheism. In its beginning, monotheism was but monolatry: for the first Hebrews, Yahweh was but a national god, alongside the protective gods of neighbouring peoples. In the more ancient interpretations of the Torah, written in the 8th century BCE, Elohim is plural: Yahweh is but the *El*[3] or *Eloah* of the Israelites, an *El* which they have placed above the others. This is what Moses affirms: "Who is as you among the gods, Yahweh? Who is as illustrious as you in godliness?"[4] Yahweh himself does not deny the existence of other gods. He only forbids that one bow down before them, since he is a "jealous" god (*quana*).[5] His very name is Jealous.[6] The notion of monotheism does not properly come to the forefront until the Exile, through an unknown prophet who has been named the Second Isaiah. In its fullest scope, this notion implies that there exists a universal God, a one and only God with the double meaning accorded to such a notion: being at once without rival as well as the 'All Other.' From this moment on, the rule is clear: "Without monotheism, there is no salvation."

The most celebrated of the Ten Words (or Ten Commandments), "Thou shalt not kill," has nothing to do with an absolute moral imperative which proclaims the sanctity of all human life. That which is solely sacred is the life of the orthodox believer. Proof of this is seen when Moses, barely having descended from the mount where God has entrusted him with the Decalogue, rushes to have 3,000 idolaters put to death.[7] "Thou shalt not kill," however, rates only as seventh in position on the Tablets of Stone. The first decree, that which dictates all others, is "You shall have no other gods before me."[8] This first commandment establishes a Covenant (*B'rith*), an exclusive contract between Yahweh and his People. With Hebrew sacred space being above all structured along vertical lines, this covenant elevates the Jewish people. With respect to other peoples, this covenant holds the Jewish people to certain duties as well as offering certain rights. The covenant creates a "nation of priests" destined to guide humanity towards a more just world. Ethnocentrism here blossoms into universalism.

---

3   *El* being a generic term for any number of Gods which was later, similarly to the Latin *deus*, given to refer to the one God of Judaism—trans.
4   Exodus 15:11.
5   Deuteronomy 5:9 and 6:14; Exodus 20:5.
6   Exodus 34:14.
7   Exodus 32:28.
8   Exodus 20:3.

The idolatrous peoples are doomed to the *herem,* a term which at once denotes exclusion, isolation and eradication. God demands that the Hebrews exterminate the idolaters,[9] while the Hebrews themselves request God to make their adversaries perish. The ungodly, henceforth, can and must be killed. Yahweh declares to his people: "No one shall be able to stand against you until you have destroyed them."[10] "The (other) nations, the *goyim,*" writes Jean Soler, "represent evil for the sole reason that they are other."[11] Here we find the root of "*alterophobia,*"[12] linked to the dread of mixing (to begin with, the dread of mixed marriages, cf. 1 Esdras 9): the Other is "impure." That it be foreign or simply deviant, evil is otherness. And the only way to triumph over evil is to eradicate it, roots and all.

Upon having ordered the massacre of the Midianites, Moses criticizes the Hebrews for having left the women unscathed and has them, and their male children, killed.[13] Following this comes a near uninterrupted series of massacres. Once the Midianites are taken care of, attention is then turned towards the Hittites, the Girgashites, the Amorites, the Canaanites, the Perizzites, the Hivvites, the Jebusites, the Philistines, the Moabites. Genocides and ethnic cleansings are perpetrated by the Hebrews—all resolute in making idolaters pay for "the reward of Yahweh's vengeance."[14] As Jehu, so are David and Saul responsible for causing streams of blood. Joshua destroys Jericho: "Then they devoted all in the city to destruction[15], both men and women, young and old, oxen, sheep, and donkeys, with the edge of the sword."[16] He goes on to destroy the entire nation: "He left none remaining, but devoted to destruction[17] all that breathed, just as the LORD God of Israel commanded."[18]

Historical Judaism will never abandon its war against "idolatry" (*avodah zarah*). It will proselytize in one negative fashion however: conversions will be discouraged but "the nations" will have to submit to the Seven Laws of Noah[19]

---

9 Deuteronomy 7:1-6 and 20:10-13.
10 Deuteronomy 7:24.
11 Jean Solet. *L'invention du monothéisme* [The Invention of Monotheism]. (Paris: de Fallois, 2002), 59.
12 See translation notes below—trans.
13 Numbers 31:15-17.
14 Numbers 31:3.
15 In the French, the terms 'anathema' (*herem*) are used instead of the word 'destruction'—trans.
16 Joshua 6:21.
17 Again, 'anathema' is used instead of 'destruction'—trans.
18 Joshua 10:40.
19 The Noahide Laws or Noachide Code—trans.

which command the renouncement of other forms of religion.

Islam, which equally proceeds from Biblical monotheism (via Judaeo-Christian communities founded during the first centuries CE), would, by its part, exhibit an uncompromising and missionary universalism, never shying away from recourse to force in order to win over new followers. In this way, Islam would assert itself as a masterful religion. Nevertheless, of the 6,000 verses which comprise the Koran, we can but count 200 which maintain a repressive legal content, "and, of these 200 verses, if we dismiss those which have been repealed by later revelations, we are left with but 80 which are still in effect."[20]

With Christianity, the viewpoint changes. The fundamental unity of the human species is always forcefully declared, but there is no longer a chosen people: it is on an equal footing that God calls all men to him. With respect to Judaism, Christianity corresponds to a complete universalization of the notion of "us". Love (*agapé*) prevails over the Law, atonement becomes a value, at times to the detriment of the notion of "justice" as understood by the Torah. The key notion therefore becomes that of *conversion*. In proper theology, the non-Christian can only enjoy an imperfect dignity. Tolerance is at best but a provisional compromise, an instance of patience which will know its end. From an eschatological point of view, the co-existence of Good and Evil, of Truth and Error, is ultimately impossible. Only good has the theological right to exist. To enjoy perfect dignity, the "idolater" (or the "pagan") must therefore abandon his specific native beliefs in order to adopt an identity designed to correspond to the notion of absolute Truth and Good. In the universal Church, the differences in faith must yield their places to Sameness. Wanting to be heir to the apostles, missionaries would devote themselves at the risk of making all the peoples of the world adapt to a distinctive model of civilization.

At the same time, the theology takes on a dogmatic form. Contrary to Talmudic commentary, Christian dogma seeks to be unequivocal, therefore providing new motives for exclusion. Similar to the foreign "Crusades" (in the Holy Land) or the domestic "Crusades" (against the Albigensians), the denouncement of schisms and heresies would justify new massacres. The "just" war is above all else a war which is morally justified. Delivered in the name of Good, the just war transforms the adversary into the figure of Evil, that is to say into the absolute enemy. Thus exists the ruthless character of "religious wars." The Inquisition will become the judge of its own heart of hearts, that is to say with respect to thought and ulterior motives.

---

20 Muhammad Saï al-Ashmaway. *L'islamisme contre l'islam* [Islamism Against Islam]. (Paris: Découverte, 1990).

Arthur Schopenhauer, in his *Parerga und Paralipomena*, well summarized the problem when he wrote:

> As a matter of fact, it is only to monotheism that intolerance is essential; an only god is by his nature a jealous god, who can allow no other god to exist. Polytheistic gods, on the other hand, are naturally tolerant; they live and let live; their own colleagues are the chief objects of their sufferance, as being gods of the same religion. This toleration is afterwards extended to foreign gods, who are, accordingly, hospitably received, and later on admitted, in some cases, to an equality of rights; the chief example of which is shown by the fact that the Romans willingly admitted and venerated Phrygian, Egyptian and other gods. Hence it is that monotheistic religions alone furnish the spectacle of religious wars, religious persecutions, heretical tribunals, that breaking of idols and destruction of images of the gods, that razing of Indian temples, and Egyptian colossi, which had looked on the sun three thousand years; just because a jealous god had said, *Thou shalt make no graven image.*[21]

We should not however forget, as Régis Debray has recently commented, that "religion is that which at once permits men to live, to love and to give of themselves as well as that which pushes them to hate, to kill and to take."[22] This ambivalence is a component of who they are. As sacred as their foundational texts may be, all faith remains inseparable from a hermeneutic. None can be reduced to the interpretation that literalists and fundamentalists wish to bestow upon it (a *jihad* which refers to a "holy war" in Classical Islam, also signifies "to concentrate on one's self" in Sufi mysticism). Moreover, there is no lack of contradictions, contained within these sacred texts. Jesus seems to caution against violence when he states: "Blessed are the peacemakers."[23] But he also states: "Do you think that I have come to give peace on earth? No, I tell you, but rather division."[24] From one and the same Church hail Torquemada and Francis of Assisi, the incestuous popes of the Renaissance and Mother Theresa.

---

21 Arthur Schopenhauer. *Parerga and Paralipomena: A Collection of Philosophical Essays*. trans. T. Bailey Saunders. (New York: Cosimo Classics, 2007), 37-38.
22 Commenting on his book *Le Feu sacré: Fonctions du Religieux* in the December issue of *Figaro Magazine*.
23 Matthew 5:9.
24 Luke 12:51.

Translation Notes:

1. With respect to the word alterophobia, I have taken the liberty of translating the French word *altérophobie* into its literal form alterophobia despite the latter's inexistence in the English lexicon. A precedent seems to have been set by the following source: WAIS Conference—World Association of International Studies, Stanford University re: "USA: One Race or None at All?" (Alain de Benoist, France), a post and reply-to-post regarding the use of the term alterophobia (October, 2006) :

> Alain de Benoist comments: "As you know, race is a very complicated matter. After World War II, UNESCO adopted the 'there are no races' strategy to fight against racism, of which Nazism has demonstrated the horrible consequences. This position is still shared by some scientists. But other scientists view the phenomenon differently. If there are 'no races', there are still different genetic pools and different collective phenotypes. Even to praise race-mixing implies that there is something to mix. Anyway, the main problem is not the 'objective' existence of races, but the subjective (and quasi universal) perception of the differences. It is clear that any kind of perceived difference can support *alterophobia* [my italics] (of which racism is one category). But if we were all alike ('the same'), humanity would lose its diversity. Racism does not result from saying that races exist, but from considering race as the most important thing to explain human history and to draw the conclusion that some races are 'superior' to others (which means nothing, because there is no objective criteria for such an evaluation). Today, the main trend is not to say that all members of human species are alike, but rather to praise differences and diversity, which seems to me more fitting."

> John Eipper (moderator of the WAIS Conference) comments: "Alain de Benoist's eloquent essay merits our attention–certainly to celebrate cultural/ethnic ("racial?") difference is even better than to deny its existence. As a dyed-in-the-wool "word guy," I am intrigued by the term "alterophobia": fear of difference or fear of the other. I checked my sources, and *it appears that English does not actually "have" this word* [my italics—trans.] —though French and Spanish do (alterophobie/alterofobia). Of course, xenophobia exists in English (as it certainly does in reality), but this is a more nationalistic, and thus more restrictive,

term than "alterophobia." I very much like its usefulness and its Gallic sophistication, and thus have left the word intact in Alain's post."[25]

2. Where needed for ease of translation and understanding, I have used the English Standard version of Biblical translations as opposed to having myself translated those Biblical quotations utilized by the author. Where a particular difference in wording has been noted and is key to the translated work itself, indications have been made in brackets. The English Standard version (as well as others) can be viewed online at: http://biblios.com

---

25 http://cgi.stanford.edu/group/wais/cgi-bin/?p=6075 (Accessed: April 09, 2010).

ODINIC RITE
FAITH FOLK FAMILY

Odinism for the Modern World

www.odinic-rite.org

An Interpretation of Germanic Mythology

by Kris Stevenson

Introduction

> *I believe that legends and myth are largely made of "truth", and indeed present aspects of it that can only be received in this mode; and long ago certain truths and modes of this kind were discovered and must always reappear.*[1]
>
> —J.R.R. Tolkien

One of the very first things I learned on my path as an Odinist—and the most enduring lesson of all—is that myths, far from being childish stories or the superstition of "false" belief are, in fact, a form of language. A different form of language from that of everyday communication or the language of mathematics, but a language none the less, a language composed of allegorical symbols designed to convey "truth" in a palatable form. A way of understanding this that I find helpful is to consider what are termed "popular science" books. These works are largely written for people, such as myself, who have no grasp of higher mathematics; they provide a "lay man's" understanding of the concepts and ideas that scientists wish to put across to us. In its own way this is exactly what mythology is, a lay man's guide to truths revealed. All religions are "revealed" religions to some extent; Nietzsche once wrote:

> Indeed it might be a basic characteristic of existence that those who would know it completely would perish, in which case the strength of a spirit should be measured according to how much of the "truth" one could still barely endure-or to put it more clearly, to what degree one would require it to be thinned down, shrouded, sweetened, blunted, falsified.[2]

Nietzsche's comment stands as a useful example for the point I am making, which is that mythology is watered down truth, watered down enough for most of us to be able to handle and comprehend. I believe that all sacred texts reflect this principle to varying degrees. I remember perfectly well the confusion I often felt

---

1 J.R.R. Tolkien, eds. Christopher Tolkien and Humphrey Carpenter. *The Letters of J.R.R. Tolkien.* (New York: Haughton Mifflin Co., 2000), 147.
2 Friedrich Nietzsche, ed. and trans. Walter Kaufman. *Beyond Good and Evil.* (USA: Vintage Books, 1989), 239.

reading the Eddic lays in a mindset that was geared to the literal. It took me some time to come to the realization of what it was, in fact, that *I was looking at.*

This level of understanding can serve us perfectly well in our lives: If we study the lays or just *Hávamál* we can come to a reasonably satisfactory state of awareness...but why stop there? The Eddas may be "watered down truth" as I term it, but for me, they are an enticement; a door ajar enough to let a chink of light through. The depth of understanding that we can gain from the Eddas is only limited by our willingness to make the effort to understand. Do we all have the same depth of understanding? Obviously not, we are all constrained by our own abilities, such is reality. However, the achievement never stands in attaining goals, but in having goals in the first place and the way in which we go about attempting to realise them. I have come to the belief that the Eddic lays contain a philosophy; a body of "truth" that can (and already has) enriched my existence and my understanding. I decided to make the effort and how far that takes me is really down to my own ability and my will to progress...

While researching the study that follows, I began to wonder about the nature of truth within mythology. What I mean is, are these objective truths, external facts and realities or are they subjective and conditioned by ourselves? I am leaning more to the conclusion that it is a bit of both. The Eddas "speak to me." If they did not I would question whether Odinism[3] was my path. I believe they speak to everyone...but that they do not necessarily say the same things to each. Out of the many things that appeal to me about Odinism, near the top of the list is the encouragement to understand and interpret the Eddas in our own way, develop our own *gnosis,*[4] and to build a "relationship," if you will, with the texts.

I say "research," but this is probably not strictly accurate. I am something of a prolific note taker. Practically everything I read I will take notes from. Over the years that I have been reading the Eddas, among other texts, I have built up a body of notes of points that have interested me. There was no actual aim in mind beyond my own curiosity. I had begun tentatively to frame some kind of picture of my own understanding and awareness regarding our lore, but it was only after I was asked if I would like to contribute to this journal that I really bent myself to it. What follows is very much a work in progress. I hesitate to call it a philosophical tract (although I am reliably informed that I am practising a branch of philosophy known as hermeneutics). It is rather my relationship to the Eddic

---

3 Now is as good a time as any to state that I call myself an Odinist. It is a term pretty much used exclusively by members of the Odinic Rite. Its relevance for us is to reflect a forward thinking movement, not one bound by restriction to the "lore."

4 *Gnosis* is an ancient Greek word and means "knowledge," as in a personal, transcendent knowledge.

lays and what they say to me. At present, I am increasingly inclined to the view that our interpretation may well alter with time and will inevitably be added to as we grow as individuals. If truth is as much subjective as objective then my understanding may well say more about me than what lies in the Eddas!

To reiterate, this is very much a work in progress. I make no claim to scholarship or expertise and I have no doubt that more experienced students of the Eddic lore will find errors, misunderstandings, and maybe even have knowledge I myself am unaware of. Any errors are, of course, down to me alone.

Throughout my study of Germanic mythology I have come to an intense appreciation of the depth of understanding of the human condition that is contained within. Central questions to most thinking people such as 'why do I exist at all?' 'what is the purpose of my existence?' 'is there such a thing as destiny?' are readily found explored within the Eddic lays. This, in itself, is doubtless something of a revelation for those who do not understand the purpose of allegory. My understanding of the lays has, perhaps, been shaped by my own outlook as well as shaped by the content within, but certainly they have affected me deeply.

Primarily, I will be looking at the creation story as regards man, the three primary phases of spiritual attainment involving Odin and what I believe to be an attempt at human apotheosis in Baldr. Throughout, I will be looking at Loki and his role in these situations. Obviously this is a study based upon my own understanding and assumptions but I have tried to refrain from imparting my own beliefs regarding deity as such and of ethics in particular. All I have attempted is to see what is there *in my eyes*. In other words, I have deliberately avoided comment on the nature of the Gods as either real beings or as Jungian archetypes reflecting elements of the human psyche. This is still an area of debate for me personally and is largely irrelevant to my interpretation of the lore. I hope, at least, it provides food for thought.[5]

Loki and Creation

---

5 Unless otherwise indicated, I have used *The Eddas: The Keys to the Mysteries of the North* by James Allen Chisholm (http://home.earthlink.net/~jordsvin/Norse%20Texts/The%20Eddas.htm [accessed: 5 January, 2010]) as the source of my passages from the Eddic poems. For the *Hávamál* quotes, I have used the above work as well as the *Masks of Odin: Wisdom of the Ancient Norse* by Elsa-Brita Titchenell (Pasadena, CA: Theosophical University Press, 1985) and *The Nature of Asatru: An Overview of the Ideals and Philosophy of the Indigenous Religion of Northern Europe* by Mark Puryear (Lincoln, NE: iUniverse, 2006).

As Bor's sons walked along the sea shore, they came across two logs and created people out of them. The first gave breath and life, the second consciousness and movement, the third a face, speech and hearing and sight...[6]

—Gylfaginning

From the host came three, mighty and powerful Æsir to the coast. There they found an ash and an elm of little might, and lacking Orlog. They had neither breath nor wit nor life hue nor manner nor good looks. Odin gave them breath of life, Hoenir gave them wod, Lothur gave them life and good looks.[7]

—Völuspá

What makes us human? This is a question that has exercised the human mind and soul throughout history. At root, it is a question of consciousness. What separates man from other animals is this sense of "knowing" or self-awareness:

> Although I do not see consciousness as the pinnacle of biological evolution, I see it as a turning point in the long history of life. Even when we resort to the simple standard dictionary definition of consciousness-as an organism's awareness of it's own self and surroundings-it is easy to envision how consciousness is likely to have opened the way in human evolution to a new order of creations.[8]

Most of us are aware of the Biblical exegesis regarding the creation of human awareness. Eve, tempted by the Serpent, eats from the tree of knowledge and persuades Adam to eat of the fruit as well. Their "eyes are opened" and they become aware of their nakedness. They are expelled from Eden before they partake of the tree of life and become immortal.[9] Our own lore has a somewhat different account and is rooted in older Indo-European legend. The Iranians have an account in the *Bundehesh* that the first man and woman grew from *Rheum ribes* (a plant commonly found in Western Asia). Ahura Mazda made them into human beings.[10] This creation of man from some form of vegetation is really a

---

6 Snorri Sturluson, trans. Anthony Faulkes. *Edda*. (London: Everyman, 1987), 13.
7 *Völuspá*, stanzas 17-18.
8 Antonio Damasio. *The Feeling of What Happens: Body and Emotion in the Making of Consciousness*. (USA, Harcourt, 2000), 4.
9 Genesis 3:4, "But the serpent said to the woman, 'You will not die, for God knows that when you eat of it your eyes will be opened, and you will be like God, knowing good and evil.'"
10 Viktor Rydberg. *Teutonic Mythology*. (London: Norroena Society, 1907), 127.

An Interpretation of Germanic Mythology

symbol of man's separation from the natural order. He has been set aside, but for what purpose? I believe to answer that question we need to understand who Lothur/Lóðurr is:

> Lodur is unknown, and the etymology is unclear. Many attempts have been made to understand Lodur as an alternate name for some god, most often Loki. The main argument in favour of Loki is that he is known to travel with Odin and Hœnir, as when they encounter Thjazi or Andvari. Odin is also known as "Lopt's friend," and Lopt is definitely a Loki name.[11]

Here we see Loki as one possibility among other suggestions, such as Heimdall and Freyr.[12] Lóðurr gave Ask and Embla *litr goda* (good colour). This is the image or appearance of the gods. The name Loki has also been related to *liechan/liuhan* (enlighten) and to the Old English *leoht* (light).[13] What conclusion can we draw (if we accept Lodur as Loki) from this? The very existence of human consciousness is the workings of a deity whose role in the mythology is as protagonist of the gods and the inspirer of evil deeds? It does not sound appealing to suggest, but perhaps it is worth considering.

My thought is based upon an opinion that human consciousness is as much a curse as it is a gift and that this "gift" was not inspired from love but from malice.[14] In my thesis, the theory of Lodur in fact being Loki makes sense.

Let us make no mistake here. I am not suggesting Loki is a Promethean figure[15] taking pity upon man. He is within us and without us (the son of a giant father

---

11 John Lindow. *Norse Mythology: A Guide to the Gods, Heroes, Rituals and Beliefs*. (New York: Oxford University Press, 2001), 212.
12 It is fair to note that opinion on Lodur's identity with Loki is not unanimous. Davidson was unconvinced by the case. Lindow himself suggests Freyr as another possibility on the premise of a fertility deity, whilst Heimdall is put forward by the Odinic Rite.
13 Titchenell. *The Masks of Odin*, 67.
14 "This view of things already provides us with a profound and pessimistic view of the world...the fundamental knowledge of the oneness of everything existent, the conception of individuation as the primal cause of evil, (Friedrich Nietzsche, trans. Kaufmann. *The Birth of Tragedy*. contained in *The Basic Writings of Nietzsche*. [USA: Random House, 2000], 74).
15 Prometheus is a Titan in Greek mythology who stole fire from Zeus and gave it to man. As punishment, Zeus bound him to a rock where an eagle would, each day, eat his liver, which would regenerate that night.

and goddess mother).[16] He is the archetype of destruction[17] and from a human perspective he is the very epitome of evil. Loki made us aware of *what we are and of what life is*. Sit and think upon that for a moment...Loki sundered man from nature, he shattered our innocence and *made us aware of it*. We are no longer just another animal. We are now beings of choice and warring within us are our former natural instinctive urges and our knowledge *of this fact*. We are schizophrenic beings capable of understanding and creating concepts of good, evil, morality and immorality. We are no longer wholly instinctive. We are creative and contemplative. *We are often afraid*. Consciousness may, or may not, be a "gift" worthy of itself, but it's also a source of pain and suffering inspired by a malicious act committed against us by a force that wills us not to just play the game but understand we are in the game itself. The awakened man is aware, in the Nietzschean sense, of the Dionysian suffering[18]...it is hardly surprising that when Heimdall came to our people we were in such a state of chaos.

> That one is also reckoned among the Æsir whom some call the Æsir's calumniator and originator of deceits and the disgrace of all gods and men. His name is Loki or Lopt, son of the giant Farbauti, Laufey or Nal is his mother...Loki is handsome in appearance, evil in character, very capricious in behaviour.[19]

Perhaps no greater evil has Loki wrought than what he did to man. Yet from that evil there is *potential and hope* that Loki could not have imagined and, indeed, he spends much of the rest of the mythological cycle attempting to make sure that man never reaches that potential. Throughout the lore we see Loki engaged in various acts of mischief from the kidnap of Idunn to cutting Sif's hair to the darker episodes surrounding the Æsir and Vanir conflicts and the eventual conflagration of Ragnarok. The tragedy is that the price of man's fulfillment of his potential is our suffering. Not the suffering of all mortal beings doomed to illness and death, but the suffering that is intrinsic to the knowledge brought by self-awareness. Loki introduced us to the moral positions of good and evil within our own personality. My belief is that these concepts simply exist nowhere else

---

16 It is possible that Loki's mother is a Goddess, hence Snorri's claim that he was counted as one of the Æsir. Of course, that his father was a giant is not unique; Odin himself is of giant ancestry.
17 "Loki is manifest in each of us and must be fought there—in our minds and souls," ("Loki." *The Odinic Rite*. http://www.odinic-rite.org/Loki.html [accessed: December 31, 2009]).
18 Nietzsche, *The Birth of Tragedy*, 73.
19 Faulkes, *Edda*, 26.

except in the human mind. Jung believed that "good" and "evil" are simply moral judgements and have no relation to the nature of *Being* itself.[20]

Fortunately, Loki does not have it all his own way. Of his companions in the creation of man, there is interest in the enigmatic figure of Hœnir. Odin gave the breath of life to Ask and Embla and kindled the sacred flame of being. It is to Odin that we owe the beat of our hearts and the breath we draw. Hœnir's gift is harder to understand. It is defined both as spirit and as motion. Davidson emphasises the importance placed upon silence in Old Norse texts as a sign of wisdom.[21] This is an interesting idea that leads to the notion that if Loki presented man with awareness and the choice between "good" and "evil" then maybe Loki and Odin represent those choices personified. If this is the case, then Hœnir may well represent the *human conscience personified*, the arbitrator of human guilt, compassion and love, the tool that enables us to carry out actions and to justify them. Hœnir is that restraint and contemplation that the truly wise possess.

This theme of man's estrangement from the natural order being the work of Loki is something I wish to continue with here when we consider the role of the giants and the conflict between the Æsir and Vanir. Heimdall may well have prevented humanity's collapse into anarchy (we will look at this in the next chapter) but Loki does not stop with his assault upon man. Indeed, what he has created is an aberration and I think this is important when we come to understand the nature of the giants.

The relationship between the giants and the Æsir in particular is a complex one that is generally seen as mutual hostility between two opposing forces.[22] The earth itself was created from the body of the giant Ymir[23] by the agency of at least one of the Æsir, Odin, and throughout the mythology the theme of the giants being evil forces that the gods fight against in order to protect man[24] is balanced

---

20 In 1952, Jung published a tract called *Answer to Job* (New York: Routledge), discussing the nature of evil and how, if the Biblical God is omnibenevolent and omnipresent, evil came into the world.

21 A clue, perhaps, may be sought in the value put upon silence in Old Norse literature; it was thought to be a sign of wisdom, and conceivably some form of mantic was represented by the figure of Hœnir the silent.

22 I doubt I need to highlight the instances where Gods clash with Giants but Thiazi's kidnap of Idunn, and Thor's continual conflict with Giants such as Utgard-Loki, Thrym, Hymir, etc. highlight his central role as a Giant slayer.

23 Odin's grandfather.

24 "Not at all do we acknowledge him (Ymir) to be a god. He was evil and all his descendents," (Faulkes, *Edda*, 11).

by others like Ægir who acts as host to the gods. What the giants actually represent is an important question. Clearly, they are the most ancient beings existent in the cosmos; primal forces and creators and guardians of its laws.[25] In *Völuspá* stanza 8[26] we read of three maidens of giant-kind who come to the gods, who are often taken to be the Norns.[27] The purpose of their visit is debatable, but I believe they came as a warning to the Æsir regarding the nature of *ørlǫg* and regarding humanity. *Ørlǫg* is the primal law first laid when the gods sacrificed Ymir, creating an ordered material world from chaos and setting in motion a temporary period of growth from entropy. Alas, it is the fate of our universe to return to entropy, and it may well be that the Norns were warning the gods of this fact.[28] It may well also be that they were afraid of the appearance of humanity, as a result of Loki's actions. If we therefore see the giants as representative of the primordial cosmos itself and as its guardians then we may begin to understand their hostility to the gods (the Æsir in particular) and man by extension.[29] Man simply *shouldn't have been*, yet he is, and the giants now have a potentially destructive force at work within the material realm, but potentially on all levels of existence as well.

Heimdall's fortuitous adoption of wayward man may have stemmed off the "cleansing" forces of the guardians but there are still elements within the Jotun race that would see this "abomination" destroyed and it is these that Thor spends his time fighting against. He is *our* guardian against the primordial guardians who would see us destroyed. What Heimdall gave to us was time and opportunity to prove ourselves as worthy beings despite our origins. The Æsir represent our defenders against (what we perceive to be) a harsh universe populated by "giants" ever on the lookout for an opportunity to snuff out our fragile existence. Yet Loki, the architect of this tragedy, would not stop with setting giants against Æsir. He would now turn man against his own world…

---

25 Mark Puryear writes that the Norns are descendants of the "higher Jotun clan," which includes Mimir, (Puryear. *The Nature of Asatru*, 18).
26 "They played tables in the garth and were blissful.
None of them lacked gold, until three maidens
came from the Thurses. Their might was awesome,
they came from Ettinhome."
27 Chisholm argues they may have been three Giantesses (including Gulveig) who attack Asgard before the walls are built.
28 It may also be that the Giants (as inert matter) wished to share in the creative process (Titchenell, *The Masks of Odin*, 33).
29 The Vanir as earth deities tend to have better relationships to an extent with the Giants (i.e. Freyr and Gerd).

The war between the Æsir and the Vanir forms one of the central episodes in the early mythological cycle. Four stanzas (21-24) in *Völuspá* give us an overview of these events:

> I recall the first battle in the world.
> There they stabbed Gullveig with spears,
> and burned her in Har's hall.
> Thrice she was burned, thrice she was born.
> It happened often, and yet she lives.
>
> She is called Heith, who comes to houses,
> the far seeing spae woman.
> The wise volva knew gand magic, she understood seith.
> She played with minds by her seith.
> She was always dear to evil women.
>
> Then all the Regin went to the doom chair.
> The Ginn Holy Gods held moot
> as to whether the Æsir should pay tribute
> or whether all the gods should have a wassail.
>
> Odin sped a shot into the host.
> That was the first battle in the world.
> The board wall was broken, the fortification
> of the Ases. The fighting Vanes trod the battlefield.[30]

From these we learn that the conflict between the two families of the gods was precipitated by the murder of the being known as Gullveig. The Æsir were deemed to be in the wrong by the Vanir, who demand that the Æsir pay compensation for Gullveig. Odin casts a spear into the Vanir host and the two families go to war. Who is Gullveig? A popular interpretation is that Gullveig is really Freyja, the Vanic goddess who teaches Odin *seiðr*.[31] Another possibility is that Gullveig-Heid is actually the feminine aspect of Loki.[32] Gullveig-Heid is most likely one being. Rydberg writes that Gullveig was the name of this being whilst in Asgard,[33] but that she went by the name Heid whilst in Midgard where

---

30 Chisholm, *The Eddas*.
31 Lindow notes that many scholars have concluded Gullveig-Heid is Freyja and that her corruption of the Æsir by teaching Odin *seiðr* is the cause of the conflict (*Norse Mythology*, 52).
32 Rydberg sees Gullveig-Heid as the feminine counterpart of Loki and that the two eventually become one being (*Teutonic Mythology*, 205).
33 Ibid., 207.

she travelled around promoting the "black arts" and encouraging the evil passions of mankind.[34] As a result she attracted the hatred of the Æsir who punished her by burning. Three attempts were made to burn Gullveig-Heid yet she came away unscathed each time, because each time she regenerated.[35] Of course, Odin himself practices magic similar to that of Gullveig-Heid and it is thought by Rydberg that the mention of this fact by the Vanir compels the otherwise calm deity to hurl his spear into the ranks of the Vanir.[36] The difference here, though, is that Odin's use of *seiðr* is born of need, even desperation, where as the use of magic by the Gullveig-Heid-Loki being is one purely motivated by malice. It is, perhaps, worth drawing attention to the theory developed by Rydberg regarding the reason that the Vanir side with Gullveig-Heid.[37] Whilst both the Æsir and Vanir are horrified by the use of dark magic, the Vanic deity Freyr married to the giantess Gerd[38] is actually related to Gullveig-Heid whom Rydberg identifies with Aurboda (Gerd's mother) and, thus, Freyr's mother-in-law. Of course, chronologically this may be inconsistent but it is well to remember that mythology is often something of a paradox when it comes to chronological progression. Rydberg then goes onto identify Aurboda with the giantess Angrboda mentioned in *Hynduljóð* stanzas 38 and 39:

> Loki begat the wolf
> with Angrboda,
> but Sleipnir he begat
> with Svadilfari:
> one monster seemed
> of all most deadly,
> which from Byleist's
> brother sprang.
>
> Loki, scorched up
> in his heart's affections,
> had found a half-burnt
> woman's heart.
> Loki became guileful
> from that wicked woman;

---

34 A fitting companion of, or aspect of, Loki indeed! One can imagine this Lokian agent tempting man towards chaos either before or after Heimdall's intervention.
35 Itself a Vanic property.
36 Rydberg, *Teutonic Mythology*, 210.
37 For a more detailed assessment I refer the reader to Rydberg's investigation starting on page 213.
38 See *Skírnismál* in the *Poetic Edda*.

>   thence in the world
>   are all giantesses come.[39]

Here then we learn Loki consumes Angrboda's heart and, according to Rydberg, imbibes the evil nature of the giantess as well as becoming an androgynous being in the process.[40] He is now possessor of the evil woman's soul and goes onto father monstrous beings such as Fenris, Jormungandr and Hel. I believe this paragraph from Rydberg is worth quoting in full:

> The activity of the evil principle has, in the great epic of the myth, formed a continuity spanning all ages, and this continuous thread of evil is twisted from the treacherous deeds of Gulveig and Loke, the feminine and the masculine representatives of the evil principle. Both appear at the dawn of mankind: Loke has already at the beginning of time secured access to Allfather (Lokasenna, 9), and Gulveig deceives the sons of men already in the time of Heimdal's son Borgar. Loke entices Idun from the secure grounds of Asgard, and treacherously delivers her to the powers of frost; Gulveig, as we shall see, plays Freyja into the hands of the giants. Loke plans enmity between the gods and the forces of nature, which hitherto had been friendly, and which have their personal representatives in Ivalde's sons; Gulveig causes the war between the Asas and Vans.[41]

It is Angrboda who nurtures the beings whose hatred for the gods is their most prominent characteristic. It is Angrboda who receives Freyr's sword given as bride price for her daughter Gerd and that would be later used by the fire giant Surtr to slay the "world god" Freyr himself at Ragnarok.[42] It was Angrboda who may well have been a maid servant of Freyja and the possible source of her knowledge of *seiðr*.[43] Clearly we can see the depth of involvement and interaction between the Lokian forces and the Æsir and Vanir reaching back into the primordial mists. Loki (in both his masculine and feminine guises) is not just

---

39 Trans. Benjamin Thorpe. "Hyndluljóð." *The Poetic Edda*. (Laneer, MI: Northvegr Foundation Press, 2004), 178.
40 Presumably this explains Loki's later feminine feats such as giving birth to Odin's horse Sleipnir.
41 Rydberg, *Teutonic Mythology*, 220.
42 Surely one can see in this the earth consumed by the expanding sun billions of years hence…
43 Plausible if we see *seiðr* as some form of primal "magic" that the Vanic deities (representatives of the earth) learn from the giants (cosmic overlords) and then a skill later learned by the Æsir/human deities. See Rydberg.

responsible for the very "awakening" of man he is also responsible for the conflict between the Æsir and Vanir and ultimately will lead the gods to their doom at Ragnarok. Viewed neutrally, we can see Loki as just representative of the destruction from which all creation is born and the seed which lies in all creation, which is a necessary part of the cycle of creation and destruction. Seen from a human perspective, the hatred Loki displays for the gods and for man is the epitome of evil at work in the mythology. Yet just as Loki's manipulation of man had unforeseen consequences so does his creation of antagonism between the Æsir and Vanir lead to an outcome less desirable for him in the reconciliation of Æsir and Vanir in the form of Kvasir, a figure we will return to when we look at Odin.

Of course, the Æsir-Vanir conflict has been interpreted in other ways, Dumézil[44] saw it as a conflict between the "gods of magic" (Æsir) and the "gods of nature" (Vanir), whilst Grigsby interprets the conflict as one of a militaristic cult of the Æsir imposed by a warlike elite upon the agricultural religion of the farming communities of northern Europe.[45] None of these are necessarily incompatible with my view. After all, I am not viewing the myths as a source of historical development,[46] or as some form of religious study *per se*, but more as a theological interpretation of the myth itself. And my interpretation leads me to conclude that what we really see in the Æsir-Vanir conflict is a war between man and his world. A war that is really still being waged today because we have still not come to terms with our separation from the earth and we have been, consciously or not, attempting to return to some kind of "ego oblivion," either of the earth itself yielding to the domination of man or abnegation of our own individuality and identity.[47]

Only in Heimdall do we see a solution to our crisis and it is to him we now turn.

---

44 H.R. Ellis Davidson. *Gods and Myths of Northern Europe*. (England: Penguin Books, 1964), 167.

45 "In seeking a motivation for Beowulf to seek to end the tyranny of the dark goddess and her hideous son, it is the actions of Odin, the chief god of the Æsir, whose victory over the Vanir was well known throughout the north, the provided the prototype for the heroic deeds of Beowulf in vanquishing the power of these nightmares" (John Grigsby. *Beowulf and Grendel: The Truth Behind England's Oldest Legend*. [Great Britain: Watkins Publishing, 2005], 171).

46 "Georges Dumézil argued forcefully that the story of the war need be no more historical than any other myth" (Lindow, *Norse Mythology*, 53).

47 "Concerned but not disconsolate, we stand aside a little while, contemplative men to whom it has been granted to be witnesses of these tremendous struggles and transitions. Alas, it is the magic of these struggles that those who behold them must also take part in the fight" (Nietzsche, *The Birth of Tragedy*, 98).

Heimdall

There is one called Heimdall. He is known as the white As. He is great and holy. Nine maidens bore him as their son, all of them sisters...He is the god's watchman and sits there at the edge of heaven to guard the bridge against mountain giants.[48]
—Gylfaginning

Heimdall is something of an enigmatic figure in our mythology yet he is surely one of the most important figures of all. I got to thinking about Heimdall when I began to think about human consciousness and the role Heimdall plays in the ordering of human society.

He has similar attributes to the Vedic deity Agni,[49] the personification of the sacred flame,[50] and both he and Loki can be interpreted as the dual nature of fire at once both harmful and destructive yet also both a source of warmth and the foundation of technological development. Fire's dual nature is, of course, familiar in other Indo-European myths, particularly that of Prometheus. Another association with Heimdall can be observed in that Agni as the sacred flame of the sacrifice and the cremation fire acts as the messenger to the gods as his smoke rises heavenwards.[51] Heimdall is warden of Bifrost, the bridge between the mortal and immortal realms. He came to man in his time of chaos and taught him civilization and is our channel to the god forces. As a force of order, he is our tutor that our sacrifices act as harmonisations between men, gods and the cosmos itself. In the *Rig Veda*, Agni is described as "the first born child of order."

Within our lore Heimdall's position in the family of the gods has been debated. Was he a Vanic deity or does he belong to the Æsir? Davidson has argued that Heimdall seems to have powers that link him to the Vanir and the underworld,

---

48 Faulkes, *Edda*, 25.
49 "In him I saw the Lord of All Tribes (Agni) with his seven sons." This fits with Heimdall's role as the father of the Teutonic Peoples. Interestingly enough, seven sisters are mentioned further on (Trans. Wendy Doniger. *The Rig Veda*. [England: Penguin Books, 1981], 76).
50 "For Yama press the soma; to Yama offer the oblation; to Yama goes the well prepared sacrifice, with Agni as it's messenger," (Ibid., 44).
51 "Do not burn him entirely, Agni, or engulf him in your flames. Do not consume his skin or his flesh. When you have cooked him perfectly, O knower of creatures, only then send him forth to the fathers" (Ibid., 46).

particularly his association with the nine daughters of Ran and Ægir.[52] Lindow[53] has also pointed out that Heimdall seems to be very much a figure linked to peripheral locations suggesting boundaries. He is a boundary figure not just in terms of location, but also time. I might add, Heimdall very much occupies the role of myth/historical figures that we find in other mythologies, the most well known being Jesus Christ. The Vanic deities are very much aligned with the earth itself, the natural order of our planet, whilst the Æsir represent human forces. They are our ancestral deities. I find the idea of a deity associated with the natural order we were unwillingly pulled from aiding us in our hour of need and showing us "salvation" or the possibility of it to be somewhat warming. Of course, my view is entirely subjective and Heimdall remains an elusive figure. Yet I believe the possibility is there.

Perhaps more intriguing is the association between Heimdall and the World Tree itself, Yggdrasil. The Finnish scholar Pipping[54] has equated Heimdall with the ram sacrifice described in Ibn Fadlan's description of the heads of sheep and cattle hung by the Rus on trees by the river Volga in 922.[55] Consequently, Heimdall has come to be seen as symbolic of Yggdrasil itself. Pipping uses Finno-Ugric parallels to claim that Heimdall was imagined as a pillar reaching up from the earth to the pole star above.[56] North has also pointed out that there is a possible connection between Heimdall's nine mothers and the nine worlds' "roots"[57] that the *völva* remembers in the poem *Völuspá*. Davidson points out that amongst the Yakut there is the legend of the "White Youth,"[58] who is the father of the human species and is nourished by the spirit of the World Tree. Of course, the creation of Ask and Embla from logs has a parallel to this suggestion. As North goes onto write:

> In *Völuspá* and other sources, Heimdall is the father of mankind, protecting, listening and warning, while Yggdrasil is pictured as the groaning support of the world. Thus it is reasonable to

---

52 "The link with the Vanir seems the most helpful clue to our understanding of him, since these would account for the different aspects in which he appears, his association with the protection of Asgard, with the sea, with the World Tree and the underworld, and finally with the fathering of mankind," (Davidson. *Gods and Myths*, 176).
53 Lindow, *Norse Mythology*, 170.
54 Davidson, *Gods and Myths*, 174.
55 Richard North. *Heathen Gods in Old English Literature*. (New York: Cambridge University Press, 1997), 284.
56 Ibid., 284.
57 Ibid., 285.
58 Davidson, *Gods and Myths*, 174.

suppose that the personality of this tree was emphasised, contained and then isolated in Heimdall, while its phenomenon was largely restricted to Yggdrasil.[59]

Davidson also supports this theory, seeing the tree[60] as the guardian of the dwelling of the gods, which would account for Heimdall's unceasing watch over their realm.

If we accept Heimdall as a Vanic deity or as symbolic of the World Tree, we are still left with the question of who, or what, exactly do these nine mothers represent? The most common theory is that the nine mothers of Heimdall are in fact the nine daughters of the sea god Ægir and his wife Ran.[61] These daughters mostly have names associated with the sea and it is generally taken that they represent waves. Another reference is found in the *Hyndluljóð,* which would seemingly associate Heimdall with the sea shore.[62] Here his mothers are giants and, as Lindow suggests,[63] there is the possibility of Odin being the father of Heimdall. Links to the sea and the sea shore make sense as well if we also accept that Heimdall has links to the moon.[64] The tidal forces controlled by the moon were a factor in the formation of life on earth. Minerals were pulled from the shore and into the depths of the oceans beginning the process of forming more complex molecules. Life began in our planet's oceans. We are children of the sea as much as we are "star dust" and it is telling that many of the world's mythologies speak of a being or beings from the sea who came to bring order and civilisation to man...

As with mythology in general, I believe the question mark around Heimdall's mothers may well contain more than one possibility. The number three and multiples thereof are sacred in our faith. The creator gods were three, there are

---

59 North, *Heathen Gods,* 287.
60 For a couple of excellent articles looking at the symbolic meaning of Yggdrasil I refer the reader to the Odinic Rite website and the following essays: "Yggdrasil—The Tree of Life and Death" and "Yggdrasil and the Individual," parts one and two (http://www.odinic-rite.org/yggdrasil%20and%20the%20individual.htm [accessed: 5 January, 2010]).
61 Their names are Hefring, Unn, Hronn, Bylgia, Bara, Kolga, Himinglaeva, Dufa, and Blodughadda (Faulkes, *Edda,* 91).
62 "A certain one was born in days of yore, with greatly increased power, of the race of gods, nine bore him, a man full of grace, Giant maidens on the edge of the earth," (*Hyndluljóð,* stanza 35).
63 Lindow, *Norse Mythology,* 169.
64 Timothy J. Stephany. *Reconstructing Rig.* http://timothystephany.com/papers/Article08-Rig.pdf (accessed: 5 January, 2010).

nine worlds existing on three planes, and Heimdall had nine mothers. These are just a few examples. In Celtic mythology the god Arawn owns a cauldron and this cauldron is guarded by nine maidens whose breath keeps the cauldron boiling.[65] Cauldrons in Celtic lore and, indeed, in Vedic mythology are often the source of rebirth and initiation into higher states of consciousness. It is this that I believe Heimdall's mothers represent; the nine worlds themselves as states of consciousness. In Heimdall we have those nine worlds concentrated within one being. In our time of chaos brought about by Loki's division of man and by his destruction of our innocence, Heimdall came to us to show us the way to integrate our conflicting personalities. He showed us order from chaos. In the Eleusinian Mysteries, the human soul, *psyche,* was personified by the goddess Persephone. For the philosophers of these mysteries, birth into the material world was in itself death. The belief was that the soul descended through eight higher realms to reach our ninth lower/material realm.[66] The mysteries taught that the human soul was of two parts: the *eidolon* (ego) and the *dæmon* or immortal stem. The *dæmon* was a shard of the original god that evil forces had divided into individual pieces.[67] By recognising that the ego was mortal the Eleusinian initiate would develop a disregard for the individuality of himself and come to view life on a greater level. A similar theme is found in the rites of Bacchus where man is once again considered to be a composite being. Bacchus was torn to pieces by the Titans. He was dismembered and boiled in water and finally he was roasted. Bacchus' heart was saved by Pallas, from which Bacchus was reborn, and the enraged Jupiter slew the Titans from whose ashes (which also contained a portion of Bacchus' flesh) the human race was brought forth. Consequently, man can either follow his rational (Bacchic) nature or his irrational (Titan) nature. The act of bringing Bacchus back together represents the rejection of the ego and unity of the whole in spiritual fulfillment.

Another interesting passage I came across in my research is this from the Anglo-Saxon "Nine Herbs Charm":

---

65 Excerpt from the *Preiddeu Annwn* in John Grigsby's, *Warriors of the Wasteland: A Quest for the Pagan Sacrificial Cult Behind the Grail Legends*. (Great Britain: Watkins Publishing, 2003), 194.

66 This descent was mirrored by the nine days of initiation into the mysteries. Of course, there is also the nine months of pregnancy in the human female. (Manly P. Hall. *The Secret Teachings of all Ages: An Encyclopedic Outline of Masonic, Hermetic, Qabbalistic and Rosicrucian Symbolical Philosophy*. [New York: Tarcher Penguin, 1928], 71).

67 For Grigsby, this represents the true meaning of the vegetal myth, the corn threshed with its seeds scattered was akin to us each with a divine seed within us (Grigsby, *Warriors of the Wasteland*, 93).

> A serpent came crawling [but] it destroyed no one when Woden took nine twigs of glory, [and] then struck the adder so that it flew into nine (pieces)...[68]

The passage has also been translated as the serpent tore a man in two.[69] The tearing of a man in two by the serpent has obvious echoes to the *eidolon* and *dæmon* aspects of man. Serpents as sources of knowledge and rebirth are common in mythology. They represent knowledge itself as a neutral substance used by man based on his disposition. They also have other meanings. For Jung, the serpent/dragon represented the "mother" out of which emerged a strong independent ego from a state of unconsciousness. For Jung, this was the "hero."[70] Possible analogies in our own mythology can be found in Beowulf and Sigurd Volsung. John Grigsby has interpreted the story of their dragon slaying exploits as the destruction of the old Neolithic agricultural faiths with their communal centred nature in ancestral tombs by the more individualistic religion of the Aryan invaders of Europe.[71] Woden's splitting of the serpent into nine parts is also, once again, a use of the number nine, nine worlds, nine states of consciousness...

So it is then that Heimdall, who represents the nine states of consciousness embodied comes into our world as a child:

> One day it came to pass that a ship was seen sailing near the coast of Scedeland or Scani and it approached the land without being propelled either by oars or sails. The ship came to the sea-beach, and there was seen lying in it a little boy, who was sleeping with his head on a sheaf of grain, surrounded by treasures and tools, by glaives and coats of mail. The boat itself was stately and beautifully decorated. Who he was and where he came from nobody had any idea, but the little boy was received as if he had been a kinsman, and he received the most constant and tender care. As he came with a sheaf of grain to their

---

68 Bill Griffiths. *Aspects of Anglo-Saxon Magic*. (England: Anglo-Saxon Books, 1996), 193.
69 North, *Heathen Gods*, 86.
70 Ruth Snowden. *Teach Yourself Jung*. (London: McGraw-Hill, 2006), 68.
71 "For them the idea of immortality came not from the realization that man was a splinter of an undying god but from the belief that the mortal personality could survive death. This engendered a new horror- an intoxicated warrior unafraid of death. Their ideal was a warrior-like Achilles or Cu Chulainn-whose aim in life was to make a name for himself, the very antithesis of the mysteries that sought to kill off the eidolon," (Grigsby, *Warriors*, 133).

country the people called him Scef/Sceaf. Scef grew up among his people, became their benefactor and king, and ruled most honourably for many years. He died far advanced in age. In accordance with his own directions, his body was borne down to the strand where he had landed as a child. There in a little harbour lay the same boat in which he had come. Glittering from hoar-frost and ice, and eager to return to the sea, the boat was waiting to receive the dead king, and around him the grateful and sorrowing people laid no fewer treasures than those with which Scef had come. And when all was finished the boat went out upon the sea, and no one knows where it landed.[72]

In *Rigsthula*, we have the tale of how Rig (Heimdall)[73] organised the human social classes. The identity of Heimdall as Scef/Sheaf rests upon a passage in the genealogy of *ealdorman* Aethelweard from AD 975.[74] On his journeys he elopes with three women in turn and from them are born the three social classes: Thrall, Karl and Jarl. Once again we see the significance of the number three, three women, each of which he spends three nights with and who give birth to three social classes, obviously after a term of nine months. Titchenell interprets the lay as a description of how humanity attained free will, destiny and responsibility from a vegetated state. In her interpretation, Rig (meaning 'a descent' or 'an involvement') descended upon man to aid in awakening his potential as an *asmegir* or godmaker.[75]

I believe that another way of interpreting this lay is as the stages of initiation that we find in *Hávamál*.[76] In my theory then, Thrall represents the fundamental basic level of human awareness. The equivalent in the *Hávamál* would be the rules on

---

72 Rydberg, *Teutonic Mythology*, 131.
73 As Larrington warns us, the identity of Rig as Heimdall is not completely certain based just upon a prose introduction but the "offspring of Heimdall" referred to in *Völuspá* seems to suggest the God as the same progenitor mentioned in *Rigsthula* (Carolyne Larrington. *The Poetic Edda.* [Oxford: Oxford University Press, 2009]).
74 "This Sheaf came to land in a light boat, surrounded by weapons, on an island in the ocean which is called Scani. He was indeed a very young child and unknown to the folk of that land. However they took him up and looked after him as carefully as if he were one of their own kin and afterwards elected him king." For Viktor Rydberg's argument in favour of Scef's identity as Heimdall see: *Teutonic Mythology*, 137.
75 Titchenell, *Masks of Odin*, 181.
76 "*Hávamál* is generally interpreted as practical advice for a young man on matters of life, love and travel with a little bit of magic and religion thrown in. It is actually the initiatory sequences of the winning of the runes and the poetic mead that are at the heart of the *Hávamál*," (Chisholm, *The Eddas*, 38).

everyday social intercourse and how to look after one's self and interests in the material world, which act as the foundation for any further work on advancing one's spirituality.

> Joth and Edda sprinkled water
> on a dark linen clad boy named Thrall.
>
> He began to grow and throve well.
> Rough the skin of his hands,
> gnarled the knuckle,
> fingers were thick, his back was bent
> His heels were long.[77]

The second level is represented by Karl, which is the nascent awareness of one's soul and the willingness to progress in its development.

> Amma bore a boy. She sprinkled him with water.
> She named him Karl and clothed him in linen.
> Wild eyed, red and ruddy he was.
>
> He began to grow, he waxed well,
> he tamed oxen and made plowshares,
> timbered houses and built sheds,
> fashioned carts and drove ploughs.[78]

Finally Rig enters the home of "father" and "mother."

> He walked in and the floor was strewn with straw.
> Man and wife sat there, gazing at one another's eyes.
> Father and Mother were playing with their fingers.
>
> The house-master twisted bow string
> and bent elm. The lady of the house
> looked to her arms, she smoothed the skirt
> and pleated her sleeves.[79]

Born to them is Jarl.

---

77 Chisholm, "The Lay of Rig," *The Eddas*, stanzas 7-8.
78 Ibid., stanzas 20-21.
79 Ibid., 26-27.

> Mother bore a son and clothed him in silk.
> She sprinkled him with water and called him Earl.
> He was fair of hair, bright of cheeks,
> and his eyes pierced like an adder's.
>
> Earl grew up there at the hall.
> He began to shake linden shields
> He fixed bow strings, bent elm,
> shafted arrows flung spears, sped lances,
> rode horses, hunted with hounds,
> swung swords and swam the sound.
>
> Then Rig came walking from the grove.
> Walking Rig came, taught him the runes
> and granted his own name,
> saying it belonged to his son. Rig bade him take
> possession of odal vales and old halls.[80]

The above passages indicate the aristocratic pursuits of the Germanic ruling classes, who were trained to be warriors and leaders. They were men who would have had more time to contemplate (man and wife sat there, gazing at one another's eye) existence and being, who would have been capable of understanding the nature of the runes. That Odin was the benefactor of the nobility is a subject I will address later in the article. For now it is of interest to note that Rig bestows upon Jarl his own name.[81] Does this imply the granting of godhood or the potential for deification upon Heimdall's human descendents? Kon (King?), son of Rig-Jarl, understands the runes from birth and assumes the title of Rig:

> He contended in runes with Earl Rig.
> He battled him in wits, and knew the runes better.
> So he came to have for himself
> the name Rig and runelore.[82]

We also learn in stanza 43:

> He understood the chirping of birds, he quenched

---

80 Ibid., 33-35.
81 It is of interest to read Viktor Rydberg's study of Heimdall's sons in his *Teutonic Mythology*, starting from page 143.
82 Ibid., stanza 44.

fires, calmed the seas, and soothed sorrows.
He had the strength and endurance of eight men.

It is of interest to compare these attributes to the ones Odin gains when he acquires the runes. From this, though, it seems obvious that the runes were an ancient property of man, a gift imparted by our "father" Heimdall to our folk. Odin may well have won the runes for the Æsir and, by extension, man, but men are likely to have been aware of them from very early on in our history. Can we assume that this was knowledge lost and re-acquired by Odin? Or rather that Heimdall as teacher showed the way that Odin, as a pathfinder, would later follow upon?

What we have in Heimdall is a deity born of the earth itself who takes pity upon the lost people abused and tortured by Loki, a people that would doubtless have fallen to mindless destruction and eventual extinction if not for the love of Heimdall.[83] He gave us the gift of opportunity, the opportunity to turn our tragedy into something greater. He represents what we could become. Never again will we be innocent and lost in the embrace of the world, but we can reach a point of synthesis with our dueling personalities.

Mimir and the Mead of Inspiration

> *Poetry is called sea or liquid of the dwarves, because the liquid in Odrerir was Kvasir's blood before the mead was made, and it was made in that cauldron, and hence it is called Odin's pot-liquid...*[84]
>
> —Skaldskaparmal

At the end of the war between the Æsir and Vanir the two families of the Gods came together to make a lasting peace between them. All of them spat into a cauldron and from their spittle was created the wisest of the Æsir,[85] the being called Kvasir.[86]

> His name was Kvasir, he was so wise that no one could ask him
> any questions to which he did not know the answer. He travelled

---

83 Heimdall represents purposeful, ordered consciousness and Loki, destructive and chaotic.
84 Faulkes, *Edda*, 72.
85 Ibid., 51.
86 Snorri Sturluson writes that Kvasir was one of three hostages exchanged by the Vanir at the end of their war with the Æsir, the other two being Niord and Frey (trans. A. H. Smith. *Heimskringla*. [New York: Dover Publications Inc., 1990], 3).

> widely through the world teaching people knowledge, and when he arrived as a guest to some dwarves, Fialar and Galar, they called him to a private discussion with them and killed him. They poured his blood into two vats and a pot, and the latter was called Odrerir, but the vats were called Son and Bodn. They mixed honey with the blood and it turned into the mead whoever drinks from which becomes a poet or scholar. The dwarves told the Æsir that Kvasir had suffocated in intelligence because there was no one there educated enough to be able to ask him questions.[87]

Davidson states that the name Kvasir comes from *Kvas,* a word meaning strong beer and used in Jutland to refer to crushed fruit.[88] This would seem to fit with the myth surrounding Kvasir. Clearly then, Kvasir is the origin of the mead of inspiration, the quest for which forms probably the most important tale of the god Odin. This Kvasir would seem, to my mind, to be symbolic of a first attempt at the reunion of man with the earth. His murder by the dwarves Fialar and Galar[89] prematurely end any such happy conclusion to Loki's mischief. What follows instead is the attempt by the Æsir to obtain the very substance of which Kvasir is made from.

After Kvasir's murder the dwarves invite the giant Gilling and his wife to stay at their home. Whilst on a fishing expedition Gilling falls from the boat and is drowned. Offering to show where Gilling had died the dwarves kill his wife because they became tired of her pining for her husband. Along comes their son Suttung looking for his parents. Discovering what the dwarves have done he drags the pair out to sea meaning to drown them in turn. The terrified dwarves offer Suttung anything he wishes in recompense for his parents. Suttung decides to take the mead as his compensation.

Some time later Odin on his travels comes across nine slaves mowing hay. He asks if they would like to sharpen their scythes. The men agree and Odin casts a whetstone into the air where upon the nine men manage to cut each other's throats in an attempt to get at it. Odin arrives at the abode of the giant Baugi (Suttung's brother) and Baugi is in a terrible strait as his nine slaves have all mysteriously died. Odin offers to help him out claiming to be able to do the

---

87 Faulkes. *Edda*, 62.
88 She writes it was used by the "eastern neighbours of the Germans" presumably Slavs (Davidson, *Gods and Myths*, 167).
89 It is interesting to note that Titchenell sees Dwarves as less evolved humans, this theme of a "divine" human murdered through ignorance is one I will address when looking at Baldr.

work of all nine of those men through the summer months. In exchange all he wants is a draft of his brother Suttung's mead, to which Baugi agrees. Come winter Odin's work is done and he calls in his favour. He and Baugi set off to visit Suttung. Baugi explains to Suttung the agreement he has with Odin, but Suttung is none too happy about it and refuses to give Odin a single draft of his precious mead. Not put off, Odin decided to resort to trickery in order to obtain the mead. Odin asks Baugi to drill a hole into the side of Suttung's mountain home and Baugi does so, but when Odin blows into the hole the shards blow outwards and Odin realises that Baugi is trying to trick him. He asks him to drill the hole again and Baugi does so and this time when Odin blows into the hole no shards blow out. Transforming himself into a snake Odin wriggles into the hole but he has to be quick because Baugi, now attempting to kill Odin, is drilling after him. Odin manages to make it through unscathed and finds himself confronted by Gunnlod, Suttung's daughter. Odin seduces Gunnlod and sleeps with her for three nights in return for a draft of the mead. Gunnlod lets him drink three drafts for three nights.[90] In his first draft, Odin drains Odrerir, in his second Bodn and in his final draft Son. With all the mead inside him he turns into an eagle and flies like the wind back to Asgard. Suttung, discovering what has happened, also transforms into an eagle and sets off in hot pursuit. Odin manages to reach Asgard and spits the mead out into three waiting containers. However, in his haste, some of the mead is lost and falls down to Midgard where anyone who wishes to may acquire it.

Thus Odin wins the mead for the Æsir, the mead of inspiration. This tale, I feel, really encapsulates much of what we know about Odin and his role in the mythology. Odin is the god who sacrifices an eye in Mimir's Well, who uses Mimir's head as a source of wisdom, who learns *seiðr* magic from Freyja, who sacrifices himself on the world tree Yggdrasil for nine nights in order to obtain the runes and who seduces Gunnlod to win the mead of inspiration. Clearly, he is an important figure and central to the whole theme of the mythology, but what do these attributes mean?

I would like to start by looking at the meaning behind the tale of Odin's winning of the mead and go from there. Here in *Hávamál* we have stanzas 104-110:

> The old ettin I sought, now I am back
> I would have gotten little, had I been silent.
> I spoke many words to work my will
>   in Suttung's hall.

---

90 There is the number three again!

> The auger bored and made me room
> gnawed through stone,
> over and under were
> the ettin ways.
> Thus I risked my head.
>
> Gunnloth gave me, as I sat on her golden seat,
> a drink of the dear won mead.
> An evil reward I dealt her afterwards,
> for her goodwill, and her heavy-heart.
>
> Dear bought, I put it to good use.
> For the wise little is lacking.
> Othroerir has been brought up
> to the ve of the gods.
>
> I would hardly have come out alive
> from the garth of the ettins,
> had I not enjoyed the good woman Gunnloth
> in whose arms I lay.
>
> The next day rime Thurses
> strode out to ask rede
> of Har in Har's Hall,
> asking about Bolverk, whether he was among the Gods
> or had been slain by Suttung.
>
> I know that Odin swore an oath on a ring,
> How shall his troth be trusted?
> He robbed Suttung and took his sumble.
> To Gunnloth he brought sorrow.[91]

The above stanzas are crucial to our understanding of not only how Odin won the mead but of Odin himself. It would seem apparent looking at the whole episode that Odin can only come out of this in a less than noble light. He seduces and lies to Gunnlod, just as he seemingly tricks Baugir, before finally stealing Suttung's mead! Such antics would lend credence to the statement made by

---

91 Chisholm, *The Eddas*.

Davidson that Odin was a deity few could really trust.[92] Certainly Chisholm[93] sees Odin's betrayal of Gunnlod as the highest betrayal of all not just to a Giant but to his own Fetch.[94] As Chisholm explains, "Odin's sexual conquests are not mere hedonism, but efforts to drastically raise his level of consciousness by welding it with supra and sub-conscious parts of his soul. The broken oath explains Odin's name Bolverk (Evil-Doer). Odin's crime was all the more heinous that the oath was made to a high and holy part of himself."[95] This seems a reasonably satisfactory explanation if we accept my premise in this study that an important, perhaps the most important, knowledge one can derive from our mythology is this quest for a re-union of the conflicting personalities *within* man. The Fetch may well represent our own personal Norn, but then again Gunnlod could well have been any denizen of the spirit world that Odin encountered whilst on some shamanic quest and whom he tricked. Perhaps this paints him in a negative light, then again if we remember stanza 45[96] of the *Hávamál* we could well argue that Odin is simply using cunning to get around a hostile enemy (Gunnlod is the daughter of a giant after all and probably a Frost giant at that), and Odin himself was betrayed by Baugi. It would be foolish to argue that spiritual attainment will necessarily always be a wholesome experience or pleasant.[97]

The mead of Kvasir then is a potent drink of inspiration, immortality and a substance partaken of by all (gods and men) desiring spiritual enlightenment. We learn in Saxo Grammaticus' *The History of the Danes* how Odin refreshed the hero Hadding[98] with a potion (mead) of inspiration before returning him to the world of the living on what must surely translate as a spirit quest. The drink (Leifner's Flame)[99] gave Hadding enhanced strength and the ability to break

---

92 "Woden and Odin are reproached on many occasions for fickleness and treachery," (Davidson, *Gods and Myths*, 60).
93 Chisholm, *The Eddas*, 40.
94 The Fetch is a being in its own right attached to an individual at birth. Often appearing either as a member of the opposite sex and/or an animal. It may well be an individual's own Norn, and has similarities to a "guardian angel." In this instance, though, Chisholm sees the Fetch Gunnlod as Odin's higher self.
95 Chisholm, *The Eddas*, 40.
96 "If you know one who evil thinks but you desire his goodwill, speak him fair though you falsely feel; repay lies with cunning."
97 Rydberg argues that Odin's theft of the mead by seducing Gunnlod is a deliberate attempt to stir up a need for revenge from the Giants. The episode lies at the heart of Teutonic ethics, as Odin motivated by the will to do good is morally reprehensible (*Teutonic Mythology*, 226).
98 Saxo Grammaticus, trans. Peter Fisher. *The History of the Danes: Books 1-1X*. [Cambridge: D.S. Brewer Publications, 1979], 25.
99 Rydberg, *Teutonic Mythology*, 259.

bonds.[100] Hadding had been ensnared by his own ego (Loki) but through his spirit quest Odin helps him to escape these bonds. In Vedic lore, the "fathers"[101] are ancestors, priests, poets and sages who have passed before on the path to enlightenment who themselves have partaken of Soma[102] and are themselves immortal as a result. Yet the mead was not strictly a property of the Æsir and of men. One other source was found with the shadowy figure of Mimir...

> They (Vanir) therefore took Mimir and beheaded him and sent his head to the Asaland people. Odin took the head, smeared it with such herbs that it could not rot, quoth spells over it and worked such charms that it talked with him and told him many hidden things.[103]

In this passage, we learn that Mimir was beheaded by the Vanir and his severed head sent back to the Æsir. Mimir had been a hostage along with Hœnir, but Hœnir had proven to be an indecisive prisoner when asked for counsel and only made decisions when Mimir was present.[104] Odin preserves his decapitated head and uses it as an oracle of wisdom.[105] Mimir is a somewhat enigmatic figure. Sometimes claimed as a member of the Æsir, the bulk of evidence supports his true origin amongst the giants.[106] We know that Mimir's Well was situated in the land of the Frost Giants. Clearly, he would have to be a descendant of Ymir and some have claimed he is even identical to the cosmic progenitor Ymir himself.[107] His relationship with Odin, at least, is somewhat clearer. He is the source of Odin's initial awakening. There appear to be a number of versions about how this event transpired, though. The most common version is that Odin sacrificed

---

100 Comparable to the rune spells learned by Odin.
101 Doniger, *The Rig Veda*, 45.
102 There is no clear consensus on what the Soma plant actually was. Amongst the runners are Psilocybin mushrooms, Blue Lotus and Cannabis. Whatever its source its equivalent in the Celto-Germanic tradition of northern Europe is mead.
103 Sturluson, *Heimskringla*, 3.
104 "But when Hœnir was at the thing or gatherings, where any difficult matter came before him he always answered the same (unless Mimir was present), 'Now get the counsel of others' said he," (Ibid., 3).
105 Orpheus is another example in Indo-European mythology of a severed head acting as a source of wisdom.
106 "If Mimir was the power who possessed inspiration before the Æsir, it is among the giants rather than the gods that we should expect to find him," (Davidson, *Gods and Myths*, 168).
107 Timothy J. Stephany. *Odin, The Well and the Mead: The Theft of the Drink of the Gods*. http://timothystephany.com/papers/Article07-Mimir.pdf (accessed: 5 January, 2010).

an eye in order to obtain a draft from Mimir's Well.[108] Another version is that the theme of the lay *Vafþrúðnismál* is really a contest between Vathrudnir (Mimir) and Odin; the two engaging in a verbal struggle which ends with Vathrudnir/Mimir losing his head as forfeit to Odin.[109] In the lay *Grímnismál*, we learn that Odin was responsible for slaying the Giant Sokkmimir (Deep Mimir).[110] In this version of events, the Vanir do not execute Mimir. Odin himself carries out the grisly task. Stephany also points out that a passage in the Sigdrifumal[111] can be interpreted as Mimir teaching Odin the use of the runes. This would suggest an alternate or supplementary account to the well known tale of Odin's self-sacrifice on Yggdrasil. Stephany goes onto suggest that Suttung is Mimir's father and that, in an alternate version of the Gunnlod episode, Odin wins the mead from Mimir in a contest.[112] These are interesting interpretations and largely rest, I believe, on Stephany's association of Odin's sacrificed eye with the phases of the moon. Hence the moon represents Odin's sacrifice and the source of his wisdom, whilst the sun represents Odin's remaining eye. Once again it is worth emphasising the multi-layered nature of mythology and the importance of self-*gnosis* when interpreting mythological texts.

Another possibility is that Odin's "eye" that he sacrifices is not, in fact, an eye but another organ that one could interpret as a "seeing" mechanism, namely the pineal gland.[113] The pineal gland has often been referred to as the "third eye" and has had various mention in philosophical studies.[114]

---

108 "She sat out, all alone, there, where the old ones came, the awesome Ase looked in her eyes. "What do you ask of me? Why test me? I know well, Odin, where your eye is hidden—in the water of Mimir's well. Mimir drinks mead each morning from Valfather's pledge. Do you want to know more, or what?" (*Völuspá*, stanza 28).

109 "Although the giant's name given is Vafthrudnir (great riddler) this might be another epithet for Mimir. The hall Odin arrives at is one that belongs to Im's father, either implying that Vafthrudnir is Im's father or that Im is Vafthrudnir. If it means that Im is his name, this too could be equivalent to Mim. Of further relevance is that Vafthrudnir like Mimir is a wise giant and that he and Odin both wager their heads, suggesting that the fate of Vafthrudnir is the same as Mimir," (Stephany, *Odin*, 9-10).

110 "Svithar and Svithrir I was called at Sokkmimi's, the time I hid the old ettin and had slain the famous son of Mithvitnir," (stanza 51).

111 "Mind-runes you must know if you want to be wiser in spirit than every other man; Hropt interpreted them, cut them, thought them out, from that liquid which had leaked from the skull of Heiddraupnir and from Hoddrofnir's horn," (Larrington, *The Poetic Edda*, stanzas 14-15).

112 Stephany, *Odin*.

113 A small endocrine gland located towards the base of the brain which produces melatonin, a hormone responsible for regulating sleep patterns.

114 René Descartes called it the "seat of the soul."

Odin's sacrifice of his pineal gland led him to a state of permanent awakening, his draft from Mimir's Well now gave him complete understanding of creation itself as well as his own immortality.[115] Mimir's name means memory or fate[116] so, essentially, what happens to Odin is that he remembers what has come before right back to the beginning of creation. There are similar tales of heroes drinking from sacred pools/wells. In Celtic lore, such as the tale of Fionn mac Cumhaill, we have the "salmon of wisdom"—a source of unlimited knowledge:

> "Fish are the treasures of the water," said Bruach. We were sitting together looking into a deep pool. "But none are as precious as the salmon, because of its remarkable endurance. For it swims for miles upstream to find its spawning ground, which is why it has been chosen by the gods to carry the deepest wisdom."[117]

The salmon is itself, as a fish, amongst the oldest life forms on earth, a denizen of the oceans, the cauldron of life itself.[118] The whole episode surrounding Mimir and the mead is little short of a shamanic vision quest to higher realms in order to obtain secret knowledge. Odin, in the guise of a snake and an eagle (the shaman turning himself into some form of animal is an integral part of this rite), wins the mead of inspiration from which he learns the reality of existence and his own place within it. He is on the way to his ascent to godhood and the status of "All Father." His final task is the integration of his psyche and it is to Odin's winning of the runes, his attainment of higher consciousness and his role as a shaman that we now turn.

> Bruach leaned forward and cupped some water in his hands. "Once" he said "you asked me where the Well of Wisdom can be

---

[115] "Odin preserves his (Mimir's) head with oils and spices and sets it in a well at the foot of Yggdrasil where he gives him his eye in return for other-worldly knowledge! The imagery is clear: the other-worldly wisdom of immortality could be gained from the severed head kept in the well. And by receiving this knowledge, Odin becomes one-eyed...and an initiate of the knowledge of the unity of all things," (Grigsby, *Warriors*, 200).

[116] "An attractive derivation of his name is that linking it with Latin *memor*, although attempts have also been made to establish a connection with Old English *meotud*, "fate," (Davidson, *Gods and Myths*, 167).

[117] Claire Hamilton. *Tales of the Celtic Bards*. (Singapore: Tien Wah Press, 2003), 122.

[118] "The symbol of the fish-an alternate symbol for the god of the deep-had a specific shamanic meaning beyond simply a "dweller in the water," for fish were the oldest animals, alive from the start of time, and that is why their knowledge of history was unsurpassed," (Grigsby, *Warriors*, 182).

found." He drank the water. "Now I am asking you the question. Where can such a well be found?" He looked at me expectantly. I wanted to please him with a clever answer. But my mind suddenly became as blank as the surface of the pool itself. We sat in silence while he waited for my answer and I waited for the pool to clear. At last, because I could think of nothing better, I said: "I think the pool that is in front of us is the well." To my surprise he nodded encouragingly…"And what about the salmon itself?" he asked. I looked around me. I could see nothing that seemed a symbol for the salmon. I closed my eyes and stopped thinking of the salmon and thought of its knowledge and wisdom instead. Suddenly I looked at Bruach. "Your teaching and the inner knowing it awakes in me," I said. "That is the salmon."[119]

The Sacrifice of Odin

> *Odin often changed himself; at those times his body lay as though he were asleep or dead, and he then became a bird or a beast, a fish or a dragon, and went in an instant to far-off lands on his or other men's errands. He could do this also: with sacrificial words he stoked fire, stilled the sea or turned winds in what way he could.*[120]
>
> —Heimskringla

In chapter four of the *Ynglinga Saga*,[121] we learn that Freyja was a priestess and it was she who first taught the Æsir "wizardry", which "was in use with the Vans." In *Völuspá*, we learn that Gullveig practiced *seiðr*.[122] Whoever we accept Gullveig to be, it is, none the less, clear that the Æsir, specifically Odin, learned the secret of *seiðr*/shamanic magic from a female deity. Freyja's link with Odin goes beyond this, though, and I believe the evidence[123] suggests that Freyja was, in fact, the wife of Odin and that Frigg and Freyja represent aspects of the same

---

119 Hamilton, *Tales*, 128.
120 Sturluson, *Heimskringla*, 5.
121 Ibid., 3.
122 See the "Loki and Creation" section of this dissertation.
123 "Freia is highest in rank next to Frigg. She was married to someone called Od…Od went off on long travels, and Freia stayed behind weeping," (Sturluson, *Edda*, 29-30). "Seid, like the dead, is something that Freyja and Odin share. It may thus be pertinent to recall here Odin's sexual promiscuity and his many names. Finally, the names Óð and Óðinn look like a doublet…and Saxo has a story in Book 1 of Gesta Danorum about a long absence of Odin from his realm, which some scholars think is parallel to Od's absence," (Lindow, *Norse Mythology*, 107).

earth mother goddess. One may speculate that this union between earth mother and the chief representative of the human gods is the attempted reforging of man's original primal bond to the earth. What Freyja[124] is offering is the means to reforge that relationship and it is exactly this "magic," specifically its property of regeneration, that enables Odin to do so.

Odin's winning of the runes comes about directly from his knowledge of *seiðr*/shamanism.

> I know that I hung, on a wind-swept tree
> for all of nine nights,
> wounded by spear, and given to Odin,
> myself to myself,
> on that tree of which no man knows
> from what root it rises
>
> They dealt me no bread, nor drinking horn.
> I looked down, I drew up the runes,
> screaming I took them up,
> and fell back from there.

From these two stanzas in *Hávamál*[125] we learn that Odin paradoxically sacrificed himself to himself for nine nights upon the world tree Yggdrasil. After nine nights of no food or drink he spied the runes and took them. I will return in a moment to the meaning behind these passages but first I want to focus on *seiðr*/shamanism as a process of initiation and regeneration. As Davidson notes,[126] shamanic[127] sacrifices usually entail great suffering for the initiate because what is being attempted is no less than a rebirth of the initiate into a higher state of being. This is what Odin is undergoing upon the world tree; a sacrifice in order to acquire hidden knowledge. This is not the only occasion that Odin undergoes a shamanic[128] style initiation. In *Grímnismál*, Odin is tied

---

124 Remember in the opening chapter I raised the possibility from Rydberg's study that Gullveig may well have taught Freyja *seiðr*.

125 Chisholm, *The Eddas*, stanzas 137-138.

126 *Gods and Myths*, 142-143.

127 "A shaman is a man or woman who enters an altered state of consciousness-at will-to contact and utilize an ordinarily hidden reality in order to acquire knowledge, power, and to help other persons. The shaman has at least one, and usually more, 'spirits' in his personal service," (Michael Harner, *The Way of the Shaman*, [New York: Harper & Row, 1980], 20).

128 "It seems possible that *seiðr* and *spae*-working may form part of the rather scattered remnants of shamanic techniques in Norse culture and have been related to the

between two fires by Geirrod and denied food and drink. This is another example of a shamanic ritual.[129] This time Odin acts as the teacher of a would-be initiate. As Davidson writes,

> the hanging of Odin on the World Tree seems indeed to have two main conceptions behind it. First, Odin is made into a sacrifice according to the accepted rites of the god of death, who is Odin himself. Secondly, Odin is undergoing a ceremony of initiation, gaining his special knowledge of magic by means of a symbolic death.[130]

That Odin survives the experience seems to be because of the regenerative properties within *seiðr*. From earliest times, *seiðr* magic of the Vanir was regarded as an instrument of regeneration.[131] As John Grigsby writes: "The old magical practices do not die out, Odin becomes the divine magician par excellence. He hangs on the world tree Yggdrasil for nine nights and days, a spear thrust in his side, a regenerating self sacrifice in the Vanir mould that allows him to learn the magic of the runes. Odin, as a warrior and shaman, bridges the gap between the two cults."[132]

So what is it that Odin actually achieves and what purpose do the runes serve? The runes themselves seem to be of ancient provenance. In *Hávamál* stanza 143 we learn that the runes are known to and used by a variety of beings from Giants to dwarves and elves as well as the Æsir.[133] Seemingly Odin wasn't the first being to acquire these tools. The Old English word *rúna* means mystery and deliberation. Its equivalent in Old Norse (same spelling) also means mystery and secret wisdom.[134] As for their application, runes were used as a writing system amongst the Germanic peoples and they were also used as a system of divination

---

    shamanic practices of other cultures," (Jenny Blain, *Nine Worlds of Seid Magic: Ecstasy and Neo-Shamanism in North-European Paganism*, [New York: Routledge, 2002], 19).

129 "Geirrod's methods of torture, starvation and heat have been thought to recall shamanistic rituals, allowing access to arcane knowledge kept hidden from the uninitiated; such practices could have been known to the Scandinavians from their northern neighbors, the Lapps," (Larrington, *The Poetic Edda*, 50).

130 Davidson, *Gods and Myths*, 142-143.

131 North, *Heathen Gods*, 28.

132 Grigsby, *Beowulf and Grendel*, 192.

133 "Odin among the Æsir, but Dain for the elves, Dvalinn for the dwarves, Asvith for the ettins. I carved some myself."

134 D.H. Green, *Language and History in the Early Germanic World*, (United Kingdom: Cambridge University Press, 1998), 255.

in gealdor magic.[135] With the runes, Odin now has the capability to manipulate the world around him and to gain some insight into future events. Along with *seiðr* practically conferring immortality, he effectively becomes a god. From *Hávamál* 140,[136] we read that Odin learns "Fimbul" spells from the father[137] of Bestla, Bolthor's son. Bestla is Odin's giantess mother, so he effectively learns the rune spells from his giant grandfather.[138] Presumably these are the ones who also deny Odin food and water during his sacrifice on Yggdrasil. Here then we have giants actively aiding the ascent to godhood of a human deity. The runes, seemingly, are won only when Odin obtains insight into the nature of reality. It is my contention that Odin is the first of his folk to achieve the integration of the various states of consciousness into himself, the lesson that Heimdall first taught our people when he came to us from the ocean.[139] Odin hangs from the World Tree for *nine* nights and Geirrod tortures him between two fires for *nine* nights before he reveals himself. As I pointed out with the Eleusinian Mysteries, the descent of the soul through to the ninth material realm, the *nine* mothers of Heimdall in chapter two and with the *nine* worlds of our cosmos, these are all reflections of the various states of consciousness[140] within the human psyche, which have to be integrated in order to achieve the reunion of one's self with the world.

Now we turn back to Loki whose person is integral to that of Odin. If we accept that Lodur is Loki then we see him accompany Odin right from the start of our existence. Loki, according to Snorri, was counted amongst the Æsir and, more to the point, he was Odin's blood brother. As we read here in *Lokasenna*:

---

135 It is not my intention to go into depth regarding the runes. For those who are interested I would recommend the following works: Stephen Pollington, *Rudiments of Runelore*, (Anglo-Saxon Books, 1995); Edred Thorsson, *Northern Magic: Rune Mysteries and Shamanism*, (St. Paul, MN: Llewellyn Books, 1992) and Guido Von List, trans. Stephen E. Flowers, *The Secret of the Runes*, (Smithville, TX: Runa-Raven Press, 1988).

136 "Fimbul spells I got from the famous Son of Bolthor the father of Bestla. I had a drink of the dear mead that was drawn from Othroerir."

137 *Hávamál* stanzas 146-163 detail the eighteen runic spells Odin learned from his grandfather. In *Sigdrifumal*, Sigdrifa teaches Sigurd about runic spells stanzas 5-19, (See Larrington).

138 Interesting to compare this with Stephany's belief (detailed in Chapter Three) that the Giant Mimir taught Odin use of the runes.

139 See the "Heimdall" chapter in this dissertation.

140 It is interesting to note that both Freud and Jung believed that the human mind was a tripartite division. Freud believed there was the conscious, unconscious and preconscious. Jung labeled them the conscious mind, personal unconscious and the collective unconscious.

> Remember this Odin, that we blended
> our blood together in days of yore.
> You said you would not taste ale,
> unless it were born to both of us.[141]

Loki is, essentially, Odin's mirror opposite.[142] He is a dual deity, one side of which (Odin) represents the ego enlightened and ennobled, the other (Loki) representing the unrestrained, selfish, ignorant and immature ego. Loki represents the quality of chaos that ensnared human kind before the arrival of Heimdall. In some respects, along with Thor, they represent the triune deity of Hindu mythology Brahma (Odin) the creator, Vishnu (Thor) the preserver and Shiva (Loki) the destroyer.[143] If Odin represents what the human mind can achieve then Loki represents the depth it can fall to. Loki is also a practitioner of *seiðr*. Like Odin he has the ability to change his shape. As a mare he distracted the giant's stallion and prevented him from building the walls of Asgard on time. He adopted the form of an eagle to search for Thor's hammer, a flea to steal Freyja's necklace, and a salmon to avoid capture after the murder of Baldr. He also adopted the guise of an old woman in order to deny Baldr return from the underworld. Loki and Odin also share another attribute linked to the practice of *seiðr* magic, a feminine aspect.

> Odin said:
> "If I have given victory to those to whom
> I should not have, to lesser men,
> you know that for eight winters
> you were under the earth giving milk as a cow
> or a woman, and you bore babies.
> I think that these were womanish ways."
>
> Loki said:
> "But they say you worked seith magic on Sam's Isle,
> that you plied magic like a volva,
> that you fared among men in the form of a vitki.
> I think that those were womanish ways."[144]

---

141 Chisholm, *The Eddas*, stanza 9.
142 "Davidson points out that Loki and Odin have a resemblance to the creation story in some North American Indian cultures. One creator is good and impressive, the other, the trickster, appears as a parody of him; a creator whose schemes go awry, so Loki would be an Odin figure in reverse," (Davidson, *Gods and Myths*, 181).
143 Davidson also points out that Odin, Loki and Thor are the most sociable deities in the mythology, (Ibid., 177).
144 *Lokasenna*, stanzas 23 and 24.

An Interpretation of Germanic Mythology

Within Heathenism past and present there has been much debate over the role of men within *seiðr*. It is not my intention to get into this argument as it is thought of today but I feel it is pretty much evident that *seiðr* magic was *predominately* a feminine form of magic in the time of our pre-Christian forefathers and that its practice amongst males was, to say the least, frowned upon.[145] The accusations by Loki against Odin seem to lie in the belief that homosexuality[146] was a part of the role played by male practitioners of *seiðr*. Shamanism has often been associated with cross-dressing and trans-sexual behaviour.[147] Grigsby claims that the origin of this belief regarding Odin lies within the sacrifice of the king within the cult of the Vanir deities. The king died at the hands of a priestess often in a sexual position involving strangulation. The male is subservient to the female and in effect takes on a passive sexual role and is "mounted."[148] Another possibility is that *ergi* doesn't mean unmanly/homosexual but unmanned,[149] an entirely different meaning. *Seiðr* often involved possession and was an active attempt to enter higher realms of consciousness. As a result, one lost control over one's own mental and physical faculties. Odin's sacrifice on Yggdrasil, and shamanic initiation in general, involves the deliberate infliction of suffering upon the body in order to access other levels of consciousness. Odin was, effectively, unmanned during this ritual, *he was no longer in control of himself.*

Loki is accused by Odin of bearing babies, i.e. of being a mother. In *Gylfaginning*, we learn that after Loki had enticed the stallion Svaðilfari belonging to the giant away from building the walls of Asgard he "had such dealings with Svaðilfari that somewhat later he gave birth to a foal."[150] This foal

---

145 "Ragnald Rettlebone had Hadeland; there he learned magic and became a wizard. King Harald did not like wizards. In Hordaland there was a wizard called Vitgeir. The king sent him a behest to leave off his wizardry. He answered and sang: It is little strange if we do wizardry, who are the sons of Carls and low-born mothers, when Ragnvald Rettlebone, Harald's noble son, can be a wizard in Hadeland. When king Harald heard that said, Eric Blood-Axe went by his counsel to the upland and came to Hadeland. There he burned his brother Ragnvald and eighty wizards with him and that work was much praised," (Sturluson, *Heimskringla*, 68).

146 *Ergi* was an Icelandic term denoting a feminised man and often directed towards male *seiðr* practitioner. "Possibly because it included female receptive sexual activities," (Blain, *Nine Worlds*, 116).

147 Grigsby, *Beowulf and Grendel*, 191.

148 Ibid.

149 "There is no evidence that the practice of *seidh* makes you 'unmanly'...but because these practices involve being 'possessed'...there is plenty of evidence that you can be 'unmanned'...Any genuine psychic experience can 'unman' anyone (male or female)," Blain, *Nine Worlds*, 120.

150 Faulkes, *Edda*, 36.

was Sleipnir,[151] Odin's eight-legged horse, which he uses to traverse the nine realms.[152] Loki's possible androgynous nature has already been mentioned in chapter one along with his fathering of Fenris, Jormungandr and Hel. From Snorri we learn that Odin summoned Loki's three children to him and cast them out of Asgard. Jormungandr[153] became the world serpent, Hel gained dominion of the nine worlds, ruler of all those who die in sickness and old age, and Fenris wolf is the cosmic destroyer bound until the time of Ragnarok.[154] Odin, however, may also have borne a child; Vali, the avenger of Baldr. North states that "if Loki's taunts against Óðinn and Frigg[155] are to be read as pointed rather than as broadly offensive, it seems that Óðinn must become a *seiðmaðr*,[156] a man with a woman's procreative powers in order to produce Vali."[157] For North, Odin's bearing of Vali represents the "crucial contribution of the Vanir." A point of interest from all this is that Carl Jung developed the theory that an integrated personality was one that first began to confront its shadow element. The next layer in his psyche was the *anima/animus*, i.e. the opposite sex image. Once a man accepted his *anima/animus* it led to greater reconciliation between his inner and outer selves.[158] Remember as well that the Fetch is often thought to appear in the guise of a member of the opposite sex. Seemingly Odin's practice of *seiðr* was part of the process of his initiation and deification. The initiation may have unmanned him but it was far from a homosexual act. It was simply Odin coming to terms with his own personality.

> Thus it is intimated that this dismemberment, the properly Dionysian suffering, is like a transformation into air, water, earth, and fire, that we are therefore to regard the state of individuation as the origin and primal cause of all suffering, as something

---

151 "The eight legged horse of Odin is the typical steed of the shaman. In his journeys to the heaven or underworld, the shaman is usually represented as riding on some bird or animal," (Davidson, *Gods and Myths*, 142).
152 Sleipnir's eight legs also put one in mind of a spider, factor in the web of wyrd, the web of consciousness and it is an almost plausible analogy!
153 Jormungandr is another symbolism of the serpent, biting its own tail. Here it is a symbol of cycles and evolutionary growth.
154 Faulkes, *Edda*, 26.
155 North is referring to stanza 28 in *Lokasenna*: "If you like, Frigg, I shall speak more of my harm-staves. I planned it such that you do not ride behind Baldr to the halls."
156 A male practitioner of *Seiðr*.
157 North, *Heathen Gods*, 109.
158 Snowden, *Teach Yourself Jung*, 71.

objectionable in itself. From the smile of this Dionysian sprang the Olympian gods, from his tears sprang man.[159]

Odin's Deification

The next day Rime Thurses
strode out to ask rede
of Har in Har's Hall,
asking about Bolverk, whether he was among the Gods
or had been slain by Suttung.[160]

—Hávamál

In *Hávamál* stanza 109, we learn that Odin receives a deputation from the frost giants. These giants wish to enquire whether Odin has managed to overcome Suttung and steal the mead of inspiration. The frost giants are one of the two[161] primordial families of giants and are usually a force hostile to the gods. Interestingly enough, we learn from Snorri[162] that "All Father" was with the frost giants before creation...it is to this question of Odin as "All Father" that we now turn. It is my contention that Odin was not always the "All Father", but that through the seizing of the mead of inspiration and his sacrifice upon the World Tree he attained godhood and through these acts of shamanism he became the "All Father." This is the crux of stanza 109 dealing with the frost giants. The implacable enemies of the Æsir wish to know if Odin has now become a god and if the humans who the giants have feared since Loki's intervention have now realised their potential.

Inevitably this leads to some confusion because how can *this Odin* who has just attained divine status be the *same Odin* who, along with Hœnir and Loki, created man and also be the *same Odin* who helped shape the earth itself? Chronological irregularity within the mythology is not uncommon. Kvasir is an example,[163] but this is still a major problem if we accept my thesis to start with. We are dealing with mythology here and so the question of how much we can actually treat it in a literal chronological sense is an open one.[164] There is also the possibility that

---

159 Nietzsche, *The Birth of Tragedy*, 73.
160 *Hávamál*, stanza 109.
161 The other being the Giants of Muspelheim (Fire Giants).
162 Faulkes, *Edda*, 9.
163 "Here we have one of those discrepancies in chronology that characterize myth in general and this mythology in particular." Lindow is referring to Kvasir's appearance in the episode surrounding Loki's capture after Baldr's death, even though Kvasir dies in the "mythic past," (Lindow, *Norse Mythology*, 206).

the linear progression in Norse mythology is due to later Christian influence.[165] The answer may well lie in our Heathen ancestors conception of time itself, which was very different from the Biblical influenced linear progression of Christianity. The Heathen understanding of time begins with the three Norns. Urðr is the Norn of being, that which has become, Verðandi is the Norn of becoming, whilst Skuld is the Norn of what is owed, duty, obligation, debt.[166] Urðarbrunir is the well where the waters of *magan* accumulate after traveling from the primordial kettle Hvergelmir and through Mimisbrunir. The three Norns draw the water and mud from this well and water the World Tree Yggdrasil. The mighty World Tree draws this water upwards through the nine worlds and up into the branches where it finally accumulates in its leaves. Drops containing new *magan* of deed and word drawn from the process of life lived within the nine realms then fall from the leaves right back down into Hvergelmir, where the process begins again.[167] In this we can see a feedback loop from primordial time into an ever changing present. I believe that Odin's attainment of divine status on Yggdrasil itself instigated a transition and that this world-changing deed of *magan* altered the very foundation of primordial time itself. Odin is responsible for his own creation. He is *the creature turned creator.* Heathen time is cyclical. We learn this from *Völuspá* stanzas 2 and 59.[168] What has happened will happen again. Think of Jormungandr, the World Serpent, biting its own tail, a symbol of the cycle of time. Odin may be as much a concept as the name of a god-man. Consider the number of names he held in *Grímnismál*:

> I am called Grim, and Gangleri,
> Herjan and Hjalmberi,
> Thekk and Thrithi, Thuth and Uth,
> Helblindi and Har.
>
> Sath and Svipal and Sanngetal,
> Herteit and Hnikar,
> Bileyg, and Baleyg, Bolverk and Fjolnir,
> Grim and Grimnar, Glapsvith and Fjolsvith,

---

164 For an overview of mythology and time see the entry, "The Nature of Mythic Time" in Lindow's *Norse Mythology* (39).
165 Ibid.
166 James Hjuka Coulter. *Germanic Heathenry.* (USA: 1st Books Library, 2003), 49.
167 For a more detailed explanation see Ibid., 49-50.
168 "I recall the children of ettins, who in the days of yore, brought me to life…I recall the nine worlds, the nine steads, of the Glorious Meting Wood, beneath the ground. She sees another rise up, earth from the ocean, all agreen. Torrents flow and the eagle flies above scanning the fells and hunting fish."

Sithott and Sithskegg, Sigfather and Hnikuth,
Allfather and Valfather, Atrith and Farmatyr.
There is one name I have never been called
since I have fared among the folk.

They call me Grimni at Geirroth's
and Jalk at Asmund's.
I was called Kjalar when I drew the sled,
and Thror at things,
Vithuth in battles,
Oski, Omi, Jafnhar and Biflindi,
Gondler and Harbarth among Gods.

Svithar and Svithrir I was called at Sokkmimi's.[169]

In stanza 54 of *Grímnismál* we read that he is called Odin but was known as *Ygg before and Thund before that*. Clearly, we are dealing with an individual known by many different names and who probably wasn't always known as Odin. Is Odin a title? Or a name newly acquired by this initiate become a god? Lindow[170] has pointed out that Ygg may refer to Odin being born of Yggdrasil, in which case Yggdrasil is the same as Odin's giantess mother Bestla. Titchenell[171] has equated Thund with the river of time surrounding Valhalla. Chisholm translates three of Odin's names from stanza 54: Vak (Wakeful), Svafnir (One who puts to sleep) and Ofnir (Weaver). The first two seem resonant of the pineal gland and also the ability to remove fetters[172] using *seiðr*. The latter may be interpreted as the use of runes by Odin to manipulate *wyrd*.

Our sources also suggest that Odin wasn't always seen as the primary god. Davidson[173] points out that the belief that Thor is Odin's son is questionable. In Snorri's prologue in the Edda, we learn that Odin is, in fact, a distant descendent of Thor.[174] Of course, Snorri's whole prologue has been explained as little more than Christian propaganda,[175] but we also learn from Adam of Bremen that Thor

---

169 Chisholm, *The Eddas*, stanzas 46-50.
170 Lindow, *Norse Mythology*, 77.
171 Titchenell, *The Masks of Odin*, 162.
172 Probably the ability to remove or place mental blocks rather than physical constraints. (Davidson, *Gods and Myths*, 63).
173 Ibid., 140.
174 Faulkes, *Edda*, 3.
175 "I have shown that they do not belong to the Teutonic Heathendom but that they were born, as it were of necessity, in a Christian time, among Teutons converted to

An Interpretation of Germanic Mythology

was seen as the ruler of heaven.[176] Davidson[177] goes on to point out that Odin shares many similarities with the Roman god Mercury. Richard North[178] also argues that Odin is related to Mercury and, as a result, is in actual fact a later foreign import into the Germanic-Norse pantheon. Whether we accept this, or not, there is one piece of evidence that Davidson cites that I find interesting; the role of Mercury as a psychopomp, guiding souls to the underworld. It is Odin's role as a god of the underworld that we now turn to.

> Yama was the first to find the way for us, this pasture that shall not be taken away. Where our ancient fathers passed beyond, there everyone who is born follows, each on his own path.[179]

In this passage from the *Rig Veda*, we learn of a man called Yama who was the first mortal to reach the realm of the dead. He is the Vedic equivalent of Odin and like Odin he also becomes a king of the dead. Odin, like Yama, was the first of his people to break the cycle of rebirth, to transcend illusion and now rules an abode of the enlightened. In effect, Odin is a pathfinder, but who are the people who follow him?

> All the einherjar slay one another
> in Odin's field each day.
> They choose the slain, then ride from the fight,
> and sit as friends.[180]

The Einherjar (One Harriers)[181] are Odin's followers, a warrior band who enter the hallowed halls of Valhalla via death in combat or by sacrifice.[182] Symbols, particularly animals,[183] were equated with Odin in his aspect of the war god.

Christianity, and that they are throughout the work of the Latin scholars in the middle age," (Rydberg, *Teutonic Mythology*, 97).

176 "Thor, they say, rules the heavens; he is the god of thunder, wind and rain, fair weather and the produce of the fields. The second god, Othin, is the god of war, and he provides man with courage in the face of his enemies," (Adam of Bremen. "Gesta Hammaburgensis Ecclesiae Pontificum." *Northvegr Foundation*. http://www.northvegr.org/lore/gesta/index.php [accessed: 5 January, 2010]).

177 Davidson, *Gods and Myths*, 140.

178 North, *Heathen Gods*, 78.

179 Doniger, *Rig Veda*, 43.

180 *Vafþrúðnismál*, stanza 41.

181 Titchenell, *The Masks of Odin*, 161.

182 Davidson, *Gods and Myths*, 149.

183 Stephen Pollington. *The English Warrior From Earliest Times to 1066*. (England: Anglo-Saxon Books, 1996), 49.

An Interpretation of Germanic Mythology

Ravens and wolves, animals that frequented the sites of battles, were especially associated with him, as was the horse,[184] and they were also associated with his followers. Odin took an active interest in his initiates. In Saxo Grammaticus,[185] we learn how Odin enlisted the aid of Hadding in his war against "Loker," (Doubtless Loki) King of the Kurlanders. After Hadding was defeated in battle, Odin brought him back to his home on the back of his horse. Once there, Odin gave Hadding a refreshing potion and returned him to the world of the living.[186] We also learn that Odin taught Hadding the tactic of the swine head formation. Odin also exhorts Hadding not to waste his time in petty conflict but to wage war beyond his borders and to win glory.[187] North[188] interprets *Hávamál* 49[189] as Odin arming two men in his own armour and creating "demons" of battle. Seemingly though, not all who fought and died in battle were destined for Odin's hall.

In *Harbardzljod*,[190] Harbarth (Odin) explains that he takes the earls that fall in battle whilst Thor takes the thralls. Thor was indeed the god of the common man and the rank and file warriors. Farmers recruited for a campaign rather than "career" warriors would doubtless have worshipped him, whilst the Germanic nobility—those expected to be leaders and warriors - would have worshiped the more aristocratic Odin.[191] However, on the battlefield we find that the fallen are divided equally between Odin and Freyja. From Snorri we learn that "there is a place called Folkvang, and there Freyja is in charge of allotting seats in the hall. Half the slain she chooses each day, and half has Odin.[192] The boar (a symbol both of Freyr and Freyja) was a particularly potent emblem for the Germanic warrior. It was seen both as a symbol of procreation and also of masculinity. In *Beowulf*, we learn of its significance as a totem of protection:

---

184 "The horse and rider motif in Germanic art and the legends surrounding Odin as leader of the Wild Hunt are examples," Ibid.
185 Saxo Grammaticus, *The History*, 24.
186 Interestingly, we may presume that Hadding underwent a shamanic experience himself, traveling on Odin's steed Sleipnir, where he was given the mead of inspiration. Hadding could have been dead, in which case Odin used *seiðr* to regenerate him.
187 The ravens give Kon similar advice in *Rigsthula*.
188 North, *Heathen Gods*, 93.
189 "I gave my clothes to two tree-men in the field. Men they seemed with clothes. Shameful the naked hero."
190 "I was in Valland waging wars. I goaded wild boars and never made peace. Odin takes the earls who fall in the slaughter but Thor takes the kin of thralls."
191 Pollington, *The English Warrior*, 51.
192 Faulkes, *Edda*, 24.

> Boar-shapes flashed above their cheek-guards, the brightly forged work of goldsmiths, watching over those stern-faced men.[193]

In *Hyndluljóð*, Ottar (a devotee of Freyja) is turned into a boar (Freyja owns a boar called Hildisvin, "battle pig") and accompanies the goddess to the spirit world. The boar may well have been a symbol particular to followers of the Vanic cults in the same way that the wolf and bear were associated with Odin's warriors.[194] In *Hávamál* 129, Loddfafnir is warned against warriors who seem like boars and are enchanted in battle.[195] What we seem to have here is a link to the use of *seiðr* magic. North points out that Odin does not just use *seiðr* to regenerate himself after his sacrifice upon the world tree, but also uses it to regenerate his dead followers who, in turn, seem to become minor deities in their own right.[196] This rite of regeneration continues within Valhalla itself:

> High said: "Each day after they have got dressed they put on war-gear and go out into the courtyard and fight each other and they fall upon each other. This is their sport. And when dinner-time approaches they ride back to Val-hall and sit down to drink."[197]

The process of regeneration also applies to the nourishment of the Einherjar. The boar Saehrimnir is cooked in the kettle Eldhrimnir above the fire Andhrimnir. Saehrimnir is cooked each day and is whole again by the evening. For drink the Einherjar are supplied with mead from the goat Heidrun whose udders fill a vat each day.[198] Titchenell[199] sees Saehrimnir, Eldhrimnir and Andhrimnir as mind, desire/will and breath, respectively. In this respect "One Harriers" means the conqueror/harrier of one's own desires. Hadding, on another trip to the underworld, witnessed the spectacle of two armies of men who had died by the

---

193 Seamus Heaney. *Beowulf*. (USA: W.W. Norton & Co., Inc., 1999), 21-22.
194 Chisholm, *The Eddas*, 132.
195 "I give you rede Loddfafnir, heed it well! You will use it, if you learn it and it will get you good if you understand it. Do not look up in battle. Sons of men become like hogs, when warriors enchant you."
196 "To the extent that Óðinn immortalises the dead warrior kings by regenerating them in Valhöll, he is imagined as the father of such asmegir, who count as minor gods themselves," (North, *Heathen Gods*, 110).
197 Faulkes, *Edda*, 34.
198 Ibid., 32-33.
199 Titchenell, *Masks of Odin*, 161.

sword continuing to fight as they had done in life.[200] Hild (who may be Freyja) also regenerates two feuding armies in a never ending battle.[201]

So, from the above we know that Odin's followers were "princely warriors,[202] kings and distinguished leaders," heroes who pledged their service to the god for his help. Yet Odin, it seems, was a fickle god and mistrusted. That Odin was thought mendacious seems to be implied in *Hákonarmál*:

> Surely we have deserved victory of the gods...
> Odin has shown great enmity towards us...
> we will keep our war gear ready to hand.[203]

Loki also accused Odin of double dealing in *Lokasenna*:

> Silence Odin! You never could
> deal victory to men.
> Often you did not grant victory to him
> whom you should have, but to duller men.[204]

When Odin withdrew his favour from Harald Wartooth (King of the Danes) he created strife between him and his friend King Ring. As Harald rode out to face Ring in battle he recognised Odin in place of his own charioteer. He begged Odin for more victories and promised to dedicate all who fell in the battle to him. But Odin was relentless and even as Harald pleaded he flung him from the chariot, to be killed upon his own sword.[205] Odin was to slay Sigmund Volsung, Sigurd's father, in a similar fashion, breaking his sword with his spear.[206] Along with those who died in battle Odin was a God of the hanged and particularly those sacrificed to him. North[207] notes that in AD 59 a mass sacrifice of war captives was made to "Mercury" and "Mars" by the Hermunduri. Procopius in *The Gothic War* mentions prisoners hung from a beam and Adam of Bremen writes of men and animals hung around the temple of Uppsala in Sweden.[208] It was the fate of Hadding himself to die by hanging, apparently in a self sacrifice

---

200 Saxo Grammaticus, *The History*, 31.
201 Davidson, *Gods and Myths*, 152.
202 Ibid., 48.
203 Ibid.
204 Chisholm, *The Eddas*, stanza 22.
205 Davidson, *Gods and Myths*, 48.
206 J.R.R. Tolkien, ed. Christopher Tolkien. *The Legend of Sigurd and Gudrun*. (USA: Haughton, Mifflin, Harcourt, 2009), 95.
207 North, *Heathen Gods*, 104.
208 Davidson, *Gods and Myths*, 48.

to Odin,[209] whilst the Swedish king Hunding (believing Hadding to be dead) drowns himself in a vat of mead.[210] Finally, another example of Odin's maliciousness is found in *Gutrek's Saga* where Starkad, a warrior dedicated to Odin, takes part in a mock sacrifice that becomes chillingly real:

> In the morning the king's counselors held a meeting to discuss their plans. They agreed that they would have to hold a mock sacrifice, and Starkad told them how to set about it. There was a pine tree nearby and close to it a tall tree trunk. The pine tree had a slender branch just above the ground, but stretching up into the foliage. Just then the servants were making breakfast. A calf had been slaughtered and its entrails cleaned out. Starkad asked for the guts, then climbed up the trunk, bent down the slender branch and tied the calf guts around it.
>
> "Your gallows is ready for you now my lord," he said to king Vikar, "and it doesn't seem all that dangerous. So come over here and I'll put a noose around your neck."
>
> "If this contraption isn't any more dangerous than it looks," said the king, "then it can't do me much harm. But if things turn out otherwise it's a matter for fate to decide."
>
> After that he climbed up the stump. Starkad put the noose round his neck and climbed down.
>
> Next Starkad stabbed at the king with the reed stalk and said, "Now I give you to Odin."
>
> Then Starkad let the branch loose. The reed stalk turned into a spear[211] which went straight through the king, the tree stump slipped from under his feet, the calf guts turned into a strong withy, the branch shot up with the king into the foliage and there he died.[212]

---

209 Saxo Grammaticus, *The History*, 31.
210 Seemingly reminiscent of the cauldron of rebirth.
211 Note that Odin was also sacrificed with a spear in his side.
212 *Gautrek's Saga*. http://aj69.tripod.com/ancestry/gautreksaga.html (accessed: 5 January, 2010).

Odin is not unique in mythological texts as a being that seems purposefully to bring conflict to man. In the Gospels, Jesus states quite explicitly that he has come to sow division amongst man.[213]

Here again, though, we may well be misunderstanding the motive behind Odin's actions. The Einherjar are Odin's warriors that he will lead out at Ragnarok to confront the chaos powers. It stands to reason that Odin will want the best warriors he can acquire and those most committed. The stakes at Ragnarok are high, no less than the rebirth of the cosmos in a new cycle. If Odin seems to "betray" the likes of Harald Wartooth, Hadding or Sigmund it is because they have reached a level of attainment where they can rightfully take their place on the mead benches at Valholl and begin to prepare themselves mentally and physically for the coming ordeal. We lose sight of Odin's purpose and neglect the fact that Odin cannot be constrained by our morality and virtues. He is working for the greater good and, sometimes, that requires the sacrifice of all that one holds dear, not least integrity in the eyes of others. Odin may have been hated and mistrusted—how many other heroes do we know of, from all manner of tales, whose true motives are misunderstood—but his purpose has always been the survival of our folk.

The ideals of the Einherjar are heroic ones and it is hardly surprising that the hero has been idealised in much of the surviving lore of Northern Europe.[214] We see the social stratification apparent in *Harbardzljod*. Odin's path, in any guise, is one that requires courage, honour, confidence and self-reliance, exactly the kind of qualities that were expected of Germanic society's elite, the warrior noble class. Society was far more violent in those times and it stands to reason that these qualities would be more apparent on the field of battle than in the daily grind of subsistence agriculture that most people were engaged in. In *Grímnismál*, we read of the rivers that flow out of the primordial cauldron of creation, Hvergelmir. These are the streams of consciousness that separate the worlds and also link them together. Many of their names have been translated:

> Vino (Wine stream/inspiration), Leipt (Lightening), Thithunna (People Swallower), Not (Burning), Hrith (Storming), Ylgr (Wolf), Gjoll (Frenzied).[215]

---

213 "Do not think I have come to bring peace to the earth; I have not come to bring peace, but a sword," Matthew 10:34.
214 Davidson, *Gods and Myths*, 153.
215 Chisholm, *The Eddas*, 161.

Clearly, these are quite combative names. This may explain why Valhalla was traditionally perceived as an abode of the warrior because of the strength, determination and dynamism needed to follow Odin's example. In some cases, this cult of the warrior could be taken to extremes. Berserkers (Bearshirts) were especially fearsome warriors set apart from other warriors by their frenzied state of mental ecstasy in battle. Often without armour, these warriors would race forwards utterly crazed. As Davidson[216] notes, Odin had the ability not only to place bonds in men's minds but also to remove them. With Berserkers, the spirit of Odin was thought to have entered them with their mind separated from their body.[217] Indeed, the Old Norse *óðr* from which Óðinn stems means raging, furious and intoxicated.

Yet it would be wrong to suggest that only a warrior could enter Valhalla. It is thought a woman could enter Valhalla if she suffered a sacrificial death[218] and others could enter Valhalla by being remarkable men honoured by their community.[219] Snorri[220] also mentions that when Odin died he was marked with a spear as a dedication to himself, which may suggest that a man could be marked as one of Odin's own. It would also be incorrect to believe that the heroic code is limited to those who pursue a warrior lifestyle. As Puryear writes, "so, exactly what is the Teutonic warrior ethic? Today it could best be expressed as a creed of inner-strength and courage, which does not necessarily have anything to do with violence."[221] Puryear also cautions us against misconceptions that one could only enter Valhalla through violent death.[222] Whilst I believe he is correct here I feel it is evident that Odin's path was not meant for all. His path was a hard one to follow. Indeed, he cautions us against it in *Hávamál* stanza 55:

> Middle wise should each man be
> and not over wise.
> He who knows not his orlog
> may sleep untroubled.[223]

---

216 Davidson, *Gods and Myths*, 63.
217 Pollington, *The English Warrior*, 72.
218 Davidson, *Gods and Myths*, 146.
219 "He (Odin) said that every man should come to Valhall with such riches as he had with him on the firebale and that each should use what he himself had buried in the earth. For a renowned man they should build a howe as a mark of remembrance, and for all men in whom there was some manliness they should raise standing stones," (Sturluson, *Heimskringla*, 6).
220 Ibid.
221 See Mark Puryear's chapter on "The Warrior," (62-74) in *The Nature of Asatru*.
222 Ibid., 65.
223 Chisholm, *The Eddas*.

This would seem an odd warning to give to a would-be initiate, one looking for transcendence. Surely one should look for wisdom in all things? Odin's path is one towards truth. Many labour under the misconception that truth is necessarily *a good thing*, but this is a major assumption. In fact, I would argue that most people *can only exist* with a web of fantasies constructed to protect themselves. To know too much is often detrimental to one's health and sanity.[224] I am not suggesting that people should live a lie or be content to be gullible and led by the nose, but I am suggesting that not everyone is ready at the right time to follow Odin to Valhalla. Odin is offering you a warning that *this may not be your time but if it is be warned*!

For those that do choose to follow Odin, we find in *Hávamál* what is, essentially, a guide to spiritual progression on three levels:

> The same three natural divisions may be discerned in any system of thought or religion. There are always large numbers who are uninspired and self-centred, content to make the most of their circumstances and enjoy life. They generally adhere to conventional norms, demanding and presenting an appearance of respectability. There is a second, fairly numerous group who enjoy speculating on the unseen causes of observed phenomena and who may dabble in a variety of superstitious practices. Among them are many who yearn for greater knowledge and recognise that the universe holds mysteries to be discovered, but they often lack the needed insight and perseverance which is achieved by self discipline. The third group has little popular appeal. It is composed of those who have penetrated the sanctuary of their soul and at first hand verified some truth. These are the elect, the few who work for spiritual nature, indifferent to praise or blame, and without regard for their own ends, knowing that they are bound up with the larger, universal destiny. There is for them no pandering to personal satisfaction though, paradoxically, their altruism forms the backbone and stamina of the human evolutionary impulse for all mankind, the advancement of which must bring the greatest satisfaction of all.[225]

---

[224] Let us not forget Nietzsche's warning quoted on this dissertation's first page.
[225] Titchenell, *The Masks of Odin*, 106.

Once again, in stanzas 11-14 of *Hávamál* we are warned over the dangers of imbibing too much of the mead of inspiration:

> A man bears no better burden,
> when on the wilderness ways
> than great wisdom. One can have no worse fare,
> on road or field, than too much ale.
>
> Ale is not so good as they say
> for the sons of men.
> A man's mind knows less,
> the more he drinks.
>
> The heron is called mindlessness
> who hovers over men stealing their minds
> I was bound by that fowl's feathers
> when I was in Gunnloth's garth.
>
> I became drunk, roaring drunk,
> with wise Fjalar.
> The best wassail is that
> which a man leaves with his wits.[226]

Of course, warriors were not the only ones who found favour from Odin. Odin was the god of poets, skalds and other people we would consider of a scholarly nature. Egil Skallagrimson was both a warrior and also a poet who found favour with King Athelstan of England. Athelstan rewarded Egil both for his work with sword and with word.[227] Poets were given their gift of inspiration from Odin himself, and there is evidence that Odin directly inspired them rather than this being an impromptu exercise. In *Egil's Saga*, again we have Egil break into verse when asked his opinion about launching an attack against the town of Lund:

> Out shall our swords come glittering, warrior, we have deeds to perform this summer; let each traveller go to Lund straightaway; let us there before sun's setting make a terrible battle.[228]

---

226 Chisholm, *The Eddas*.
227 Trans. Jane Smiley. "Egil's Saga." *The Sagas of the Icelanders*. (USA: Penguin Books, 2000), 3-185.
228 Pollington, *The English Warrior*, 65.

Another example of seemingly divine inspired verse is found in an account by the English monk Bede. In the *Ecclesiastical History of the English People*, Bede writes about a monk named Cædmon:

> In this monastery of Streanaeshalch lived a brother singularly gifted by God's grace. So skilful was he in composing religious and devotional songs that, when any passage of Scripture was explained to him by interpreters, he could quickly turn it into delightful and moving poetry in his own English tongue. These verses of his have stirred the hearts of many folk to despise the world and aspire to heavenly things. Others after him tried to compose religious poems in English, but none could compare with him; for he did not acquire the art of poetry from men or through any human teacher but received it as a free gift from God.[229]

Amongst the Celts, the Vates were a Druidic order known for their skill at prophesy and divination. They were inspired by dream, touch and *poetic composition*.[230] Clearly, Odin was attracted not only to those with the qualities of courage and heroism but also those capable of intellectual endeavour. But what exactly did these would-be initiates face on their journey to Valhalla?

In *Grímnismál*, we read of Odin visiting the court of king Gunnlod. Once there Gunnlod ties Odin between two fires to learn more about him. None would give him food or drink until Agnar, Gunnlod's son, intervenes and one night gives Odin a drink...

> Hail Agnar! Veratyr
> bids you greetings.
> You will never get
> better payment for a single drink.[231]

In Vedic lore, soma was an exchange between men and gods, a ritual drink that empowered both. Agnar is an initiate on the path of Odin. He represents the ordinary unenlightened soul, whilst Gunnlod represents the enlightened soul overcome by his own ego. Odin goes on to give Agnar an education in the

---

229 Bede, trans. Leo Sherley-Price. *Ecclesiastical History of the English People*. (London: Penguin Classics, 1955), 248.
230 Claire Hamilton. *Tales of the Celtic Bards*. (Hampshire: O Books Publication, 2003), 19.
231 Chisholm, *The Eddas*, stanza 3.

Germanic cosmos, particularly of the abode of the various gods. Our interest begins from verses 26, 27 and 28:

> Eikthyrnir the hart is called who stands
> in warfather's hall and eats of Laerath's limbs.
> Drops fall from its horns to Hvergelmir.
> From there all waters have their ways.
>
> Sith and Vith, Soekin and Eikinn,
> Svol and Gunnthro,
> Fjorm and Fimbulthul,
> Rin and Rennandi,
> Gipul and Gopul,
> Gomul and Geirvimul,
> turn about the hof of the Gods
> with Thyn and Vin, Tholl and Holl,
> Grath and Gunnthorinn.
>
> One is called Vina, another Vegsvinn,
> a third Thiothunna.
> Nyt and Not, Nonn and Hron,
> Slith and Hrith, Sylg and Ylg,
> Vith and Van, Vond and Strond,
> and Gjoll and Leipt flow among men
> and thence to Hel.[232]

As mentioned above, Hvergelmir (roaring kettle) is the primordial well of time and space, filled by the waters created when the realms of fire and ice met in Ginnungagap at the beginning of creation. It is from this well that all the rivers begin to flow. These rivers are streams of consciousness separating the nine worlds and acting as conduits between them. Titchenell[233] believes them to represent streams that animate the worlds, perhaps as actualisations from potentialities. Verses 27 and 28 also indicate that two different types of river flow from Hvergelmir, one from the primordial well to heaven and one from Hvergelmir to our world (Midgard) and Hel...perhaps these represent different levels of consciousness? The latter being of a more commonplace kind through which most people with at least some modicum of spiritual awareness can avoid oblivion and be reborn into and out of the lower kingdoms, while those streams leading to Asgard represent the enlightened higher consciousness.

---

232 Ibid.
233 Titchenell, *The Masks of Odin*, 169.

Moving on from these connecting streams of consciousness we discover how the gods work within them in verses 29 and 30:

> Kormt and Ormt, and the two Kerlaugs,
> these Thor shall wade each day
> when he fares to doom at the ash Yggdrasil.
> The bridge of the Gods
> is all ablaze with fire
> and the holy waters seethe.
>
> Glath and Gullir, Gler and Skeithbrimir,
> Silvertop and Sinir, Gisl and Falhofnir,
> Golltopp and Lettfeti,
> these steeds the Æsir ride
> when they fare to doom
> each day at the ash Yggdrasil.[234]

The Æsir (human deities) all seem to have steeds[235] with which they traverse between the nine realms. Thor, by contrast, seems to wade through the rivers.[236] All the gods ride over Bifrost/Bilfrost[237] each day to where it enters Asgard at the well of Urðarbrunir.[238] Urðr's well is the well of becoming or actualisation. It inherits the potentiality of Hvergelmir and Mimisbrunir.

Of course, there are dangers on this road leading to Valhalla. In verse 21 we discover the river Thund that surrounds Valhalla, guarded by Thjothvitnir:

> Thund roars and fish live
> in the flood of Thiothvitnir.
> That river's current seems too strong
> for the throng of the slaughtered to wade.[239]

---

[234] Chisholm, "Lay of Grimnir," *The Eddas*, stanzas 29-30.
[235] Clearly reference to a spirit animal guise of the shaman.
[236] I am not entirely sure on the meaning of this.
[237] One possible translation of the bridges name is "stopping current," (Lindow, *Norse Mythology*, 80).
[238] Snorri mentions that Bifrost appears as a rainbow and the red in it is fire in order to keep the Giants out of heaven, (Faulkes, *Edda*, 18).
[239] Chisholm, *The Eddas*.

Thjothvitnir (people swallower) is probably another name for Fenris.[240] Here he is fishing[241] in Thund for souls on the path to enlightenment, ready to pick out or wash away those without the necessary discipline to make the crossing.

For those that make the perilous crossing, the next ordeal is that of the threshold. They now are faced with a warg that guards the doors of Valhalla and an eagle that sits above:

> It is well known to those
> who come to Odin to see his hall
> that a warg hangs before the west door
> and an eagle hovers above.[242]

The warg represents man's lower, baser nature, whilst the eagle represents his enlightenment.[243] Once inside, our would-be initiate is faced by Odin's own hounds, Geri and Freki, who represent greed and gluttony.[244] In verse 42, Agnar completes his initiation:

> Ull and all the Gods will befriend him
> who first takes it off the fire,
> for the worlds are opened to the sons of Ases
> when they heave off the kettle.[245]

Agnar saves Odin from the fire, he pulls the kettle off and the wisdom of Odin is laid before him. This removing of the kettle is symbolic of Agnar removing the cauldron of rebirth. He no longer needs it. He is now one of Odin's chosen and abides in the hall of the enlightened, Valhalla. This is the gift Heimdall first brought to us and that Odin was the first to recognise. We are all "sons of the Æsir." We all have the potential to enlightenment in our own time.

However, we are not alone in our quest to reach Valhalla:

---

240 Titchenell, *The Masks of Odin*, 162.
241 Chisholm believes these fish represent swords drawing blood from Fenris and washing away the weak. Personally, I believe they represent our own salmon of wisdom swimming against the tide of the river and the claws of the wolf.
242 Chisholm, "Lay of Grimnir," *The Eddas*, stanza 9.
243 One is reminded of Dante's Divine Comedy where our hero is faced by the lion (pride), Leopard (sensuality) and the she-wolf (materialism).
244 Titchenell, *The Masks of Odin*, 161.
245 Chisholm, "Lay of Grimnir," *The Eddas*.

> There are also other Norns who visit everyone when they are born to shape their lives, and these are of divine origin, though others are of the race of elves, and a third group are of the race of dwarves...[246]

> There are still others, whose function is to wait in Val-hall, serve drink and look after the tableware and drinking vessels...These are called Valkyries. Odin sends them to every battle. They allot death to men and govern victory.[247]

Valkyrie means "chooser of the slain" and, as Davidson[248] notes, they are something akin to the Norns and other powerful female guardian spirits. In fact, they seem to have much in common with the Dísir (collective female spirits). In *Grímnismál* 54, the doomed Geirrod is told:

> A sword mown man will Ygg now have.
> I know your life is through.
> there are many Dises. Now you will be able
> to see Odin—Move against me if you dare.[249]

Lindow writes that the Dísir often appear as Valkyries.[250] He mentions how in the *Thidranda thattr ok Thorhalls*, Thidrandi—the son of Sidu-Hall—is attacked by nine women dressed in black, whilst *nine* dressed in white rode come to his aid. This is taken as representing a change in religion. The Dísir in black represent Sidu-Hall's family *fylgjur*/fetches departing from the family to be replaced by Christian representatives. Grigsby[251] believes that the Valkyries were originally an aspect of the Vanic goddess Freyja and that they were later appropriated by Odin. This would make some sense given that Odin was likewise a beneficiary of the goddess's *seiðr*. Grigsby has also likened the Valkyries to the keres of ancient Greek mythology. The *keres* were originally spirits of the dead[252] who became associated with illness and misfortune. Like

---

246 Faulkes, *Edda*, 18.
247 Ibid., 31.
248 Davidson, *Gods and Myths*, 61.
249 Chisholm, *The Eddas*.
250 Atlamal 28: "I thought dead women came hither into the hall, not poorly decked out. They wished to choose you, would have invited you quickly to their benches; I declare of no value these dísir to you," (Lindow, *Norse Mythology*, 95).
251 Grigsby, *Beowulf and Grendel*, 112.
252 It is interesting to note that Grigsby believes that the Elves were in fact spirits of the ancestral dead who lived within communal burial mounds and that some of these dead may well have been deified, which is similar to North's view that the Einherjar were

the Valkyries, they would hover over the field of battle waiting to satiate themselves on the blood of the fallen. This association seems quite probable given that the common perception of Valkyries as buxom blonde maidens waiting to ferry the dead off to Valhalla for an afterlife of drinking and whoring is a misconception probably born in Wagnerian opera and not true to the picture of what the Valkyries were, omens of fighting and death, drenching the battle field with blood and riding across it on wolves ready to devour the fallen warriors. In *Njal's Saga*, a dream vision depicts three women weaving a loom of men's entrails and weighed down with severed heads. To me, the representation of Valkyries, Norns and Dísir is clear, these are all aspects of one's own *fylgjur*/fetch. This independent guardian is man's aid and guide in his spiritual progression but it should not be lost sight of that this guardian can also be harmful to us if we persist in going against our own progression and working harm. On the field of battle a man's *fylgjur* becomes a *dæmon* and one wonders if this is not the ultimate test of one's courage and integrity to face one's spirit self, as Jung believed one must come to face one's own anima/animus in order to truly progress.

In the final stanza of *Grímnismál*, Odin reveals himself to Agnar and Geirrod:

> I am called Odin and was called Ygg before.
> I was named Thund before that.
> Vak and Skilfing, Vafuth and Hroptatyr,
> Gaut and Jalk I was called by Gods.
> Also I was called Ofnir and Svafnir.
> I think they are all one in me.[253]

They are "all one in me," Titchenell translates this as "opener and closer all are one in me."[254] Odin acknowledges that all realms of consciousness are one in him and he is the path to it, but this translation of Titchenell's got me wondering about his son Baldr. In Valhalla, the Einherjar are the enlightened, the ones who have successfully followed Odin's path, and have reunited their ego with the cosmos. They now spend their time fighting and feasting[255] and the ego is submerged. They are preparing for Ragnarok, where they will give their lives for the creation of a new world out of the old. They are the ones who will help the gods stop the cosmic destroyer. Once in Valhalla this is not "and they all lived happily ever after," not at all. They will be called upon to give the ultimate

---

seen as deified mortals (Ibid., 103).
253 Chisholm, "Lay of Grimnir," *The Eddas*, stanza 54.
254 Titchenell, *The Masks of Odin*, 163.
255 Davidson interprets the fighting and feasting as forgetfulness of one's self (*Gods and Myths*, 70).

sacrifice...oblivion...for new life, new creation to emerge. We know from the sources that Baldr was to return from Hel after Ragnarok. What if Baldr was Odin's plan for the future of man? A plan that did not come to fruit in this cycle but may in the next?

Baldr

> *Odin's second son is Baldr, and there is good to be told of him. He is so fair in appearance and so bright that light shines from him, and there is a plant so white that it is called after Baldr's eyelash. It is the whitest of all plants and from this you can tell his beauty both of hair and of body. He is the wisest of the Æsir and most beautifully spoken and most merciful, but it is one of his characteristics that none of his decisions can be fulfilled.*[256]
> —Gylfaginning

Baldr is one of the most important characters in our mythology. The central myth surrounding Baldr is that of *Baldrs Draumar*. In this tale we learn that Baldr has been suffering disquieting dreams of his own impending death and the Æsir gather around to debate the problem. The upshot of the discussion is that Odin rides to Hel and there raises up a *völva* from the dead[257] and questions her about Baldr's fate, at the end of the exchange both make a discovery:

> "As I thought, you are not Vegtam.
> Rather you are Odin, the old god."
>
> "You are no volva, nor wise woman
> but rather the mother of three thurses."[258]

Here the tale in *Völuspá* ends and we have to go over to Snorri[259] to learn more. After Baldr tells the Æsir his dreams they decide to make all things of "fire, water, iron, all kinds of metal, stones, earth, trees, diseases, animals, birds, poison and snakes" declare an oath not to harm Baldr. Once this was done the gods celebrated by throwing objects at Baldr who was now unable to be harmed as he

---

256 Faulkes, *Edda*, 23.
257 The ability to raise the dead by *seiðr* is another property Odin shares with Freyja.
258 Davidson believes this "mother of three thurses" to be none other than Loki. The three giants being Jormungandr, Fenris and Hel. This would make sense if we remember Rydberg's suggestion of Angrboda being Loki's feminine aspect. It is also worth noting here that Rydberg sees Hyokkin as another aspect of Angrboda/Loki (Davidson, *Gods and Myths*, 188).
259 Faulkes, *Edda*, 48.

was immortal. The only one who did not see cause for celebration was Loki Laufeyiarson. In the guise of an old crone, he came along to watch the merriment and there questioned Baldr's mother, Frigg, about what was happening. Frigg told the old woman of Baldr's dream and the oath she had extracted from all things. The old woman pressed her to know if all things really had sworn an oath. Frigg, seeing no harm in her, let on that only the mistletoe, too young to swear oath, had not. At that the old woman went her way and changed back into Loki. He went off to pick the mistletoe and returned to the celebration where he saw the blind god Hod standing alone. Enquiring why he was so, Hod explained he had neither thing to cast nor sight to see. Loki offered to provide him with both and with his guidance Hod cast the mistletoe at Baldr, piercing his heart. Baldr fell dead.

None of the Æsir could take in what they saw but Odin was most grieved of all, understanding the loss the Æsir had just suffered more fully than most. At Baldr's funeral, Odin lays his sacred arm-ring Draupnir on Baldr's pyre. This is the ring made by the dwarf Sindre[260] in his contest with Ivalde. Draupnir sheds eight gold rings every ninth night. I believe this represents the nine worlds united within Baldr and will sustain Baldr through Ragnarok in preparation for his rebirth in the new world to come.[261] Baldr's ship (Hringhorni), which he was to be burned on, was too heavy to move (even for Thor), so they sent for a Giantess called Hyrrokkin. When she arrived on a wolf she dismounted and with one push set the boat rolling in flames and all the earth quaked.

Meanwhile, Odin rode off to the hall of Hel to plead for Baldr's release from the halls of the dead. Hel agreed but only if "all things alive and dead" wept for Baldr. After this the Æsir went out into the world and demanded that all things weep for Baldr. All things did except one giantess who said her name was "thanks" but was Loki in disguise, "thanks will keep dry tears for Baldr."

This, in summary, is the story of Baldr but what exactly does this myth represent? Probably the most common interpretation is that of a myth of seasonal change. Baldr representing the dying sun in winter. An interesting take on this basic format is Stephany's[262] article linking Baldr and Hod to agricultural practices coming from the Near East. In this, Baldr would correspond to the Syrian god Bel, Hod represents winter/darkness and Nanna (Baldr's wife) is the Syrian

---

260 Rydberg, *Teutonic Mythology*, 172.
261 Snorri also tells us that Odin rode for nine nights until he reached the river Gioll, where he spoke to the *völva* in *Baldrs Draumar*.
262 Timothy J. Stephany. *Brother Gods of Light and Darkness: Origins of the Baldr Myth*. http://timothystephany.com/papers/Article04-Baldr.pdf (accessed 5 January, 2010).

goddess Inanna. An interesting association he makes with mistletoe is that of redemption of life and the promise of spring.[263] Another interesting possibility is Baldr's links with the Vanir. Both Baldr and Freyr mean "lord" but the similarity does not stop there. In Saxo,[264] we read that Baldr was transported around in a cart just like Freyr was in Sweden. Connection[265] has also been made with Freyr's killing of Beli with a stag's antler and the slaying of Baldr with mistletoe. Davidson has also linked Baldr's myth, in part, to the Vanir.[266] For Titchenell,[267] the lay is one that simply describes the end of human innocence. In her thesis, Baldr is the serene and stagnant humanity of the primordial state. An utopia of a sort, but without growth or change, living in perfect communion with the earth. Loki shatters this innocence and introduces to man the ability to evolve as a more complex being:

> The evolutionary urge of intelligence in action-Loki, disguised as
> the aged crone-refused to mourn the passing of that golden age,
> for the real work of man's inner growth must take its place.[268]

For Titchenell, Loki is a tragic hero, a misunderstood character whose "evil" is simply to steal the knowledge of the gods and aid man's ascent to divinity.[269]

Saxo Grammaticus[270] provides us with our other major source of the Baldr myth, but with a slightly different angle. In Saxo's account, Baldr is a demigod of divine and mortal parentage whilst Hod is a human hero competing with Baldr for the love of Nanna. In this account, Hod one day comes across a band of Valkyries who tell Hod that they award victory or defeat at leisure to whom they wish. They warn Hod that Baldr has become aroused after seeing Nanna bathing but that Hod would be foolish to challenge Baldr as he is "begotten of divine seed." As I see it, this is shaping up into a contest between Baldr, representing the apotheosis of man, and Hod, who represents the highest nobility of attainment

---

263 Ibid., 2.
264 Saxo Grammaticus, *The History*, 73.
265 Stephany, *Brother Gods*, 5.
266 "It is hard to doubt that the story owes something to the cult of the Vanir, even if Baldr himself were not a true member of that family," (Davidson, *Gods and Myths*, 109).
267 Titchenell, *The Masks of Odin*, 256-257.
268 Ibid., 256.
269 "The best and highest possession mankind can acquire is obtained by sacrilege and must be paid for with consequences that involve the whole flood of sufferings and sorrows with which the offended divinities have to afflict the noble aspiring race of men," (Nietzsche, *Beyond Good and Evil*, 71).
270 Saxo Grammaticus, *The History*, 111.

in *mortal man*. Hod makes it known that he wishes to wed Nanna, but Gevar (possibly Loki) says he is afraid to go against Baldr, who has already asked for her hand. Hod learns that whilst Baldr's body is impervious to all steel, there is a sword belonging to the "wood satyr" Miming[271] which can slay him. Miming also possesses a bracelet[272] with the property of increasing its owner's wealth. What follows appears to be a shamanic spirit quest. Hod yokes a team of reindeer (perhaps a spirit animal like Sleipnir) and travels to the frozen north to await Miming. While waiting he passes the time watchful and awake, meditating. Eventually, one night[273] the satyr appears and Hod grabs him and threatens him with a spear. In order to buy his freedom Miming gives Hod the bracelet and the sword. If in the satyr we see a bestial lustful creature, does Hod's threatening him with a spear (reminiscent of Odin's sacrifice on Yggdrasil) represent his defeat of his own lower nature? Has Hod now achieved a state of psychological integration comparable with Odin and is now able to take on Baldr? Baldr enters Gevar's lands to claim Nanna. Nanna says to Baldr that "a god could not possibly wed a mortal, as the huge discrepancy in their natures would preclude any congruous union between them."[274] Hod, learning of Baldr's actions, decides to face him in a sea battle. On Baldr's side fight Odin, Thor and "battalions of deities." "Divine and human strength…[are] pitted together in the struggle."[275] Hod (clad in a sword-proof tunic) smashes aside the ranks of the gods, but it seems in vain. Inevitably the gods gain the upper hand, but just as all seems lost Hod cuts off Thor's hammer at the handle and the gods flee.[276] Hod then goes and spies on Baldr and the fugitives and whilst there learns the secret of Baldr's strength and invulnerability. His food is mixed with the venom of three snakes.[277] Eventually Hod comes face to face with Baldr and slays him with the sword taken from Miming.

---

271 Miming would seemingly be Mimir the owner of the well that both Heimdal and Odin sacrifice an ear and eye respectively at. That Miming possesses a sword with which to slay Baldr has correlations again with Freyr whose own sword was used by Surtr to slay him.

272 Draupnir?

273 One wonders if Hod waits nine nights…

274 Saxo Grammaticus, *The History*, 72.

275 Ibid.

276 Saxo states that they were not really gods and that name was given to them out of custom more than truth. One could well read this as the Christian Saxo belittling the Gods but remembrance of human defiance and defeat of deities is not alien to Indo-European myth. One prime example comes from the Iliad Book V, where Diomedes makes Aphrodite bleed and even faces up to Ares and Apollo.

277 I am assuming this has some reference to wisdom coming from the serpent of knowledge. Baldr is invulnerable because in partaking of the venom he is now an immortal, all-wise.

Odin (as in Snorri's account) approaches "seers" and "soothsayers"[278] with a view to finding vengeance for the death of his son. Rostiof[279] the Finn tells Odin he must father a child with Rinda, the daughter of the Ruthenian king. She will bear him a son to avenge Baldr. Odin visits the king in disguise, is made the king's general and single-handedly defeats an opposing army. After being rejected by Rinda several times, Odin touches her cheek with a stick carved with runic spells and makes her mad.[280] Later on, Odin puts on women's clothing[281] and pretends to be a female physician calling himself Vecha (prophetess/wizard). When Rinda takes ill, Odin prescribes a remedy that involves here being tied down onto a bed. The king agrees and once Odin has tied her down he rapes her.[282]

The aftermath of Baldr's murder sees the architect of this crime finally hunted down and held accountable for his deed. Disguising himself as a salmon in the waterfall of Franangr, Loki believes he can avoid capture, yet he reckons without Kvasir who, noticing the shape of a net burnt in Loki's fire, constructs such a device to capture him. Eventually, after dragging the net a few times over the riverbed, Loki realises he is in trouble and makes a leap for the sea. Unfortunately for him, Thor grabs hold of his tail and Loki is captured.[283]

> Now Loki was captured without quarter and taken to a certain cave. Then they took three stone slabs and set them on edge and knocked a hole in each slab. Then Loki's sons Vali and Nari or Narfi were fetched. The Æsir turned Vali into the form of a wolf and he tore his brother Narfi to pieces. Then the Æsir took his guts and bound Loki with them across the three stones...then Skadi got a poisonous snake and fixed it over him so that the poison would drip from the snake into his face...[284]

Two points interest me here. Fist Loki turns himself into a salmon...a salmon of wisdom? Second, the snake dripping poison into his face. In Saxo's version of Baldr's myth, the venom from the snake is a source of strength. For Loki, it is a source of distress, causing him to shake uncontrollably when his dedicated wife Sigyn has to empty the bowl that she holds above Loki's face. Maybe these

---

278 Saxo Grammaticus, *The History*, 76.
279 Davidson believes this Rostiof to be none other than Loki.
280 Odin is, of course, the god of madness and frenzy.
281 Obviously an allusion to the use of *seiðr*.
282 This bares some resemblance to the Gunnlod episode and the winning of the mead. It is also worth drawing attention again to Richard North's view that Odin himself bore Vali, Baldr's avenger.
283 Faulkes, *Edda*, 52.
284 Ibid.

examples are a clear indication of the nature of enlightenment...it is beneficial or harmful dependent solely on the character of the one seeking it. Loki as a salmon is captured from the water like Fenris fishing for salmon in Thrund...

For me, the myth of Baldr is essentially the story of human apotheosis. Whilst Titchenell sees in Loki a tragic hero attempting to raise humanity to godhood, I see Loki as a malicious, evil force, whose creation, man, is to suffer in order to attain godhood as its only chance at salvation.[285] This is the lesson Heimdall teaches us and is the vision that Odin is the first to achieve. If Baldr really does represent man's innocence destroyed (for whatever motive) by Loki, he also represents a new future for our people, one where the torment and suffering of transcendence is no longer needed and a new form of man is created. Loki (unrestrained ego) destroys that vision, that hope. Whether Odin knew this would be the case, we never really know, but seemingly Loki has won in this cycle. Odin's only hope is the return of his son in the next world following Ragnarok. What did Odin whisper in Baldr's ear? We have to come to our own conclusions on that, but the mounting doom we feel through the myth of Baldr leads us on inexorably to Ragnarok.

Ragnarok

Loki has one more nefarious deed to commit before he is captured and bound by the Æsir: the disruption of Ægir's banquet for the gods. In *Lokasenna*, we read how Loki, having caused uproar at the feast, is driven away but returns to cause mischief:

> I shall go in to Aegir's hall
> to see that sumble. Hate and evil,
> I will bring to the sons of Ases,
> and blend this venom into their mead.[286]

Titchenell[287] sees Loki, at this stage in the mythology, as the human ego grown arrogant, proud and selfish. Hence the reason Loki was driven from the feasting hall. However, within the hall sit the Elves. Titchenell believes Elves[288]

---

285 It is important to understand that I do not see apotheosis in Nietzschean "superman" terms as such, more an attempt to close the circle. In essence, man is attempting to go back to where he was, in union with the world, but we can never be truly "whole" again. We will always be a synthesis of individuation and the loss of the ego in the world spirit.
286 Chisholm, "Lokasenna," *The Eddas*, stanza 3.
287 Titchenell, *The Masks of Odin*, 211.
288 Ibid.

represent the highest form of humanity, one that has united their essence (*asmegir*) with their divine self. I think this is a reasonable interpretation. We could go further and say that the Elves clearly represent the Vanir (who we know are present in the hall from *Lokasenna* anyway) and the Æsir, human deities, who have now achieved godhood through the agency of Odin. Ægir is clearly symbolic of the cosmos itself, which, along with the earth, humanity has begun to achieve unity with. Loki clearly intends to sow hate and discord. He wishes to break this synthesis of man-earth-cosmos just as he originally separated man from his world. That he wishes to blend venom into the mead is interesting:

> I, Lopt, come thirsty to this hall
> from a long trip
> and bid the Æsir grant me
> one more drink of mead.
>
> Remember this Odin, that we blended
> our blood together in days of yore.
> You said you would not taste ale,
> unless it were born to both of us.[289]

In these two revealing stanzas, we discern that Loki is attempting to acquire a draft of the mead of inspiration. He claims that Odin promised not to taste of it unless Loki was granted a draft as well. If we see Loki and Odin as opposites, the unenlightened ego versus the enlightened ego, then we have a situation here where the darker side of this dual deity is attempting to gain access to the mead…with disastrous consequences.[290] Loki's aim is to poison the well of inspiration. He has already slain Baldr as he reminds Frigg in stanza 28[291] and now he intends to ensure that no more Einherjar can come forth, that no more humans can attain enlightenment. The painstaking effort Odin has gone to ensure the reunion of man with his world is now seriously compromised:

> You brewed ale Aegir,
> but you will never hold a sumble
> after this. Flames are playing
> on all that you won in her

---

289 Chisholm, "Lokasenna," *The Eddas*, stanzas 6-7.
290 Remember in the previous chapter how I drew attention to the fact that Loki turned himself into a salmon to escape the Æsir, the salmon being the oldest and wisest of all creatures…
291 "If you like, Frigg, I shall speak more of my harm-staves. I planned it such that you do not ride behind Baldr to the halls."

> and are burning on your back.[292]

Loki has now succeeded in his goal. He has sullied the mead of inspiration, destroyed the newly won synthesis, and murdered Baldr. Loki has ended whatever chance man had of peace in this cycle. Though he is hunted down and captured by the Æsir, the inevitable conclusion is that Loki has triumphed. He has achieved his goals and the gods will now go into the darkness and death of Ragnarok...

Ragnarok, "the twilight of the gods,"[293] is the end of the present cycle of existence. As mentioned previously,[294] if we take Odin, Thor and Loki to be representative of the triune deity of Hindu mythology then this is the time when the aspect of destruction in that deity comes to the fore. Translated as "god-origin,"[295] Ragnarok sees the primordial forces and the evil creations of Loki-Angrboda let loose to drive the cosmos into fire.

> He fills himself on the flesh of dead men, reddens the
> seat of the gods with gore. The sun turned swarthy in
> the following summers. The weather grew entirely
> shifty. Do you want to know more, or what?[296]

In stanza 42 of *Völuspá*, we see that Fenris is gorging himself on the souls he fishes out of the river Thund. Valhalla is drenched in their blood, Loki has tainted the mead, and no new "salmon" can come to wisdom. The hall is closed and the Einherjar wait to be lead out by Odin.

> Mim's sons play. The Meter will be set alight.
> Heimdall blows loudly on old Gjallarhorn
> with the horn aloft.
> Odin speaks with Mim's head.[297]

---

292 Chisholm, "Lokasenna," *The Eddas*, stanza 65.
293 The interpretation of the name popularised by Richard Wagner's opera *Götterdämmerung*.
294 Section one, "Loki and Creation."
295 Titchenell translates *ragna* as the plural of the Icelandic *regin* (god/ruler) and *rok* as ground, cause or origin, (*Masks of Odin*, 90).
296 Chisholm, "The Spae of the Volva," *The Eddas*, stanza 41.
297 Ibid., 46.

An Interpretation of Germanic Mythology

Yggdrasil is now aflame and the giants[298] go to war. Odin takes counsel with Mimir's head. With Loki now steering the ship bearing the fire giants to battle, Odin steps forth to face Fenris with the Einherjar:[299]

> Another sort of grief comes to Hlin
> when Odin fares to fight the wolf
> and the illustrious Bane of Beli to battle with Surt.
> Frigg's lover will then fall.
>
> Then comes the mighty son of Victory-father,
> Vithar, to vie with the deadly beast.
> He struck the heart of Hvethrung's[300] son
> and so his father was avenged.
>
> The fierce jaws of the earth encircling worm
> gaped from the hills at the holy sky.
> Then Odin's son meets the worm,
> Vithar's kinsman slays the warg.[301]

Fenris, the cosmic destroyer, slays Odin, but the Einherjar sacrifice themselves to prevent him destroying all creation and Vidar[302] slays the wolf. Thor, meanwhile, perishes after slaying Jormungandr.[303] He stumbles back *nine* steps and falls. Finally, Surtr sets all the cosmos afire and the cycle is over...

To be reborn anew:

> She sees another rise up, earth from the ocean,
> all agreen. Torrents flow
> and the eagle flies above

---

298 Lindow believes Mim's sons are the Æsir (*Norse Mythology*, 231).
299 "Interestingly enough the number of warriors issuing forth from Valhalla is 432,000, 800 men each coming out of Valhalla's 540 doors. This coincides exactly with the number of years of the Kali Yuga in Vedic lore, the time of "great sin" or the end time," (Grigsby, *Beowulf and Grendel*, 160).
300 Loki.
301 Chisholm, "The Spae of the Volva," *The Eddas*, stanzas 53-55.
302 Georges Dumézil saw Vidar as symbolic of space. Vertically with his hand on Fenris' upper jaw and his foot on his lower, and horizontally by means of his shoe (Lindow, *Norse Mythology*, 314).
303 Chisholm believes Jormungandr represents the horizontal to Yggdrasil's vertical, seemingly a take on Dumézil's theory (Chisholm, *The Eddas*, 15).

> scanning the fells and hunting fish.[304]

Not all the gods die in Ragnarok. Three pairs of brothers survive, Thor's sons Magni and Modi, Odin's sons Vidar and Vali and Hod and Baldr. Both Baldr and Hod shall live in "Hropt's"[305] victory hall (Valhalla). From Snorri[306] we also learn that two humans, a man and women called Life and Leifthrasir, survive Ragnarok. They hide themselves, according to *Vafþrúðnismál*[307] in "Hoddmimir's forest." Hodd[308] means "treasure" or "gold" whilst Mimir is obviously a reference to the giant himself. So Baldr, the human apotheosis, returns from the halls of the dead to lead the next generation of humans in the new cycle. One other god survives Ragnarok...Hœnir. We learn that this god, symbolic of the silence of contemplation, will handle the "lot wood," presumably runes. It is interesting that Hœnir is the only one not to be in a pair of surviving deities. Will he play the role of conscience just as he did during the creation of man in the previous cycle? The final two stanzas of *Völuspá* contain one mystery and one chilling statement:

> Then comes the strong one, to the doom of the gods,
> the awesome one from above who rules all.[309]

Who the *völva* is referring to here remains a mystery. It is often argued that this is a later Christian intrusion.[310] This may be plausible, but given that the gods did not create our universe and the giants are its underlying primal laws, but not creators, one wonders...[311]

> The dark drake comes flying,
> the flashing viper from under Nitha-Fells
> She sees Nithogg carrying corpses in his feathers
> as he flies over the valley. Now she shall sink down.[312]

---

304 Chisholm, "The Spae of the Volva," *The Eddas*, stanza 59.
305 Odin.
306 Faulkes, *Edda*, 57.
307 "Lif and Lifthrasir, they shall hide Hoddmimir in the woods. They shall have the morning dews as their meat. So shall mankind be nourished."
308 Lindow, *Norse Mythology*, 179.
309 Chisholm, "The Spae of the Volva," *The Eddas*, stanza 65.
310 Lindow, *Norse Mythology*, 318.
311 The idea of one primary deity is not alien to Indo-European thought. Brahman, in some Hindu sects, is seen as the all powerful deity of which all others are aspects. Plato and Aristotle believed in one primary god and Neo-Platonic belief was based on the theory of emanationism.
312 Chisholm, "The Spae of the Volva," *The Eddas*, stanza 66.

The seeds of the next destruction are already sown in the new creation. Do we see evolution in the new world? Is Baldr a better type of god-man? Are we seeing a renewal of the Odin concept? Do we see progress but within a cycle, like a DNA double helix spiralling upwards? Whatever we make of these stanzas there is one particular piece I find moving in *Völuspá*, stanza 61:

> They will again find the wondrous
> gold chess pieces in the grass,
> those they had owned in the days of yore.[313]

One pictures the next generation of gods quietly setting up the board once again and carefully placing the pieces. It is an old game. How old, no one knows, but the gods have a feeling...this has all been done before. Over their shoulders the shades of their forefathers look on. It is a new dawn and a new game. The dice roll...

Conclusion

> *Ever would Odin on earth wander weighed with wisdom, woe foreknowing, the lord of lords and beleaguered gods, his seed sowing, sire of heroes.*[314]
>
> —J.R.R. Tolkien

We come to the end of my essay. My goal was simply to provide some of my insight into the Eddas as I view them at my present level of comprehension. I am not sure I have answered my question about the nature of the messages contained within as objective and/or subjective but I know, from writing this, that I have come to some level of understanding applicable for me. Whether this meets with the agreement of others is nothing I can concern myself over. As the Stoic[315] philosopher Epictetus[316] wrote; "he not only wants to perform well, he wants to be well-received—and the latter lies outside his control." At least I hope to have provided something of interest for thought, even if it is only criticism of the piece!

---

313 Ibid., stanza 61.
314 Tolkien, *The Legend of Sigurd and Gudrun*, 65.
315 Stoicism is a philosophical system first outlined by Zeno whose ethical stance is one of meeting life with a sense of virtue and dignity in behaviour.
316 Epictetus was a Greek Stoic who ran a school at Nicopolis in the early 2nd Century AD.

It is quite probable that some will perceive my take on Germanic mythology as bleak and that my view of life is somewhat depressing. I think nothing could be further from the truth. Perhaps what has attracted me to the ways of our ancestors the most is the *life-affirming* quality of their worldview. Our ancestors did not fear life. They did not fear to accept it *for what it is*. In stanza 3 of *Völuspá*, we read the following:

> It was in the earliest times that Ymir dwelled.
> Neither sand nor sea, nor cold waves, nor earth
> were to be found. There was neither heaven above,
> nor grass anywhere, there was nothing but Ginnungagap.[317]

James Allen Chisholm, in his translation of *Völuspá*, has this to say about Ginnungagap:

> A magically charged cosmic void called "Ginnungagap" existed before creation. It may have been that the magical stuff of this gap was Ginn...The noun ginnung can mean deceit, trickery or illusion. The verb ginna means to delude or to intoxicate. In Swedish, the verb ginna can mean both to deceive and to perform magic. The title of the first part of the Prose Edda is *Gylfaginning*, which means the deluding of Gylfi. The gunnungar is the magical stuff of the world, the illusion that is the fabric of human consciousness. Human society operates by accepting shared illusions (cultural conceptual constructs) as truths...It is especially the job of the Ginnregin (Odin, Vili, and Ve) to understand the world's mysteries and to see beyond the illusions and handle the magical essence of the universe.[318]

This sense of a woven illusion was one shared by Nietzsche in which he used the Greek deities Apollo and Dionysus to represent different qualities, where Dionysus represents the primal power in which unity for man is the destruction of ego through intoxication and Apollo represented the power of illusion protecting man from nature but *without denying its true nature*. It is in this sense that I regard Heimdall as a deity that allowed man to come to terms with *his origin* and what *he was*, not to deny it or to lie about it, not to deny his true self, but to accept it and work to improve it. There are no "and they all lived happily ever afters" in our mythology. There are no gods who will hold your hands through life, although they may aid those willing to aid themselves. Our

---

317 Chisholm, *The Eddas*.
318 Chisholm, *The Eddas*, 12.

ancestors valued self-reliance, perseverance and honour. This is what Tolkien called the "spirit of courage," a sense of accepting life as it is and moulding it on our own terms. To fail is not to fail at a goal, it is not having goals to begin with. Our forefathers lived in a harsh, unforgiving environment. In many ways, their mythology reflects that reality. Their honour rested in how they approached life. I believe those characteristics mean as much today as they did in our ancestors' time. We carry their legacy, just as we carry the gift given to us by Heimdall, the ability to perceive the possibility of good in the bad and to turn a situation to our advantage. We may be an aberration in the cosmic scheme of things, but we are not without purpose nor ability. If we do, in part, owe what makes us human to such a one as Loki it is important to remember that we do not owe to him our choices. We are our own selves. It is this mistake on Loki's part that he has attempted to rectify in the cycle of our mythology.

As a people we look to the future. Heimdall, Odin, Thor and the other Æsir have given us the opportunity, but it is solely down to us, and us alone, what we make of it.

> Perched on the isthmus of a middle state, A being darkly wise and rudely great...He hangs between, in doubt to act or rest, in doubt to deem himself a god or beast...Sole judge of truth, in endless error hurled, the glory, jest and riddle of the world.[319]

---

[319] From Alexander Pope's *Essay on Man*, quoted on page 139 of Mary Midgley's *Myths We Live By* (New York: Routledge, 2004).

Book Reviews and Interviews

I speak to, and will be heard by, all those oppositional souls to the draconian duplicity of Modernity. As an inspired act of the Gods, I am I; and those who recognize things 'arcane' as *advanced*, will hear my bellow resound in their Souls. And I shall festoon my Heart with these few; and I, and We, shall lead —un-named—the league of tomorrow to its ultimate goal.

—K.S.

The Decline of the West [Der Untergang des Abendlandes]: Volume I, Form and Actuality and Volume II, Perspectives of World History
By Oswald Spengler
Translated by Charles F. Atkinson
London: George, Allen & Unwin Ltd., 1926
925 pages

Reviewed by Ben McGarr

Looking around for prophecies and reassurances in the form of scripture or Sibylline Books is not particularly a feature of the Northern tradition, but modern revivalists may at least be curious to hear that many of their hopes and ambitions find some precursors in the writings of a German philosopher immediately following the Great War, Oswald Spengler. While not fully 'of us,' Spengler put his insightful finger right on many of the urges at work behind the contemporary rebirth of Heathenry, and almost went as far as to predict its inevitability (though he did not *quite* realize it as such) against the backdrop of what might crudely be called 'historical laws.' The wary would be right to question this assertion—we've heard it all before; absolute faith in the unstoppable and deeply necessary nature of the historical movement they represented drove the actions of Lenin and Trotsky, and still inspire many more subtly dangerous ideological descendants of Karl Marx today, as well as, conversely, Hitler and the National Socialists. Why should we pay any more attention to this other prophet, crying in the wilderness?

The short answer is to read the book.[1] A longer one is somewhat beyond me, for one of its major points would have to be the manner in which Spengler towers intellectually over his would-be rivals and I readily admit to lacking the philosophical training and erudition (or simply instinct?) to adequately communicate its nature, never mind offer a worthy critique. This thinker really goes deep into human nature and beyond[2] in the interests of demonstrating the soundness of his more secondary conclusions. For the uninitiated, these aetiological forays are rather hard reading, but the cumulative effect of them, combined with the wealth of real life examples offered in illustration, do help the reader to absorb the author's main thrusts, as he leads us on by the hand to the summit of understanding. To take that metaphor a little further, the elation

---

1 Never has this been easier—two PDF documents (in several major languages) are available for free download at: http://www.scribd.com
2 Amazing as it may seem until one reads the text for oneself and sees how freely the thought process flows, Spengler dares to discuss the cognition and instincts of the animal, and even plant worlds, finding much of relevance there to the human historical plane...

Illustration 1: Volume I's cover.

accompanying this enlightenment might well be compared to the sensation of having broken the cloud cover upon scaling some lofty peak, for the 'view' earned is indeed a breathtaking one. I concede I occasionally found myself a little lost, and flipped ahead, to then realize that the foundation arguments deserved the effort of struggling through them, for the sake of the impressive virtuosities of thought built upon them later. There is nothing superfluous in this book, and patience will be fully rewarded with fuller insight and appreciation of its creator's reasoning. For another thing, Spengler's own tastes and partisanships are never too overpoweringly thrust into the foreground, more hinted at by inference, and he does not stoop to propose any detailed political programme. Those of all political dispositions might find something useful to take away with them here.

Published just prior to the national humiliation of 1918, *Der Untergang Des Abendlands* has a correspondingly gloomy title. One might expect before even getting beyond the cover that Oswald Spengler had thought to 'cash in' on the apocalyptic mood of the more reactionary part of his countrymen, by cataloguing the treasons of the reform parties that had brought the Kaiserreich to its collapse and fostered the growing sociopolitical chaos of his day, and possibly by charting a way out of the miasma as might flatter those nostalgic for the traditional certainties of the *Ancien Régime*—but no, this is no mere work of political pornography. Spengler had been contemplating its contents since long before the Great War—it was no spontaneous reaction to German defeat. Its origins are more to be found in the uneasy Silver Age, where the élites still enjoyed inherited privilege but were aware enough of their loss of control over both social trends and the new economy, to see that they were living on borrowed time. Living on the edge of an epoch often sharpens the historical sense and this perhaps goes some way to answering the question as to why this work appeared exactly when it did. That nothing of the sort was seen in the literature of the victorious allies might be apportioned to the misplaced euphoria of the time, the deceptive over-confidence of victory having blinded them to the transience of their ascendance.

Spengler's *magnum opus* is not a very large book, easily dwarfed by the dense *Das Kapital* or the repetitive *Mein Kampf*, but its two respectable volumes contain such detailed and complex argument that suitable effort is demanded of the reader who would master its contents. The explanation of the history of the entire Earth is its aim and a vast array of facts is necessarily pulled into play. But Spengler's thrust is more in the conclusions he draws from these, which in their turn are put to work in discovering the essence of world history as the birth, floruit, interaction *and death* of Great Cultures, their boiled-down internal essence and lifespan. That interwar Germany should have received some enlightenment as to its circumstances became almost incidental in the light of this aim.

Moving on to actually describe what it is that Oswald Spengler does, the central concept is that of his analysis of history, of 'destiny' even, as he does not shrink from naming it. He divides the world into great Cultures, of similar 'life history' as organisms, but 'born' at different times and with highly individual, and often contradictory, 'souls.' The modern Heathen will find much to nod to himself at in this thinker's exploration of the antagonism between the young Faustian and older Magian souls (respectively of the Western European and Middle Eastern Cultures), especially evinced in the European experience with and response to Christianity.

Steering clear of crass simplistic notions of this time-proved religion as one of 'desert Semites' which are all too often blurted out by our less subtle fellows, Spengler draws out the common features of the Byzantine, Persian and Islamic worldviews as part of one wider more fundamental 'Magian' soul-expression, with its 'cosmic cavern,' focus on the Word and idea as 'magical/divine substance,' and societal model of the 'great Consensus.' In contradistinction, he depicts our Faustian Culture as one in which the feel for infinity, historicity, and life as a dynamic interplay of forces is key. Architectural and geopolitical manifestations of this soul have both involved a vigorous striving upward and outward, from the imperialism that conquered half the world, to the soaring spires and arches and flying buttresses of our mediaeval cathedrals, to modern astronomy and the space race itself. Yes, despite the book's title, there is much in here to uplift.

More important than these character sketches of the ten or so great Cultures that have inhabited this globe, Spengler has observed and charted their common lifespan, discovering shared phases of development matching even in relative length. Though their peculiar 'prime symbols' adapt its realization, each Culture is seen to go through an almost regularly spaced series of development.

> [Corresponding phases] occur in exactly the same relative positions in their respective Cultures, and therefore possess exactly equivalent importance.[3]

Our own Faustian is the youngest he deals with (except Russia's, which he saw as yet to fully express itself beyond a few hints as to the nature of its 'prime symbol'),[4] and thus has yet to enter the later phases, or rather, in our time stands right on the edge of the coming age. Consequently, by comparison with the ancient Egyptian, Classical,[5] Chinese, Indian and Magian 'biographies,' some light can be thrown onto our own future, at least in terms of its broader tendencies. He does not omit to warn, however, that a culture is not immortal, even before it reaches maturity or advanced age, and offers the Meso-American example to demonstrate the potential risks of utter annihilation a great culture can face from without.

Most fascinating for the readers of this journal is Spengler's sketch of the future of the Faustian world, *our* world, in the religious realm. Working from analogy with the corresponding (in his own terminology 'contemporary') life-stages of the earlier Great Cultures, his predictions for our coming era of 'Caesarism' include a *Second Religiousness*, born from the dissatisfaction of our recent past's extreme secularism and an inability to keep up on a societal level with the advances made

---

3 Spengler, vol. I, 112.
4 It is interesting to consider whether or not *others* have come into being or first made themselves known to the remaining world in the decades since this was penned in the First World War Germany.
5 Also termed 'Apollonian' by Spengler, but in a wider sense than Nietzsche's more familiar usage.

in the sciences. What he meant by this he explained as a return to motifs of a particular Culture's 'springtime' or early youth, which for Faustian Man he dates to around the Ninth and Tenth Centuries AD. His own admittedly tentative attempt to hazard a guess at what concrete form this would take for *us* was one rather off-putting to the heathen thinker of our own day: Adventism?!

> It is perhaps possible for us to make some guess already as to these forms, which (it is self-evident) must lead back to certain elements of Gothic Christianity. But be this as it may, what is quite certain is that they will not be the product of any literary taste for Late-Indian or Late-Chinese speculation, but something of the type, for example, of Adventism and suchlike sects.[6]

An alternative he neglected to explore is quite simple to outline, and he had made nigh on all the groundwork for this conclusion in the same work. Considering the Germanic peoples of the early Faustian period, Spengler had lavished fit praise on the late Heathen Norse articulation of spirituality found in the Poetic Edda. He saw this as fully equal a rival to the external interference that came at this time from the Magian Culture and supposed that had our forefathers been better isolated from such older worlds, this expression of the Northern Soul had more than sufficient potential to provide the religious backbone of a wholly Faustian 'Mediaeval' civilization. Just as he charts our slow struggle against the mathematical, artistic, scientific, legal and financial inheritance[7] of the Classical Culture of Greece and Rome, so we might now suppose the time is at hand to finally take the last steps in shrugging off the other foreign inheritance we were lumbered with in our youth – that of Christianity itself.

Here Spengler articulates the vitality of the Northern tradition, subconsciously putting a return to it as a welcome alternative to the dreary 'Adventism' proposed above:

> Far apart as may seem the Christian hymnology of the south and the Eddas of the still heathen north, they are alike in the implicit space-endlessness of prosody, rhythmic syntax and imagery. Read the *Dies Irae* together with the *Voluspa*, which is little earlier; there is the same adamantine will to overcome and break all resistances of the visible. No rhythm ever imagined radiates immensities of space and distance as the old Northern does.

---

6 Spengler, vol. II, 311.
7 And Spengler has a great deal of note to say on these spheres of human endeavor and self expression…

> Olympus rests on the homely Greek soil, the Paradise of the Fathers is a magic garden somewhere in the Universe, but Valhalla is nowhere. Lost in the limitless, it appears with its inharmonious gods and heroes the supreme symbol of solitude. Siegfried, Parzeval, Tristan, Hamlet, Faust are the loneliest heroes in all the Cultures. Read the wondrous awakening of the inner life in Wolfram's Parzeval. The longing for the woods, the mysterious compassion, the ineffable sense of forsakenness it is all Faustian and only Faustian. Every one of us knows it. The motive returns with all its profundity in the Easter scene of Faust I:
>
> > *"A longing pure and not to be described*
> > *drove me to wander over woods and fields,*
> > *and in a mist of hot abundant tears*
> > *I felt a world arise and live for me."*
>
> Of this world-experience neither Apollonian nor Magian man, neither Homer nor the Gospels, knows anything whatever.[8]

With such a resource lying dusty and unused in our metaphysical attic, who now can content themselves with a return to yet another tired old rehash of the Magian borrowing?!

Spengler indeed mentions that such a reclamation of ancient cultural property is not unknown in our past, as for instance in the German response to the Reformation:

> But in the place of the mythic light-world, whose helpful nearness the faith of the common people could not, after all, forgo, there rose again out of longburied depths an element of ancient German myth. It came so stealthily that even to-day its true significance is not yet realized. The expressions "folktale" and "popular custom" are inadequate: it is a true Myth that inheres in the firm belief in dwarfs, bogies, nixies, house-sprites, and sweeping clouds of the disembodied, and a true Cult that is seen in the rites, offerings, and conjurings that are still practised with a pious awe. In Germany, at any rate, the Saga took the place, unperceived, of the Mary-myth: Mary was now called Frau Holde, and where once the saints had stood, appeared the faithful

---

8 Spengler, vol. I, 185-186.

Eckart.[9]

And Spengler insightfully points out here the fact that this trajectory in Western spirituality has far from reached its end...

Using the analytical tool of his Prime Symbol—the most boiled-down essence of a great Culture's worldview—Spengler explores what cultural expressions are more fitting for a civilisation, in distinction to those that are more properly to be considered a contamination from without. Spengler asserts that a Culture is quite capable at arriving at its own stage of maturity with all the facets of life that involves, without external input, inferring the undesirability and ultimate indurability of significant borrowing and impositions from alien sources. He goes on to demonstrate how foreign memes—to use an up to date expression[10]—are neutralized and distorted to eventually comprise quite a different set of ideas than the import did in its 'native' Culture. Christianity is the prime example of such borrowing by the early Faustian world from the Magian, and my colleague Chris Plaisance will be elaborating on the 'naturalisation' process it went through in his conclusion to this volume of our journal. The Magian and Faustian Cultures both inherited some of the dress and conceptual repertoire of their Classical predecessor, and Spengler follows the history of both in shrugging off that which was fundamentally unnatural to it. It might be taken from this that 'Destiny is on our side when we reject the borrowings of our forebears and concentrate on that which fundamentally *suits* us...

On a general bibliophilic note, this book belongs in that select category of written works wherein, regardless of topic, the prose is a sheer delight to read in and of itself. We have much to be grateful to Charles Francis Atkinson for, having translated Spengler into English with such consummate skill and digression. Atkinson's short and unobtrusive footnotes provide the occasional glimpse of the original German beneath and offer welcome indications of where the interested reader should go to chase up Spengler's allusions to obscure historical matters, and the odd extra illustrative example or update is provided in support of the author's arguments. In terms of raw factual content, the book lives up to the expectations aroused by so broad and ambitious a subject as world history, and I certainly learnt a great deal on matters hitherto little explored by myself, including higher mathematics, later Greek history and the works and thoughts of Goethe. I doubt anyone would not find something to pique his curiosity in this

---

9   Spengler, vol. II, 299.
10 A behavioral counterpart of the gene, likewise susceptible to natural selection of sorts (religion being a good example). The term was first coined by Richard Dawkins in his 1976 book *The Selfish Gene*.

Illustration 2: The author, Oswald Spengler.

work, inspiring further research into subjects so far neglected in their studies.

Spengler would hardly have welcomed comparison with the likes of Nostradamus, but it deserves passing mention that he as good as predicted plastic money back in 1918, as well as anticipated the present day interest in intellectual property rights, thereby demonstrating that he was at least 'on to something' to men of our time wondering if his works are still valid. These trivial facts may well have been 'on the cards' for some time, and not too far beyond the prescient of his day, but Spengler's distinction from the common or garden seer lies in his methodology: He 'proved' the inevitability of these developments not by gazing into crystal balls or merely extrapolating current trends, but by the internal logic of his vision of the 'Prime Symbols' unique to each culture, which must manifest itself in all facets of the civilisation its bearers create. More impressive are his socio-political forecasts, often as chillingly inhuman as Orwell's and likewise becoming ever more startlingly correct with each passing year. Unlike *1984* however, *The Decline of the West* holds its horses and keeps its feet rather more on the ground, dealing with the rise of plutocracy hand in hand with intellectual liberalism, in other words foreshadowing the 'Soft Totalitarianism' seen growing today. The monolithic political order of Orwell's cautionary tale is thus replaced with a far more subtle monopolisation of power, less obviously unappealing on the surface than Big Brother, but ultimately as ruthless and all-encompassing.[11] For those with an interest in political theory versus actuality, Spengler's analysis of the alliance between big money and socially 'progressive' neo-Marxist movements is required reading. For an Englishman to see the so-called 'Labour' Party of 2009 so accurately described in 1918 is striking to say the least:

> In the beginning the leading and the apparatus come into existence for the sake of the program. Then they are held on to defensively by their incumbents for the sake of power and booty as is already universally the case to-day, for thousands in every country live on the party and the offices and functions that it distributes. Lastly the program vanishes from memory, and the organization works for its own sake alone.[12]

Again, our author takes their reasoning far deeper than the familiar efforts of our modern sociological and political schools (which themselves should form more the *object* of such study than the subject), right back down to human nature at its very core.

---

11 It should be noted that he rules out nothing of the sort for our *coming* age.
12 Spengler, vol. II, 452.

As for the 'life' of this work since its 1918 publication, I have refrained from consulting secondary works in order to let first the book stand by itself before me, lest my impressions be falsely coloured and my attention drawn to aspects that do not shine forth themselves. I might class my approach as a testing of the book's intrinsic worth for all times, rather than evaluation of it as a historical document. There is some interest, however in the continuation of Spengler's theme by Twentieth Century Russian 'Eurasianists': I had read Lev Nikolaevich Gumilyov and Prince Trubetskoy several years prior to *The Decline of the West* and was surprised to see the same kind of approach, and though little credit is given their German predecessor, this quasi-political search for a third way between Capitalism and Marxism is probably the only significant movement to have taken much notice of Spengler's ideas, if indeed we are not dealing here with an independent, convergent, development. Gumilyov certainly goes a step further than Spengler in the attempt to discover the 'physiology' at work behind the regular cultural 'life stages' he observed. To this end, the Russian historian evolved his unique concept of *'passionarnost'* as the energy prompting the blossoming of new cultures—a synthesis of Spengler's less concrete notions of Form, Symbol and Blood. Lev Nikolaevich's struggle to find an astronomical explanation for the apparently random appearance of new Superethnoses on the Earth's surface (invoking the revolution of the Milky Way itself) had earlier received some brief attention from Spengler himself:

> [Traditional historiography] limits possible causal connexions, in the first place, to those which work out their entire course on the earth's surface; but this immediately excludes all great cosmic relations between earthly life-phenomena and the events of the solar system and the stellar universe, and assumes the impossible postulate that the exterior face of the earth-ball is a completely insulated region of natural phenomena.[13]

Gumilyov also extend the scheme to the north, taking in the peoples of the Great Steppe,[14] as well as more insignificant peoples elsewhere, thus increasing considerably the number of 'cultures,' or 'superethnoses' in his terms, well beyond the ten or so proposed by Spengler for the entire duration of human history. Where the German had seen only ahistorical irrelevance, the Russian applied Spenglerian concepts to the internal history of the Scytho-Sarmations, Huns,

---

13 Ibid., 31.
14 His main works to outline and make use of these ideas are indeed to be found in his popular *Steppe Trilogy*, comprising *The Hunnu* 1960, *The Ancient Turks* 1967, and *In search of the Imaginary Kingdom* 1970. The more theoretical work *Ethnogenesis and the Earth's Biosphere*, 1979, has been translated into English and is available online at: http://gumilevica.kulichki.net/English/index.html

Turks and Mongols. Where both find full concord, however, is in the treatment of Russia herself, both viewing that world within a world as something peculiar to itself, younger than, and borrowing much from, the Faustian/'Romano-Germanic' West, only to periodically rub off these foreign accretions as it refinds its own unique (in Spengler's words) *soul*.

The US writer Francis Parker Yockey has also built on Spengler's foundation work and his book *Imperium* may be seen as a continuation of where our author left off. Or at least so I am *told*; adequate discussion of this point is a further book review down the line. It can at least be said that Yockey's 1948 work provides a valuable example of an effort to tie in the forecasts of this 'Philosopher of the Twentieth Century' (Yockey's words for his mentor) to subsequent events, as well as identify areas in which Spenglerian concepts may hold less water, or simply be transformed from the Spenglerian vision thereof, due to the 'moving of the goalposts' that has accompanied the continuing acceleration of globalism and technological and economical intensification. Like Gumilyov, this American writer attempts to go beyond Spengler in proposing means to prevent the 'pathology' that kills a Great Culture. For this, the reader can decide for himself whether or not these 'disciples' have succeeded in eliminating one of their master's less palatable truths. Both certainly suffered for their work—the Russian left to stew in academic limbo most of his life, and the American even reaching martyrdom. Earlier still, Alfred Rosenberg's *Myth of the Twentieth Century* could also be seen as following Spengler in style, if possibly more self-consciously than the others. The most striking thing I took with me from Rosenberg (again, I had came across this derivatory work before the origin) was his refutation of the 'family' as the seed of the state rather than the warrior bands of the ancient tribes' young braves. On reading Spengler, this same notion was met with decades before:

> A people "in condition" is originally a band warriorhood, a deep and intimately felt community of men fit for arms. State is the affair of man, it is Care for the preservation of the whole...[15]

More 'liberal' thinkers have tended to give Spengler a wide berth, mindful no doubt of his all too clear insight into their own flaws, especially in his critique of the tacit modern alliance of Money and Ideology, as well as his heretical refutation of their hallowed Universalism. Indeed, Spengler's uncovering of the scandalous interrelation and tacit collaboration between these two seemingly polarized interests was to me one of the more impressive feats contained in the work as a whole, and one immensely significant to our times, wrapped up in this

---

15 Spengler, vol. II, 362.

author's own pithy style:

> [There are] two tendencies which emerge out...along with abstract concepts abstract Money...appear as political forces. The two are inwardly cognate and inseparable the old opposition between priest and noble continued, acute as ever, in the bourgeois atmosphere and the city framework. Of the two, moreover, it is the Money that, as pure fact, shows itself unconditionally superior to the ideal truths, which so far as the fact-world is concerned exist...only as catchwords, as means. If by "democracy" we mean the form which the Third Estate as such wishes to impart to public life as a whole, it must be concluded that democracy and plutocracy are the same thing under the two aspects of wish and actuality, theory and practice, knowing and doing. It is the tragic comedy of the 'world-improvers' and freedom-teachers' desperate fight against money that they arc ipso facto assisting money to be effective. Respect for the big number expressed in the principles of equality for all, natural rights, and universal suffrage...are ideals, but in actuality the freedom of public opinion involves the preparation of public opinion, which costs money; and the freedom of the press brings with it the question of possession of the press, which again is a matter of money; and with the franchise comes electioneering, in which he who pays the piper calls the tune. The representatives of the ideas look at one side only, while the representatives of money operate with the other. The concepts of Liberalism and Socialism are set in effective motion only by money.[16]

In ending, I do not offer *The Decline Of The West* merely as a pat-on-the-back to modern Heathen thinkers. I would hope that serious note be taken of the call to action and resolution contained in its message, as well as of the dangers facing us at this pivotal time in world history. Alain de Benoist has already cautioned us of the potential folly of millenarian hopes for a coming grand shift to a new religiousness, perhaps echoing Spenglerian thought, but I am veering a little more towards the optimistic viewpoint. I was even before I read Spengler, given the fact that sufficient time has elapsed since 1968 to allow for a new generation to put matters on their heads once more. De Benoist himself is wise enough to rule nothing out in the long run, even if his realism then forces him to backtrack somewhat:

> Admittedly, in the long run, human history is by definition

---

16 Spengler, vol. I, 402.

always open. But as regards the foreseeable future, I personally tend to share Gauchet's opinion that nothing allows us to foresee a "return of religion" in the phenomena most commonly alleged today as heralding such a possibility.[17]

He goes on to furnish a timely warning to premature triumphalists of the Heathen milieu as to the fact that the *old foe* has many an unexpected twist in its tail to surprise and confound us with yet:

> Ernest Renan, in an article on "The Religious future of Modern Societies" published in 1860, said that Christianity is "susceptible to infinite transformations."[18]

Our fellows would do very well to keep de Benoist's concerns fully in mind. I however, would give the last word rightly to old Oswald himself:

> History, however, teaches that doubt as to belief leads to knowledge, and doubt as to knowledge (after a period of critical optimism) back again to belief.[19]

> Money, too, is [now] at the end of its success, and the last conflict is at hand in which the Civilization receives its conclusive form—the conflict *between* money and blood.[20]

> In these conditions [of rampant plutocracy] so much of old and great traditions as remains, so much of historical "fitness" and experience as has got into the blood of the twentieth century nations, acquires an unequalled potency. For us creative piety, or (to use a more fundamental term) the pulse that has come down to us from first origins, adheres only to forms that are older than the Revolution and Napoleon, forms which grew and were not made. Every remnant of them, however tiny, that has kept itself alive in the being of any self-contained minority whatever will before long rise to incalculable values and bring about historical effects which no one yet imagines to be possible…To be "in condition" is everything. It falls to us to live in the most trying times known to the history of a great Culture. The last race to

---

17 Alain de Benoist. "Qu'est-ce qu'une religion?" trans. Ben McGarr (lecture, meeting, Paris, January 30, 2005).
18 Ibid.
19 Spengler, vol. II, 269.
20 Ibid., 506.

keep its form, the last living tradition, the last leaders who have both at their back, will pass through and onward, victors.[21]

Belief in program was the mark and the glory of our grandfathers; in our grandsons it will be a proof of provincialism. In its place is developing even now the seed of a new resigned piety, sprung from tortured conscience and spiritual hunger, whose task will be to found a new Hither-side that looks for secrets instead of steel-bright concepts and in the end will find them in the deeps of the "Second Religiousness."[22]

---

21 Ibid., 431.
22 Ibid., 455.

New Lands, New Faith: Christianity and the Vinland Voyages in Medieval Icelandic Manuscripts
By Vésteinn Ólason
Reykjavík: Árni Magnússon Institute, 2000
29 pages

Reviewed by Asseling

Vésteinn Ólason's *New Lands, New Faith: Christianity and the Vinland Voyages in Medieval Icelandic Manuscripts*, was published in 2000 as a guidebook to an exhibit of the same name at the Árni Magnússon Institute in Reykjavík. Both exhibition and book mark the 1000 year anniversary of Christian Iceland, the discovery of Vinland by Icelandic seafarers, and the commencement of Iceland's outstanding literary tradition. The purpose of Ólason's book is to act as a guide to the Institute's exhibit, and to provide the reader with a concise survey of major Icelandic manuscripts and scribes, particularly those detailing the conversion of Iceland and the discovery of Vinland.

Ólason largely discusses the work and influence of Ari Þorgilsson (1067-1148), primarily centering his text on the *Íslendingabók*, but also includes five notes on other important manuscripts such as the *Book of Haukur,* the *Book of Kálfalækur*, the *Book of Skálholt*, the *Book of Flatey*, Snorri Sturluson's *Prose Edda*, and the Melsteð *Edda*. Adam of Bremen's *Gesta Hammaburgensis ecclesiae pontificum*, and the 1969 *Vinlandspúnkta* by Halldór Laxness are also among Ólason's sources. Laxness' book is the only modern source used, and it is included to highlight the significance of Ari's writing style, avant-garde within its historical context, describing it as untainted by "fairy tales and religious verbosity." Indeed, Ólason does well to elaborate on the style that often distinguished Icelandic scribes from their Continental counterparts who rarely refrained from inserting Christian overtones in originally non-religious texts. Ólason's praise of Ari is tasteful and quite fitting considering the book was written in celebration of a millennium of Icelandic book culture. Yet, at the same time, Ólason makes clear that he is providing an objective survey, careful not to over glorify the scribes mentioned. Problems concerning Icelandic manuscripts as accurate historical sources are discussed, more specifically the mention of Ari's omissions of certain important details. Ólason treats the omission with care, and provides possible explanations for them. He likewise does not overstate the historical accuracy of all Icelandic manuscripts, mentioning narratives in which the author draws upon "fairy tales" rather than fact, or where the information is tainted by the desire to present a certain view of history. Though Ólason does not provide specific examples of tainted narratives, he does exclude Ari as one of the guilty authors.

The only point at which Ólason strays from a factual discussion of the subject is during his brief mention of the geographic location of Vinland and the extent of Norse exploration of North America, where he presents the theory that Norse explorers reached the St. Lawrence as archaeologically supported fact, rather than as speculation. While this detail has little to do with Icelandic manuscripts, it does detract slightly from the overall impression of the book as an unbiased, factual survey.

Ólason succeeds in providing a concise, accessible guide to major Icelandic manuscripts and scribes. The book is a recommendable springboard for students who wish to delve further into the subjects of Icelandic and medieval book history. Ólason's book is of interest to students of book history not only because of the valuable information it provides, but because it builds an understanding of the unique importance of book culture in both medieval and modern Iceland. Its importance is particularly demonstrated by the inclusion of Melsteð's *Edda*, which expresses Icelanders' continued appreciation of Icelandic manuscripts as displays of Iceland's unique book culture, and the intrinsic connection between that culture and the foundation and development of the nation itself.

Primordial Traditions Compendium 2009
Edited by Gwendolyn Toynton
Oxford, UK: Twin Serpents Limited, 2009
235 pages

Review by Juleigh Howard Hobson

> The Primordial Tradition describes a system of spiritual thought and metaphysical truth that overarches all the other religious and esoteric traditions.
> —*Primordial Traditions Compendium 2009*

The *Primordial Traditions Compendium 2009* contains the best of the essays and articles published in *Primordial Traditions* from 2005 through 2008.

Ranging, as it does, the full gamut of authentic religious metaphysics—from Occultism to Islam, from Paganism to Hinduism—the compendium offers up much wisdom of interest to Asatruar, Odinists and others following the Northern Paths. While it would be extremely difficult for Heathens of any stripe to feel accord with each and every piece in this 'overarching' anthology, this is an engaging and eclectic publication offered to the few who comprise the spiritually enlightened reading public, and there is much insight to be gained in its 235 pages.

Of particular interest to those of the Northern Tradition are Stephen Borthwick's "Knowledge is Power: Rune Magic in Germanic Culture," Gwendolyn Toynton's "Mercury Rising: The Life and Writings of Julius Evola," "Of Wolves and Men: the Beserker and the Vratya" and "The Black Sun: Dionysus in the Philosophy of Friedrich Nietzsche and Greek Myth" as well as Patricus Prolympia's "Son of the Sun"—a look at Sol Invictus.[1] Other essays of interest to Heathens include metaphysical musings and commentary on subjects such as statehood, aristocracy, Cúchulainn—the wolfhound of Culann, Hinduism, the cult of Mithras, and traditionalism itself. The pieces on Buddhist, Middle Eastern (Heathen author and neo-folk musician Troy Southgate offers one up here), Pagan and Mediterranean spiritual matters are of interest as small reminders that our tradition does not exist in a vacuum, and that other paths—while not ours—do share many features in common with it.

---

[1] The ancient Roman deity and associated festival, *Natalis Invicti*, not the contemporary musical project.

The lack of an index is a shortcoming (the only real shortcoming of the publication)—but the list of contents is thorough and the compendium itself is arranged alphabetically, by general spiritual discipline, which makes locating articles a fairly sensible affair.

In July 2010, *Primordial Traditions* will bring out a series of books on different Traditions, the first of the series being *The Northern Traditions*. If this worthy compendium of traditional spiritually is anything to judge them by, it is something for thinking Heathenry to look forward to.

Keep abreast at: www.primordialtraditions.com

The EDDA *as Key to the Coming Age [Die "Edda" als Schlüssel des kommenden Weltalters!]*
By Peryt Shou (Albert Christian A. Schultz)
Edited, translated and introduced by Stephen E. Flowers
Smithville, TX: Rûna-Raven Press, 2004
57 pages

Reviewed by Christopher A. Plaisance

Originally published in 1920, during the interim between the World Wars, this tract is an exceedingly interesting example of the kinds of *völkisch* texts that were being written during the phase of the Heathen revival surrounding the turn of the century. Shou's work is of particular interest due to his extensive influence within *völkisch*, Armanist and Ariosophical circles.[1] At only fifty-seven pages, the book is small, but is densely packed with historical, mythological, philosophical, scientific and occult references and allusions. While the kinds of Theosophical ideas that permeate the text are much less common among contemporary Heathens than was the case in Shou's day, his thoughts provide us with a window into a world that is still largely unknown to non-German speakers. An awareness of such writings can at least prompt modern Heathens to reflect on their own susceptibility to wider current trends in society—a susceptibility that might perhaps seems as peculiar and dated to Heathens of the future as the ideas of the Ariosophists may appear to most of us now. Dr. Flowers has done the Anglosphere a great service by providing translations of pieces by Shou, his mentor von List and other Heathen thinkers whose ideas might otherwise have been lost to the darkness of time.

The central theme of the book is the thesis that the *Hávamál* (the "Rúnatals þáttr" section in particular) provides a mythologized account of a ritual that Shou terms the "Ninth Night." He posits that the apotheotic experience of Wuotan[2] on the World Tree (which he identifies with the death and resurrection of Christ)[3] is in actuality an experience that the Germanic peoples will undergo—that they will be sacrificially destroyed and then reborn. One might at first assume that this is the

---

1 Dr. Flowers notes in the introduction that "those directly influenced by Peryt Shou include Ludwig Schmitt, Alfred Strauss, G.W. Surya…, Rudolf von Sebottendorf, Hans Sterneder, Arnold Krumm-Heller, A. Frank Glahn, Herbert Fritsche and Karl Spiesberger." He goes on to note that "Shou was in close contact with the leading Ariosophical thinkers, e.g. Rudolf John Gorsleben, Werner von Bülow and Karl Maria Wiligut," (from the Editor's Introduction, 7).
2 Shou favors this variant of Odin's name throughout the text.
3 The retroactive of Germanizing Christianity was not uncommon among Ariosophists, as can also be seen with Wiligut's "Irmin-Kristianity."

Illustration 1: The book's cover.

same type of racial mysticism that is so prevalent with other Ariosophists, such as Jörg Lanz von Liebenfels, but this is not entirely the case. Although connected to a whole host of *völkisch* thinkers, Shou, in this case particularly, displays a strong universalist streak. Although the transformative experience he describes will be undergone by the Germans, its ramifications will be global; indeed, "the Germans will be a sacrifice for a new world order"[4] and will pave the way for "a spiritual brotherhood…[that will] unify humanity."[5] In this context, he connects the cults of Wuotan to the Brotherhood of Hermes mentioned by Nostradamus— an idea which is wholly in line with that of the purported existence of various "brotherhoods" from whom originated the mass of revealed literature at the core

---

4 Shou, 9.
5 Ibid., 11.

Illustration 2: A rare photograph of the author, Peryt Shou.

of the Theosophical societies then flourishing in Shou's day.

The operation—the Ritual of the "Ninth Night"—is quite interesting both in that it tells us a great deal about the author's personal theology and in that certain technical aspects of it appear to have been independently reformulated by our very own Dan Cæppe.[6] Shou envisions the rite as transforming its participants into antennas so that they might channel the divine energy that radiates from the cosmos. He identifies this energy with the *önd*[7] of the Norsemen, the Odic force[8] of Baron Karl von Reichenbach, and the *Kuṇḍalinī* serpent[9] of the Indian Tantrikas. He describes this as being a spiritual analog to a radio-wave which can be "picked up" if one correctly performs the ritual. I was immediately struck by the similarity to Dan's comparison of theophantic exchanges to radio signals presented in his essay printed in this very journal.[10] Stemming from this, we gain

---

6 Dan assured me that he had never heard of the book prior to my mentioning it to him.
7 An Old Norse term meaning both "breath" and "spirit."
8 A type of vital energy or life force purportedly discovered by von Reichenbach in the mid-19th century.
9 A source of energy envisioned by the Indians as normally lying dormant, coiled at the base of the spine.
10 Dan Cæppe, "Wandering the Nine Worlds: Heathenism's Shamanic Origins," 105-

a bit of insight into Shou's conception of Wuotan as well. As we read on, it becomes clear that Shou does not view Wuotan as a singular entity, but rather as an aggregate of spiritual adepts who have undergone the aforementioned transformation.[11] To be sure, it is a theology that is infrequently—if ever—espoused in contemporary Heathenry.

Like nearly all works from this period, the scholarship is not quite the standard expected nowadays; logical leaps are taken to bridge the most tenuous of connections, and whenever comparative religion enters the picture, inferences are drawn based on morphological similarities rather than demonstrable genealogical links of ideas. Even with all of these flaws, this is still a piece well worth reading. If we are to be both serious and thorough in treating Heathenry with the same depth and clarity that historians and philosophers of religion treat other faiths, then we must be prepared to fully examine, analyze and come to terms with this phase of the revival. We are still looking through a glass darkly in regards to so many of the men who spent their lives working to bring about a Heathen resurgence. If fellows like Shou and von List are to be dismissed out of hand for any number of unsavory connections their names may bring to mind, then this will remain the case. But if we can look at these men and their works with open minds, then there is yet much we can learn.

124.

11 "Wuotan is not a single entity in the human sense, but rather his is the community of the Hermes-Brothers," (Shou, 28).

Confessions of a Radical Traditionalist
Essays by John Michell
Edited and introduced by Joscelyn Godwin
Waterbury Centre, Vermont: Dominion Press, 2005
352 pages

Reviewed by Henry Lauer

Confessions of a Radical Traditionalist is a curious book, being a compilation of articles written by elder Radical Traditionalist statesman John Michell (who, sadly, parted from this world in April 2009). Editor Joscelyn Godwin has sensitively assembled the articles to create coherent thematic arcs for the reader to explore. It is difficult to ascribe a genre to the text: something akin to occult-tinged philosophy (the latter meant in a very wide sense) might be the best label, though it is peppered with reflections on history, politics, science, art, music, culture, religion, and morality.

The articles are derived from Michell's writings for UK magazine *The Oldie*, a journal for senior citizens. Michell, an Englishman of aristocratic bearing, was a seminal writer on matters of the paranormal, mysterious, and plain confounding. If three principle motifs can be discerned in this anthology, they are is his breadth of reading, his erudition, and his self-effacing sense of humour.

Michell is a Platonist in the best sense: not part of the stodgy tradition of revealed Western philosophy, but rather appreciating Platonism as a mystical metaphor, a door into numinous experience. While Michell is quick to echo Socrates' claims of ignorance and uncertainty before the mysterious order of the universe, he is also more than happy to argue along with Plato that our world is threaded through with its own inherently good order, and that it is up to us to find and live according to that order. This is one reason for his famous campaign against the Metric system: the Imperial system was derived in terms of the relationships between actual objects in the world, not a disconnected and abstract principle, and for Michell it therefore retains a connection to the numinous that the humble metre and kilogram simply cannot match.

As a Radical Traditionalist, it is no surprise that Michell regards much of modernity as being very much in contradiction to the Golden Mean that Plato aspired to invoke. In his estimation it runs on principles of abstraction, instrumental hubris, ignorance, and pettiness. Michell's critique is many-faceted, and tends to violate the usual lines drawn in modern politics: he is not afraid, for example, to argue that multiculturalism has brought good things to the UK (by reinstating something akin to the spotted micro-communities of the Merrie

Illustration 1: The book's cover.

England of yore), yet he will also reject the notion of international aid to the Third World and is very keen to stick up for that mysterious thing known as 'Englishness' without allowing it to be wedded to any particular ideology. In short, this book will outrage the politically correct and the politically incorrect in equal measure, and I for one greatly enjoyed his ability to deflate such a wide variety of worldviews and ideologies.

This tendency to combine seemingly incompatible ideals makes Michell's writing most riveting, for the simple reason that it exposes the reader to their own prejudices, assumptions, biases, and blinders. One might be cheering his wholesale demolition of this or that ideal one moment, only to feel wounded and angry the next when that demolition somehow expands into shredding some other value that one holds in high sentimental regard (and in opposition to the notion that he had just previously been dismantling).

If with irony and literalism Socrates forced his Greek interlocutors to look past the narrow confines of reasoned speech—which can bend or twist into any arbitrary direction—then Michell achieves something similar with his penchant for ideological polymorphism. Many readers might be tempted to throw this book across the room at the first hint of this challenge, but to do so would be to miserably fail the dare that it presents the reader.

Nowhere perhaps is Michell more controversial than in his strident denunciation of evolutionary theory and Darwin. His arguments tend to focus on two themes: one, that the evidence is not as strong as the theory's proponents claim; two, that the theory nourishes all kinds of objectionable social phenomena such as colonialism (which he neatly thumbnails as being "a profitable racket"[1]), and racism. On the second argument, Michell seems to be arguing that evolutionary theory has nourished the scientific legitimation of prejudice since its inception (and even in Darwin's own work), and that although these legitimations have subsequently been debunked, they live on in the public consciousness.

As someone who has always accepted evolutionary theory (and actually studied it in some detail), I found his forthright assault quite confronting. Frustratingly, most of his discussion of this theme is quick, to the point, and does not at all walk the reader through the reasoning. The result is that in order to assess Michell's views one is obliged to go and do a lot of independent research—perhaps this is his intention. I ultimately was not swayed by his views on the theme as presented, but I do very much appreciate the way in which Michell's venom exposed my own dogmatic slumber, and I realise that to some extent I am guilty of holding opinions on this issue that are much stronger than I can really justify. In a way this is the recurring genius of this whole book—it makes one more tentative, and therefore more curious about the world, and *therefore* more able to learn and grow and to tend towards that hidden-in-the-open Platonic beauty to which Michell returns again and again.

Michell's views on spirituality and religion are quite at variance with that of the Heathen-flavoured Radical Traditionalism that most readers of this journal would be familiar with. Michell is a kind of non-denominational Gnostic Christian: happy to take pot shots at every institution of faith (though also, in his contrary way, reverent of various old traditions). He displays a soft spot for paganism, Islam, and all the mystic histories of England—the folk history of Joseph of Arimathea, the magic of geometrically ideal chorister monk-druids singing bliss across the isle, and so forth. His writing succeeds in blurring fact and imagination so that one cannot help but feel that the tightly clutched factuality of modernity might be the dream, and a rather dry and boring dream at that. His

---

1 J. Michell, *Confessions of a Radical Traditionalist*. Dominion Press: Waterbury Centre, 2005, p. 335.

Illustration 2: The author, John Michell.

ability to reference and allude to vastly disparate themes and figures is impressive, and as a whole this anthology evokes a horizon that is rich and heavy with mysteries and portents.

One of Michell's touchstones in his criticism of over-educated, abstract, superficial modernity is the image of *Merrie England*—a semi-mythical (*Or is it?* One begins to question this as the book wraps around one's mind.) pastoral England of benevolent Christianity, uneducated but knowledge-filled peasantry, a warmly pagan atmosphere, and bounty reigning through a land ordered in accordance with the Golden Mean in its infinite forms of manifestation. Michell dreams of a time of manly men, women filled with the full lush of their femininity, when everyone knew their place in the world and everyone lived close to the land, sea, and sky.

It is an almost fairy tale England from which he draws his inspiration, and it is certainly tempting to level the charge of irresponsible idealism at Michell. Yet here again we must be aware to keep our wits, irony, and sense of humour about us. Merrie England is deployed in Michell's writings in much the way that Plato deploys his *Republic* or Moore his *Utopia*—not necessarily to be taken literally, but to become a cipher and vessel for imagination and the questioning of one's acceptance of the obvious as though it were necessary.

Readers who lack subtlety might dismiss Michell as a simple-minded dreamer (or possibly a reprehensible reactionary), but I think they would be missing the point. He is daring us to dream, to dismantle modernity's ideology of 'progress' and take our chance to peer though the cracks. If my interpretation is correct, Michell is doing something much more profound than merely asking us to substitute one dogma (modernism) for another (traditionalism): he is asking us to peer through all dogmas and articles of faith through to the nature of reality itself, that is, to the Platonic symmetry and harmony that is hidden in plain view at every moment and in every place.

Ultimately, this book presents an aggressively confident optimism about life, the universe, and everything. I particularly admire a sentiment that appears towards the end of the book—that the mathematical order of the universe ensures that though we might despair at the world, there is a larger logic that, however mysterious, guarantees that in the grand scheme everything will be as it should be. "[T]hings are far better taken care of than we can possible imagine. So there really is nothing to stop anyone being happy," Michell declares in this vein.[2] If the reader feels tempted to scoff at this courageous positivity then I suggest they submit themselves to reading the book and exploring Michell's philosophy for themselves: *Confessions of a Radical Traditionalist* makes a powerful dare to its reader to cast off the shackles of cynicism (no matter how warranted they may sometimes be), and instead embrace a powerfully life-affirming attitude to the world. I think Michell favours action over complaining and laughter over tears, and his words make a light-footed mockery of anyone burdened by a spirit of seriousness. In a way his ideals are quite Nietzschean, though I think Michell is perhaps more gifted with self-awareness and perspective than Nietzsche. The aplomb with which Michell treats life is something to aspire to.

Complaints? I have two. Firstly, the short essays are arranged thematically without dates being provided. This is annoying because sometimes Michell references something of events current at the time of writing, but writes with the

---

[2] Ibid., p. 230.

assumption that his reader already knows what he is talking about. This might have been true when the articles were first published, but in this anthology format they are shorn of that context, and as a result some of them are perhaps less powerful than they might have been. At times I found myself quite frustrated at this short-coming. The idea of thematic arrangement is perfectly sound and indeed works very well, but I do not see why the dates could not have been retained for the benefit of the curious reader.

My other complaint is a little prosaic: there is no index. Because the book moves lightly from theme to theme, varied motifs recurring throughout its pages in an occult pattern, an index would have been extremely helpful. This seems like a cruel oversight and certainly crimps the value of the volume both as a guide to Michell's thought and as a launch pad for further research.

Like *Thus Spoke Zarathustra* this is a book for all and none, and as fond of Nietzsche as I am, I think I tend slightly towards recommending Michell's words to those of the tempestuous German. My reader is invited to take that as the kind of meant/not-meant irony that Michell (under Socrates' tutelage) excels in: *Confessions of a Radical Traditionalist* is very much worth the read, though the reader had best be ready to embrace a text far more challenging, subtle, and subversive than perhaps anything else they are likely to encounter.

Freyja: Great Goddess of the North
By Britt-Mari Näsström
Edited by Tord Olsson
Lund, Sweden: University of Lund, 1995
237 pages

Reviewed by Jordan Turner

In *Freyja: Great Goddess of the North*, Britt Näsström uses a variety of techniques to form a basis for future research on the Germanic goddess, drawing on a number of primary sources, particularly the Poetic and Prose Eddas, the Sagas, and Skaldic poetry. She also discusses Freyja's role in poems like the Hyndluljóð and Gylfaginning. To inform her thesis, namely that the nature of the goddess is multifunctional, she discusses George Dumézil's tripartite theory of ancient Indo-European society and mythology; i.e., that all Indo-European societies are divided into three classes: Priest-Kings, Warriors, and Farmers. On top of this, she discusses Dumézil's notion of *glissement* or "sliding" between classes, indicating that these three classes sometimes overlapped or were not cast in stone. Näsström utilizes the argument that Freyja was not merely to be relegated to one class as Dumézil had done—placing her in the latter agricultural function in a trinity with Odin and Thor—but rather that she combined all elements of the Dumézilian triad in her person.

Näsström makes clear that in the Eddas, Freyja is goddess of fertility, love, beauty and attraction but also a goddess of war, death, magic, prophecy and wealth. In this, we can see that Freyja subsumes all three functions, religious ritual, war, and fertility. To strengthen her argument, Freyja's relationship to other groups of Germanic goddesses are examined, namely the Disir, the Norns and the Valkyries. It is pointed out that Freyja takes an equal share of the warriors slain on the field of battle with Odin. Näsström uses linguistics to explain the function and nature of Freyja. She examines Freyja's many kennings or epithets such as Syr, "sow" Gefn, "giving" and Blótgyðja, "priestess of the sacrifice." She also draws a connection between Freyja and the goddess Frigga, with whom she shares many characteristics. It is argued that at some point in the past, the two goddesses may have originally been one on account of the fact that over time the Old Norse suffix *-jjya* evolved into *-gga*. Näsström also utilitizes archaeological evidence and toponyms to better understand the historical development of the Northern goddess. She notes that there are many place-names throughout Northern Europe with the element *dis* which may indicate cult-sites, citing the example of the Disir-sallr, "Halls of the Disir," at the temple in Uppsala. Over time the fields of archaeology, comparative mythology, and philology have diverged from one another, thus leading to a state of

Illustration 1: The cover of the original Swedish edition of the book.

fragmentation wherein the different disciplines no longer inform each other. Näsström recommends that the three disciples come together once again to form new insights into the nature of Norse religion.

Näsström rightly maintains that ancient Norse religion was for the most part, "fragmentary, unorganized, and fluid." In order to get a better understanding of Norse myth she uses the comparative method, comparing Norse mythology with the mythology of other Indo-European peoples. Referencing Hindu sources, she draws parallels between Freyja and women and goddesses in the Vedas, along with their respective functions. She notes that while Vac, or "speech," was personified as a goddess in early India, Freyja was endowed with magic words with which to form incantations. Indeed, Freyja presided over two forms of Norse magic—*seiðr* and *galdr*—both of which make use of ritual formulas and meters. As a promiscuous and independent goddess, Freyja is compared with the Vedic Draupadī who, due to a vow made by the prince Arjuna to share his wealth with his brothers, must marry the five Pāṇḍavaḥs.

Näsström goes back far in prehistory to the Bronze Age to trace the development of Freyja, noting that statues of women with golden neck-rings resembling the goddess' famed Brisingamen necklace were found to be plentiful at various ancient sites. Simultaneously, Näsström devotes considerable space to acknowledging some of the weakness of previous archaeological research. The work of Marija Gimbutas receives particular attention in this vein, the noted feminist scholar having made a number of extravagant and fanciful claims about a pre-Indo-European matriarchal order, a claim largely discredited by scholars due to a lack of concrete evidence. Similarly, previous research on the "Great Goddess" saw scholars attempt to draw parallels between the relationship of Freyja and her special devotee Óttar and the myth of Cybele and Attis. Claims were made about Cybele's eunuch priesthood in a bid to fit them into the "Dying God" model of the noted Scottish anthropologist James Frazer who had also tried to construct a theory of a sacrificed king. Such evidence for Cybele's priesthood simply does not exist and Näsström puts a definitive end to the speculation that the cult of Freyja may have had an origin in the ancient eastern Mediterranean.

Freyja does however act as a guardian and tutelary deity to Óttar who, as Näsström points out, makes frequent sacrifices at her altar in Hyndluljóð, covering the stones in blood so that they glisten like glass. Indeed, the goddess serves as a helper in Óttar's transition from boyhood to manhood. Näsström draws parallels through linguistic systemic correspondence between Óttar and the god Odin, and also shows a link between Freyja's mount Hildisvíni, "Battle-Swine," and the sow as an ancient Germanic symbol of fertility. Indeed, Tacitus points out in his *Germania* that

> [The Germans] worship the mother of the gods: as an emblem of that superstition they wear the figures of wild boars: this boar takes the place of arms, or any other kind of protection, and guarantees to the votary of the goddess a mind at rest even in the midst of foes.[1]

Näsström sees the goddess Nerthus as a possible prototype for the goddess, noting that she was widely worshiped throughout the Germanic world, as Tacitus made clear, but she also notes that the etymology of Nerthus' name is unclear and has been a subject of debate.

Finally, the author shows how certain aspects of Freyja's cult survived into the modern day, particularly in Scandinavian folk festivals, of which many were later dedicated (along with many of Freyja's previous titles, functions and attributes) to the Virgin Mary. She also cites the survival of certain old prayers and poetic devices in Scandinavian folk Catholic devotional literature.

---

1   Tacitus. "Germania." In *Dialogus, Agricola, Germania*. trans. William Peterson. (London: William Heinemann, 1914), 329.

For many, *Freyja: the Great Goddess of the North* will be a difficult read. The writing style is very dense and a large wealth of sources are referenced. If the reader is unfamiliar with the Old Norse and Icelandic languages, the material may seem rather dizzying in its breadth. The book is intended primarily for students of Old Norse and comparative religion. Indeed, the long tract was first published in a Swedish journal of comparative religion. The author goes into much detail regarding the methodology of previous researchers and mythographers, particularly George Dumézil, and discusses the different approaches and schools of thought in scholarship on Indo-European myth and society. This book can give the student a detailed background on the main sources, writers, and commentators on Old Norse poetry, religion and society. Readers will be informed of the social prejudices and influences of each researchers' time and circumstance, and the impact of these on their work. The author takes a number of seemingly disparate subjects and weaves them together into a cohesive unit. The author ultimately does a good job analyzing the sources, dispelling the errors of previous researchers, and drawing attention to questions which have hitherto been largely ignored in the study of Norse religion. Through analyzing these various schools of thought and disciplines, the author gives us a new and more complete understanding of the many functions and aspects of the Great Goddess of the North.

Songs of Sun and Hail:
A Conversation with Sonne Hagal[1]

Hailing from Germany, Sonne Hagal is currently at the forefront of the Neofolk musical movement. Like many groups within the genre, they arose out of the post-Industrial wreckage and through the combination of dark, Folk-inspired music and a thoroughly Heathen spirit have forged an identity that sets them wholly apart from the morass of soulless mainstream "music." We are very pleased to bring our readers this interview with them…

Tell us a bit about the formation of Sonne Hagal.

Sonne Hagal wasn't exactly "founded" but rather "occurred" somehow. Back in the early nineties, when all this happened in the small town that we're all originally from, it was pretty common to play in a band or to be involved in some kind of musical project. In this incestuous melting pot of Punk Rock, Metal, Industrial, Hardcore, Techno and other styles, two of us met and felt a certain relatedness. We started to play around with Medieval inspired sounds, Industrial-like soundscapes, ritualistic influences and other weird stuff. As instruments, we used human bones, scrap metal and anything that appeared useful to us. The "music" was basically improvised. Each "song" was extremely long and loud.

We radically changed our style when we met our bass player and violinist. Both inspired us, along with other friends, to write songs rather than just deafening noise. Step by step, our music became what you can hear today. Through all the

---

1 This interview was conducted by Chris Plaisance via email between 28 June and 5 December 2009.

years the basic members never changed. That means we've been making music for more than fifteen years now. We were aided by different guest musicians from time to time, but the regulars were the same the entire time. We still feel the same sense of relatedness, but have become close friends too. With Sonne Hagal, we follow no ideology nor political currents. Our music is much too valuable to be befouled with such nothingness.

What brought about your interest in Heathenry?

It was in this period of artistic redefinition and musical self-discovery when we radically changed our musical style that we got in touch with the Runes and the Northern mysteries through friends that had already been studying them for some time. We were immediately captivated by their power and radiance. They epitomized all our searching for our own origin, our love for nature and its magick, as well as our desire for freedom—both artistic and personal. But Heathenry is not only the Runes. For us it also means a certain way to conceive the world and, apart from this spiritual approach, to experience the world with all of our senses. Our Earth and the unsettled nature around us are full of secrets. Unfortunately, ninety percent of mankind is unable to feel the presence of these holy secrets and will die unaware of them. For us, Heathenry is also about individuality. You see, it is good to have a few close friends with whom to share arcane knowledge, enemies, spiritual ideas and visions. But it is important for the Heathen to bethink himself of his own strength and will. There's no need to follow other people like a sheep. Normal people have lost their ability to see beyond their own nose. If you want to transform yourself into something greater, you need to rediscover your own power and learn to trust your own instincts. Expect no support from the rank and file!

Your group's name is quite evocative, calling to mind both mythological and runic images; would you expand on its meaning and origin?

When we were thinking about how to name our musical project, we felt that its name would have to have more relevance than just to entitle the band. Our band name should be omnipotent enough to unify all of our own different personalities, all the different visions, experiences and aims that each of us had. At the same time, it should be definite enough to give a clear hint of what we're dealing with. We were looking for nothing less than a gleaming banner that we could gather ourselves round as well as all those other people in the world that not only look, but see...

We decided to combine two extremes:

The Sun itself that stands for light and the fire of knowledge—for life and noble gains—for the everlasting circle of life and nature itself. The *Hagal* Rune stands for destruction and chaos. For us, it represents man's confrontation with oneself and the world. It is part of the cultural superstructure of Norse traditions and Germanic heritage. Apart from these 'theoretical' aspects, the Rune stands for our own practical work with the Runes—for our natural grappling with European mythology and history.

As important as the Runes are to you, with which runic tradition do you work—the Elder Futhark, the Anglo-Frisian Futhorc, the Younger Futhork, the Armanen Futharkh or something else? Does your inspiration draw more from the Rune Poems themselves or from the works of Guido von List and his contemporaries?

We work exclusively with the Elder Futhark. Its inherent brilliance, magick and divine wholeness is a constant source of inspiration, a challenge, a subject of scientific research and deep veneration. We love the Rune Poems, but they are not directly to be found in our work. Maybe they are rather like a good old friend that we meet every now and then, but we don't need to meet daily to know that they are out there for us.

Concerning the works of von List, we know his writings but are concerned with different key aspects. His scientific work with the *Eddas* and the Rune Poems are brilliant, but we reject his combination of runic themes with political and racial issues.

What we are interested in is the 'natural' handling of the Runes—using them for curses, personal benedictions, protective sayings, etc. Through the years, the Runes have literally become a part of our daily life.

So, how do you incorporate all of this into a musical performance?

Two things about this:

Concerning our live show, we avoid the "big show." We always concentrated on our music, not on the great performance. We are sure that our music, lyrics and —not the least—our personalities stand for themselves and don't need much more than a few dimmed lights in a dark club to transport our message. But, what we do is to present our sound in the best possible way. We do believe that this kind of "performance" is necessary to demonstrate how important music is for us and how much it means to us. It has become pretty common to download tracks more or less legally on the web, but we see our tracks as complete *Gesamtkunstwerk*,[2] that demands and deserves nice graphic artwork to be whole. That doesn't necessarily mean to scatter Runes all over the cover of an album. If used too frivolously, their magick and beauty can easily be lost...

The same is true for our lyrics. Seeing the Runes as a daily part of our lives, we don't need to sing about them in every track. There are even more deeply moving themes that are worth being sung about.

Aside from your runic studies and practices, how involved in other aspects of Heathenry are you (i.e. the Æsir, Vanir, Landvættir, etc.)?

Dealing with the Runes brings you, sooner or later, in contact with these natural spirits. Of course we know about them and believe in the impact that these entities have on our lives. Based on our studies on the stories of the Æsir, we touch on all related characters of Norse mythology as well, but they are not our main focus.

---

2 *Gesamtkunstwerk* is a term usually associated with Richard Wager meaning, "total work of art" or "all-embracing art form."

Would it be fair to characterize your approach to Heathenry as being more in line with emulating the Master Rune Magician (Odin) than with what Westerners generally associate with religious practice, such as prayer?

See, what we appreciate in Heathenry is its individualism and the possibility to choose whether you want to share your experiences and thoughts with a group or develop your personal spirituality to reach a higher level of consciousness. To describe it more metaphorically: we don't follow Odin's footsteps, but we try to become Odin ourselves. It is always easier to follow predestined pathways, but it is more exciting to find one's own way to *satori*.[3] However, we're not so presumptuous to consider ourselves provided with an authoritarian total-knowledge. We rather see ourselves in an "inquiring and finding" way of progress. The more you're aware of your own abilities, the more you're in a position to analyze and to have an impact on your environment. We were given the Runes by Odin to study and use their ancient power. The Runes and their secret power are a perfect way for us to channel our energy and alter the world the way we want...

---

3 *Satori* is a Japanese Buddhist term meaning, "understanding" or "enlightenment."

Do you have any words of wisdom for those who would follow a similar path?

It is difficult to advise someone in such complex matters, but maybe the whole secret is to listen—to listen to what your own increased awareness tells you, or even your subconscious mind—to listen to what all the spirits and entities around tell you, and then follow your heart. A friend of mine had an inscription above the door to his study: "*Wir wissen wo, wenn wir dort angekommen sind.*"[4] Could this be the secret formula?

Do you have any forthcoming releases or projects?

Yes, there are several plans for new releases. Within a few days we will release a new 7" vinyl single named *Läuthner 2A* and a vinyl version of our last album *Jordansfrost*. We also plan to release a vinyl edition of our live show in Russia (perhaps with some bonus material) and another edition of our first album *Helfahrt*, this time in CD version. And, of course, we are working on a third album and hope to start the recordings next year.

---

4 Trans., "We will know when we get there."

Discography

Albums and EPs:

Year	Title	Format
1993	*Irrlichter*	K7 Tape
1994	*Häretische Mission*	K7 Tape
2000	*Sinnreger*	10", EP
2001	*Starkadr*	7" Single
2001	*Sinister Practices in Dark Sunshine*	12", EP
2002	*Helfahrt*	CD, LP
2002	*Sonne Hagal vs. Polarzirkel*	12", EP
2004	*Tarja*	7" Single
2005	*Dŷgel*	7" Single
2005	*Nidar*	Mini-CD, 10"
2007	*Ähren*	10"
2008	*Jordansfrost*	CD
2009	*Only Echoes Remain*	DVD-V

Compilations:

Year	Title	Format
2002	*Audacia Imperat!*	2xCD, LP
2002	*Tempus Arborum*	CD
2002	*Eichendorf Liedersammlung*	CD
2003	*The Bells Shall Sound Forever*	CD
2003	*Eisiges Licht*	CD
2004	*:Per:Version: Vol. 10*	CD
2004	*Audacia Imperat!*	CD
2004	*Ny Regret Du Passè, Ny Peur De L'Avenir...*	MP3
2005	*Looking For Europe*	4xCD
2005	*Eisiges Licht 2*	CD
2006	*Europa Aeterna*	LP
2006	*Forseti Lebt*	CD
2006	*Indaco EP*	CD, EP
2006	*The Impossibility of Silence*	2xCD
2007	*Donec Ad Metam*	MP3
2008	*Old Europa Cafe*	7xCD
2009	*The Blood of My Lady*	CD

Website: http://www.sonnehagal.de
Email: einsatzleitung@sonnehagal.de

Editorial Staff

Christopher A. Plaisance
Editor in Chief

Chris entered into Heathendom via unconventional means—the philosophy of Friedrich Nietzsche. It was his study of *Also sprach Zarathustra*, along with a cotemporal interest in genealogy that led him to the study, and eventual practice, of the pre-Christian religion of his ancestors. Correspondingly, his activities in regards to Heathenry have always tended towards philosophical analysis and development. His essay, "Why I am a Heathen," current research projects and this very journal are manifestations of this impetus to explore the overlap between Heathen religious ideas and Western philosophy. Since coming to Heathenry, he has been a member of the Wolfbund, and worked as a Folkbuilder for the Ásatrú Folk Assembly (AFA). He is currently a member of both the AFA and the Odinic Rite. Although primarily an autodidact, Chris graduated from the Defense Language Institute, during his tenure in the US Army, with a degree in Mandarin Chinese and currently studies Philosophy through the American Military University. Presently, he resides in Pennsylvania.

Ben McGarr
Editor

Ben found himself involved in matters Heathen via his interest in the history and culture of his ancestors. Comparative religion, folklore and linguistics took him from his archaeological and anthropological education back to the myths of his forebears, the internet bringing him in touch with the like-minded individuals responsible for realising this journal. As the dramatic moorland landscape of the Pennines shaped his spirituality, the post-industrial decay and metamorphosis of his native Manchester early impressed on him the transience of human endeavour. Seeing the smoke stacks of the 'dark satanic mills' topple one by one as 'Cottonopolis' faded into memory, questions arose in his mind as to the nature of history in which the old gives way to the new, prompting a re-examination of deeper, less mutable, aspects of our own nature. He hopes that his review of Oswald Spengler's work in the present volume will help draw the attention of the Heathen community to at least one grandiose attempt to tackle such fundamental matters. Ben McGarr studied at Durham University, worked abroad in Moscow for seven years, and is presently living in rural Devon.

Vincent Rex Soden
Editor

Many Heathens cite an interest in genealogy and the history of their families as a spark which led them to study the pre-Christian beliefs of their ancestors. Vince is no different in this regard. He traces most of his family back to the English settlers who came to New England during the Great Migration and the Deitsch who made their way out of the Rhineland and Switzerland in the eighteenth century. His interest in European history led him to study both the change and the continuity present between the centuries spanning from today to back then and well before. A concern for the future we are making today is never too far from his thoughts. The works of J.R.R. Tolkien, in which he sought to envision the myth and lore of the Anglo-Saxons prior to the Norman conquest of England, have also resonated deeply with him. Vince now learns as much as he can about the pre-Christian faith of his forefathers through reading and conversations with like-minded individuals such as those involved with the production of this journal. Vince was born in Lancaster, Pennsylvania and graduated from Temple University in Philadelphia with two degrees in European History and Philosophy and a minor in the German language.

Contributors

Asseling

Hailing from the pastoral beauty of rural Eastern Ontario, Canada, Asseling knows well the power and effect of the landscape upon a mindscape and the resulting flow of ideas and perceptions from mind onto paper. Fittingly, as a reflection of her expertise in Medieval Studies and her keen interest in pre-Christian and Christian thought during this time period, she contributes a book review of Vésteinn Ólason's *New Lands, New Faith: Christianity and the Vinland Voyages in Medieval Icelandic Manuscripts* for this issue.

Xenia Bakran-Sunic

Xenia was born in Croatia on November 23, 1956. She has lived part of her life in the United States of America and obtained her BA degree in the English language at the University of California in Santa Barbara. She currently resides in Croatia where she teaches English.

Alain de Benoist

Alain was born on 11 December 1943. He has studied law, philosophy, sociology, and the history of religions in Paris, France. A journalist and writer, he is the editor of two journals: *Nouvelle Ecole* (since 1968) and *Krisis* (since 1988). He has published more than fifty books and 3,000 articles. He is also a regular contributor to many French and European publications, journals, and newspapers (including *Valeurs actuelles, Le Spectacle du monde, Magazine-Hebdo, Le Figaro-Magazine* in France, *Telos* in the United States, and *Junge Freiheit* in Germany). In 1978 he received the Grand Prix de l'Essai from the Académie Française for his book *Vu de droite: Anthologie critique des idées contemporaines* (Copernic, 1977). He has also been a regular contributor to the radio program *France-Culture* and has appeared in numerous television debates.

Stephen M. Borthwick

Stephen is a graduate student at the University of Chicago pursuing his MA in History. He has a BA in History with subconcentrations in German and English language and literature from the Catholic University of America. His focus is on Central European history, with especial attention paid to the development of nationalism in the German and Habsburg lands in the sixteenth through nineteenth centuries. In addition, he works in civilizational history in the tradition of Oswald Spengler, Arnold Toynbee, and William McNeill. His spiritual experience with Germanic Heathenry began with an interest in Hinduism, which he found closed to all but those of Hindu birth. His interest in a religion involving a similar relationship of ancestry with faith led him into Odinic circles, from which he also ultimately departed in favor of his present practice as a lone devotee to the gods Óðinn and Týr. Theologically he works in scriptural studies, runic studies, and pneumatology. He is presently developing what he has named Truistic Theology, based in the concept of *trú fyrst*, or "faith first."

Dan Cæppe

Dan resides in the south of England, where he was born and raised. Despite belonging to a non-religious family, Dan was christened—though he later rejected Christianity in favor of atheism. Eventually, his life-long fascination with the supernatural led him to the study and practice of ancient and esoteric spiritual traditions. Dan works as a graphic designer and is heavily involved in music.

Juleigh Howard-Hobson

Works of Juleigh Howard-Hobson that are influenced by or examine European folklore and tradition have appeared in numerous publications, including *Hex Magazine, Idunna, The Old Heathen's Almanac, Odin's Gift, The AFA Voice, The Odinic Rite Briefing, *newWitch*, Megalithic Poems, A Devotional to Thor* (Retter) as well as in her own chapbook: *Sommer and Other Poems* (RavensHalla Arts). Similar writings have been accepted and published by a variety of mainstream literary venues, such as *Umbrella Journal, Soundzine, Lucid Rhythms, Mezzo Cammin, Bewildering Stories, Strong Verse, Brilliant, Tilt-a-whirl* and *Every Day Fiction*. Juleigh is the former editor of *The Runestone Journal* (AFA/RavensHalla), and has been nominated for both "The Best of the Net" and The Pushcart Prize. She was an invited artist in the 2005 Heathen Art Show (Portland OR); her formal poetry collection has been favorably reviewed in

Rûna.

Henry Lauer

Henry's interests include Heathenism, runes, *seidh*, magic, spirituality of many branches, music, writing, art, history, philosophy, literature, psychology, nutrition, health, environmentalism, love, hate, war, and peace. He writes for the *Elhaz Ablaze* website, and is one of the editors of *Hex Magazine*. Henry works in a range of musical guises, including Ironwood, Sword Toward Self, Ein Skopudhr Galdra, Greed & Rapacity, and Beastianity:
- http://www.elhazablaze.com
- http://www.hexmagazine.com
- http://www.ironwoodsound.com.au
- http://www.swordtowardself.com
- http://www.myspace.com/einskopudhragaldra
- http://www.myspace.com/greedrapacity
- http://www.myspace.com/httpwwwmyspacecombeastianity

Loddfafner

I have always been heathen but in a wordless manner inspired more by American Indian ideals about the sacredness of place. My identification with Norse Heathenry emerged out of the synchronicity of discovering my Swedish heritage while sheltering a mentally-wounded Odinist fresh out of prison. In the Norse traditions, especially the *Havamal*, I find the words and metaphors to guide my heathen sense. As my overt heathenism starts with the *Havamal*, I am using the name Loddfafner, arguably the everyman to whom parts at least are addressed, as a screen name on the internet forums where I found the crew that put this journal together.

Diana M. Plaisance

Born in New Orleans, Louisiana in 1978 to an old Southern family, Diana became dedicated to painting and art as a very young child. At the age of fifteen, she began painting in oils and acrylics, and has since devoted herself to the development of her unique artistic vision which is often inspired by her interest in European folklore and mythology, and her Heathen beliefs and practice. Though she considers herself to be mainly self-taught, Diana has nearly completed her university studies towards a Bachelor of Fine Arts—a degree program to be pursued once again when her youngest child enters kindergarten. Her works have been displayed in Honolulu, Hawaii and will soon be seen in and around Philadelphia, Pennsylvania. Her current portfolio can be viewed online at: http://www.dianaplaisance.net

Jennifer Roberge-Toll

An apprentice member of the Odinic Rite, where I am known as *Aemma AOR*, and a former member of the Asatru Folk Assembly and the online community called "A Heathen Thing," I am a proud fifth generation Franco-Ontarian whose direct ancestors came from Normandy, to help settle the cradle of French North America at l'Ile d'Orleans, Quebec. Add to this the recent Irish, Scottish and English ancestry in my lineage, and I am what some might accurately call the quintessential Canadian of Hugh MacLennan's *Two Solitudes* variety. Although raised as a Roman Catholic, my ties to this tradition were always more cultural than spiritual. Not until answering the call of my ancestors' heathen heritage have I been able to enjoy a more authentic sense of self through this more culturally-genuine expression of my spirituality. It is with great pleasure that I offer this first volume a translation of a work from a long-time favourite Heathen thinker of mine, Alain de Benoist.

Steven "Piparskeggr" Robinson

Steven is native of western Massachusetts, born there in early 1957. His interest in genealogy has found ancestors from Lithuania to Ireland, Italy to Denmark, and many points in between these extremes, with his first European forebears coming across the Atlantic to Massachusetts Bay Colony in the mid-1620s and Acadia in the late 1640s. He is currently living in northern Illinois with his wife of over 25 years; accompanied by four cats. Academically, while he is well-read, degree work just did not take. He has had a wide-range jobs over the years, from rake jockey to supervisor in an electronics plant, and served for 9 years in the US Air Force Reserves as a combat engineer. His interests are wide-ranging, but closest to his heart are reading, writing, conversing, cooking, brewing and dining. He is also a marksman, hunter and safety instructor. He also likes to craft things in wood, metal, leather, cloth and other materials. He awoke to the "Call" of the Northern Ancestors and Holy Powers over 20 years ago. He has gained some note as a Skald and guest since then. Within his Ásatrú beliefs, he is closest to Ullr.

Kris Stevenson

Kris has been a practicing Odinist for the last six years and is an associate member of the Odinic Rite, a UK based Odinist organization. He graduated from Leicester University in 2002 with a BA in Archaeology but spends much of his time researching topics not having a great deal to do with that discipline. His research interests within Germanic mythology currently include the study of Heathen concepts within the writings of Nietzsche, Tolkien's "spirit of courage" within Old English literature and an analysis of Vedic and Eddic creation myths. He believes it might be a good idea to write a novel that encapsulates some of his beliefs regarding the nature of existence from an Odinist, or rather his own, perspective; somebody might even want to read it.

Jordan Turner

Jordan received a BA in History from Wheaton College in Norton, Massachusetts, where he also studied German and Classics. He first discovered Greek mythology at the age of eight and from there his interest branched out into the realm of comparative religion (especially Eastern and ancient religions), history, languages and literature. He also studied at the Free University in Berlin, and has traveled to India where he studied the goddess Kālī at the Dakshineswar Mandir in Calcutta. In his spare time he enjoys reading, fine dining, and listening to medieval, folk and experimental music.

Troy Wisehart

It was the essay "What is Asatru?" written by Steve McNallen of the Ásatrú Folk Assembly that first introduced me to Heathenry. As I read that paper, it was as if I was reading what I had known all my life. I knew right then and there that I had found my religion. Not long after the discovery of my ancestral faith, Dave Taggart and I decided to form our own kindred. It quickly became evident that it was Freyja who had taken notice of us and she took us under her wing. Falcon Hill is located near to where we lived at that time—hence the name Falcon Kindred. I study everything I can get my hands on but it is the *Hávamál* upon which I base my philosophy. Over the course of the years I have met several of the founders of modern Ásatrú, including Steve McNallen, Mike (Valgard) Murray, Susan Granquist. I learned what I could from each of them but, as with all things, true learning comes only through doing. Falcon Kindred is now based out of Olympia Washington. The kindred meets for *blót*, feast, and *sumbl* every month without fail. We have 501(c)(3) tax exempt status with the IRS as a Religious Organization. Falcon Kindred also has a very busy Prison Ministry here in Washington State. The religion of Ásatrú has profoundly changed my life. I am still learning and always will be.

Hunter Yoder

Hunter was born and raised in the heart of Pennsylvania Dutch country: Berks

County, Pennsylvania. He began painting hex signs on barns at an early age before attending Kutztown University to earn a BFA in Painting. He has been involved in experimental film making and video art and has shown his works in New York City at the Museum of Modern Art's Cineprobe program and in France's Festival International du Jeune Cinema Different Programme. His current work is a culmination of his background, life experiences, and insatiable thirst for knowledge of the commonality of symbolism across all cultures. An avid Netherland Dwarf rabbit breeder, Entheologist, and father of four, he is co-founder of http://www.zaubereigarten.com and author of *The Backdoor Hexologist, Volume One*. He is a founding member of the Folkish Heathen tribe in Pennsylvania, *Der Heidevolksstamm*.

Made in the USA
Lexington, KY
01 November 2012